POEMS BY THE WAY
& LOVE IS ENOUGH

By

William Morris

British Library Cataloguing-in-Publication Data
A catalogue record for this book is available from the
British Library

Contents

William Morris

William Morris was born in London, England in 1834. Arguably best known as a textile designer, he founded a design partnership which deeply influenced the decoration of churches and homes during the early 20th century. However, he is also considered an important Romantic writer and pioneer of the modern fantasy genre, being a direct influence on authors such as J. R. R. Tolkien. As well as fiction, Morris penned poetry and essays. Amongst his best-known works are The Defence of Guenevere and Other Poems (1858), The Earthly Paradise (1868–1870), A Dream of John Ball (1888), News from Nowhere (1890), and the fantasy romance The Well at the World's End (1896). Morris was also an important figure in British socialism, founding the Socialist League in 1884. He died in 1896, aged 62.

POEMS BY THE WAY

FROM THE UPLAND TO THE SEA

Shall we wake one morn of spring,
Glad at heart of everything,
Yet pensive with the thought of eve?
Then the white house shall we leave.
Pass the wind-flowers and the bays,
Through the garth, and go our ways,
Wandering down among the meads
Till our very joyance needs
Rest at last; till we shall come
To that Sun-god's lonely home,
Lonely on the hillside grey,
Whence the sheep have gone away;
Lonely till the feast-time is,
When with prayer and praise of bliss,
Thither comes the country side.
There awhile shall we abide,
Sitting low down in the porch
By that image with the torch:
Thy one white hand laid upon
The black pillar that was won
From the far-off Indian mine;
And my hand nigh touching thine,
But not touching; and thy gown
Fair with spring-flowers cast adown
From thy bosom and thy brow.
There the south-west wind shall blow

Through thine hair to reach my cheek,
As thou sittest, nor mayst speak,
Nor mayst move the hand I kiss
For the very depth of bliss;
Nay, nor turn thine eyes to me.
Then desire of the great sea
Nigh enow, but all unheard,
In the hearts of us is stirred,
And we rise, we twain at last,
And the daffodils downcast,
Feel thy feet and we are gone
From the lonely Sun-Crowned one,
Then the meads fade at our back,
And the spring day 'gins to lack
That fresh hope that once it had;
But we twain grow yet more glad,
And apart no more may go
When the grassy slope and low
Dieth in the shingly sand:
Then we wander hand in hand
By the edges of the sea,
And I weary more for thee
Than if far apart we were,
With a space of desert drear
'Twixt thy lips and mine, O love!
Ah, my joy, my joy thereof!

OF THE WOOING OF HALLBIORN THE STRONG

A STORY FROM THE LAND-SETTLING BOOK OF ICELAND, CHAPTER XXX.

At Deildar-Tongue in the autumn-tide,
So many times over comes summer again,
Stood Odd of Tongue his door beside.
What healing in summer if winter be vain?
Dim and dusk the day was grown,
As he heard his folded wethers moan.
Then through the garth a man drew near,
With painted shield and gold-wrought spear.
Good was his horse and grand his gear,
And his girths were wet with Whitewater.
"Hail, Master Odd, live blithe and long!
How fare the folk at Deildar-Tongue?"
"All hail, thou Hallbiorn the Strong!
How fare the folk by the Brothers'-Tongue?"
"Meat have we there, and drink and fire,
Nor lack all things that we desire.
But by the other Whitewater
Of Hallgerd many a tale we hear."
"Tales enow may my daughter make
If too many words be said for her sake."
"What saith thine heart to a word of mine,
That I deem thy daughter fair and fine?
Fair and fine for a bride is she,
And I fain would have her home with me."
"Full many a word that at noon goes forth
Comes home at even little worth.

9

Now winter treadeth on autumn-tide,
So here till the spring shalt thou abide.
Then if thy mind be changed no whit.
And ye still will wed, see ye to it!
And on the first of summer days,
A wedded man, ye may go your ways.
Yet look, howso the thing will fall,
My hand shall meddle nought at all.
Lo, now the night and rain draweth up.
And within doors glimmer stoop and cup.
And hark, a little sound I know,
The laugh of Snæbiorn's fiddle-bow,
My sister's son, and a craftsman good,
When the red rain drives through the iron wood."
Hallbiorn laughed, and followed in,
And a merry feast there did begin.
Hallgerd's hands undid his weed,
Hallgerd's hands poured out the mead.
Her fingers at his breast he felt,
As her hair fell down about his belt.
Her fingers with the cup he took,
And o'er its rim at her did look.
Cold cup, warm hand, and fingers slim.
Before his eyes were waxen dim.
And if the feast were foul or fair,
He knew not, save that she was there.
He knew not if men laughed or wept,
While still 'twixt wall and daïs she stept.
Whether she went or stood that eve,
Not once his eyes her face did leave.
But Snæbiorn laughed and Snæbiorn sang,
And sweet his smitten fiddle rang.

And Hallgerd stood beside him there,
So many times over comes summer again
Nor ever once he turned to her,
What healing in summer if winter be vain?

Master Odd on the morrow spake,
So many times over comes summer again.
"Hearken, O guest, if ye be awake,"
What healing in summer if winter be vain?
"Sure ye champions of the south
Speak many things from a silent mouth.
And thine, meseems, last night did pray
That ye might well be wed to-day.
The year's ingathering feast it is,
A goodly day to give thee bliss.
Come hither, daughter, fine and fair,
Here is a wooer from Whitewater.
Fast away hath he gotten fame,
And his father's name is e'en my name.
Will ye lay hand within his hand,
That blossoming fair our house may stand?"
She laid her hand within his hand;
White she was as the lily wand.
Low sang Snæbiorn's brand in its sheath,
And his lips were waxen grey as death.
"Snæbiorn, sing us a song of worth.
If your song must be silent from now henceforth.
Clear and loud his voice outrang,
And a song of worth at the wedding he sang.
"Sharp sword," he sang, "and death is sure."
So many times over comes summer again,
"But love doth over all endure."

What healing in summer if winter be vain?

Now winter cometh and weareth away,
So many times over comes summer again,
And glad is Hallbiorn many a day.
What healing in summer if winter be vain?
Full soft he lay his love beside;
But dark are the days of winter-tide.
Dark are the days, and the nights are long,
And sweet and fair was Snæbiorn's song.
Many a time he talked with her,
Till they deemed the summer-tide was there.
And they forgat the wind-swept ways
And angry fords of the flitting-days.
While the north wind swept the hillside there
They forgat the other Whitewater.
While nights at Deildar-Tongue were long,
They clean forgat the Brothers'-Tongue.
But whatso falleth 'twixt Hell and Home,
So many times over comes summer again,
Full surely again shall summer come.
What healing in summer if winter be vain?

To Odd spake Hallbiorn on a day
So many times over comes summer again,
"Gone is the snow from everyway."
What healing in summer if winter be vain?
"Now green is grown Whitewater-side,
And I to Whitewater will ride."
Quoth Odd, "Well fare thou winter-guest,
May thine own Whitewater be best
Well is a man's purse better at home

Than open where folk go and come."
"Come ye carles of the south country,
Now shall we go our kin to see!
For the lambs are bleating in the south,
And the salmon swims towards Olfus mouth,
Girth and graithe and gather your gear!
And ho for the other Whitewater!"
Bright was the moon as bright might be,
And Snæbiorn rode to the north country.
And Odd to Reykholt is gone forth,
To see if his mares be ought of worth.
But Hallbiorn into the bower is gone
And there sat Hallgerd all alone.
She was not dight to go nor ride,
She had no joy of the summer-tide.
Silent she sat and combed her hair,
That fell all round about her there.
The slant beam lay upon her head,
And gilt her golden locks to red.
He gazed at her with hungry eyes
And fluttering did his heart arise.
"Full hot," he said, "is the sun to-day,
And the snow is gone from the mountain-way
The king-cup grows above the grass,
And through the wood do the thrushes pass."
Of all his words she hearkened none,
But combed her hair amidst the sun.
"The laden beasts stand in the garth
And their heads are turned to Helliskarth."
The sun was falling on her knee,
And she combed her gold hair silently.
"To-morrow great will be the cheer

13

At the Brothers'-Tongue by Whitewater."
From her folded lap the sunbeam slid;
She combed her hair, and the word she hid.
"Come, love; is the way so long and drear
From Whitewater to Whitewater?"
The sunbeam lay upon the floor;
She combed her hair and spake no more.
He drew her by the lily hand:
"I love thee better than all the land."
He drew her by the shoulders sweet:
"My threshold is but for thy feet."
He drew her by the yellow hair:
"O why wert thou so deadly fair?
O am I wedded to death?" he cried,
"Is the Dead-strand come to Whitewater side?"
And the sun was fading from the room,
But her eyes were bright in the change and the gloom.
"Sharp sword," she sang, "and death is sure,
But over all doth love endure."
She stood up shining in her place
And laughed beneath his deadly face.
Instead of the sunbeam gleamed a brand,
The hilts were hard in Hallbiorn's hand:
The bitter point was in Hallgerd's breast
That Snæbiorn's lips of love had pressed.
Morn and noon, and nones passed o'er,
And the sun is far from the bower door.
To-morrow morn shall the sun come back,
So many times over comes summer again,
But Hallgerd's feet the floor shall lack.
What healing in summer if winter be vain?

Now Hallbiorn's house-carles ride full fast,
So many times over comes summer again,
Till many a mile of way is past.
What healing in summer if winter be vain?
But when they came over Oxridges,
'Twas, "Where shall we give our horses ease?"
When Shieldbroad-side was well in sight,
'Twas, "Where shall we lay our heads to-night?"
Hallbiorn turned and raised his head;
"Under the stones of the waste," he said.
Quoth one, "The clatter of hoofs anigh."
Quoth the other, "Spears against the sky!"
"Hither ride men from the Wells apace;
Spur we fast to a kindlier place."
Down from his horse leapt Hallbiorn straight:
"Why should the supper of Odin wait?
Weary and chased I will not come
To the table of my fathers' home."
With that came Snæbiorn, who but he,
And twelve in all was his company.
Snæbiorn's folk were on their feet;
He spake no word as they did meet.
They fought upon the northern hill:
Five are the howes men see there still.
Three men of Snæbiorn's fell to earth
And Hallbiorn's twain that were of worth.
And never a word did Snæbiorn say,
Till Hallbiorn's foot he smote away.
Then Hallbiorn cried: "Come, fellow of mine,
To the southern bent where the sun doth shine."
Tottering into the sun he went,
And slew two more upon the bent.

And on the bent where dead he lay
Three howes do men behold to-day.
And never a word spake Snæbiorn yet,
Till in his saddle he was set.
Nor was there any heard his voice,
So many times over comes summer again
Till he came to his ship in Grimsar-oyce.
What healing in summer if winter be vain?

On so fair a day they hoisted sail,
So many times over comes summer again,
And for Norway well did the wind avail.
What healing in summer if winter be vain?
But Snæbiorn looked aloft and said:
"I see in the sail a stripe of red:
Murder, meseems, is the name of it,
And ugly things about it flit.
A stripe of blue in the sail I see:
Cold death of men it seems to me.
And next I see a stripe of black,
For a life fulfilled of bitter lack."
Quoth one, "So fair a wind doth blow
That we shall see Norway soon enow."
"Be blithe, O shipmate," Snæbiorn said,
"Tell Hacon the Earl that I be dead."
About the midst of the Iceland main
Round veered the wind to the east again.
And west they drave, and long they ran
Till they saw a land was white and wan.
"Yea," Snæbiorn said, "my home it is,
Ye bear a man shall have no bliss.
Far off beside the Greekish sea

16

The maidens pluck the grapes in glee.
Green groweth the wheat in the English land,
And the honey-bee flieth on every hand.
In Norway by the cheaping town
The laden beasts go up and down.
In Iceland many a mead they mow
And Hallgerd's grave grows green enow.
But these are Gunnbiorn's skerries wan,
Meet harbour for a hapless man.
In all lands else is love alive,
But here is nought with grief to strive.
Fail not for a while, O eastern wind,
For nought but grief is left behind.
And before me here a rest I know,"
So many times over comes summer again,
"A grave beneath the Greenland snow,"
What healing in summer if winter be vain?

ECHOES OF LOVE'S HOUSE

Love gives every gift whereby we long to live:
"Love takes every gift, and nothing back doth give."

Love unlocks the lips that else were ever dumb:
"Love locks up the lips whence all things good might come."

Love makes clear the eyes that else would never see:
"Love makes blind the eyes to all but me and thee."

Love turns life to joy till nought is left to gain:
"Love turns life to woe till hope is nought and vain."

Love, who changest all, change me nevermore!
"Love, who changest all, change my sorrow sore!"

Love burns up the world to changeless heaven and blest,
"Love burns up the world to a void of all unrest."

And there we twain are left, and no more work we need:
"And I am left alone, and who my work shall heed?"

Ah! I praise thee, Love, for utter joyance won!
"And is my praise nought worth for all my life undone?"

THE BURGHERS' BATTLE

Thick rise the spear-shafts o'er the land
That erst the harvest bore;
The sword is heavy in the hand,
And we return no more.
The light wind waves the Ruddy Fox,
Our banner of the war,
And ripples in the Running Ox,
And we return no more.
Across our stubble acres now
The teams go four and four;
But out-worn elders guide the plough,
And we return no more.
And now the women heavy-eyed
Turn through the open door
From gazing down the highway wide,
Where we return no more.
The shadows of the fruited close
Dapple the feast-hall floor;
There lie our dogs and dream and doze,
And we return no more.
Down from the minster tower to-day
Fall the soft chimes of yore
Amidst the chattering jackdaws' play:
And we return no more.
But underneath the streets are still;
Noon, and the market's o'er!
Back go the goodwives o'er the hill;
For we return no more.
What merchant to our gates shall come?
What wise man bring us lore?

What abbot ride away to Rome,
Now we return no more?
What mayor shall rule the hall we built?
Whose scarlet sweep the floor?
What judge shall doom the robber's guilt,
Now we return no more?
New houses in the street shall rise
Where builded we before,
Of other stone wrought otherwise;
For we return no more.
And crops shall cover field and hill
Unlike what once they bore,
And all be done without our will,
Now we return no more.
Look up! the arrows streak the sky,
The horns of battle roar;
The long spears lower and draw nigh,
And we return no more.
Remember how beside the wain,
We spoke the word of war,
And sowed this harvest of the plain,
And we return no more.
Lay spears about the Ruddy Fox!
The days of old are o'er;
Heave sword about the Running Ox!
For we return no more.

HOPE DIETH: LOVE LIVETH

Strong are thine arms, O love, and strong
Thine heart to live, and love, and long;
But thou art wed to grief and wrong:
Live, then, and long, though hope be dead!
Live on, and labour through the years!
Make pictures through the mist of tears,
Of unforgotten happy fears,
That crossed the time ere hope was dead.
Draw near the place where once we stood
Amid delight's swift-rushing flood,
And we and all the world seemed good
Nor needed hope now cold and dead.
Dream in the dawn I come to thee
Weeping for things that may not be!
Dream that thou layest lips on me!
Wake, wake to clasp hope's body dead!
Count o'er and o'er, and one by one,
The minutes of the happy sun
That while agone on kissed lips shone,
Count on, rest not, for hope is dead.
Weep, though no hair's breadth thou shalt move
The living Earth, the heaven above,
By all the bitterness of love!
Weep and cease not, now hope is dead!
Sighs rest thee not, tears bring no ease,
Life hath no joy, and Death no peace:
The years change not, though they decrease,
For hope is dead, for hope is dead.
Speak, love, I listen: far away
I bless the tremulous lips, that say,

"Mock not the afternoon of day,
Mock not the tide when hope is dead!"
I bless thee, O my love, who say'st:
"Mock not the thistle-cumbered waste;
I hold Love's hand, and make no haste
Down the long way, now hope is dead.
With other names do we name pain,
The long years wear our hearts in vain.
Mock not our loss grown into gain,
Mock not our lost hope lying dead.
Our eyes gaze for no morning-star,
No glimmer of the dawn afar;
Full silent wayfarers we are
Since ere the noon-tide hope lay dead.
Behold with lack of happiness
The master, Love, our hearts did bless
Lest we should think of him the less:
Love dieth not, though hope is dead!"

ERROR AND LOSS

Upon an eve I sat me down and wept,
Because the world to me seemed nowise good;
Still autumn was it, and the meadows slept,
The misty hills dreamed, and the silent wood
Seemed listening to the sorrow of my mood:
I knew not if the earth with me did grieve,
Or if it mocked my grief that bitter eve.

Then 'twixt my tears a maiden did I see,
Who drew anigh me on the leaf-strewn grass,
Then stood and gazed upon me pitifully
With grief-worn eyes, until my woe did pass
From me to her, and tearless now I was,
And she mid tears was asking me of one
She long had sought unaided and alone.

I knew not of him, and she turned away
Into the dark wood, and my own great pain
Still held me there, till dark had slain the day,
And perished at the grey dawn's hand again;
Then from the wood a voice cried: "Ah, in vain,
In vain I seek thee, O thou bitter-sweet!
In what lone land are set thy longed-for feet?"

Then I looked up, and lo, a man there came
From midst the trees, and stood regarding me
Until my tears were dried for very shame;
Then he cried out: "O mourner, where is she
Whom I have sought o'er every land and sea?
I love her and she loveth me, and still

We meet no more than green hill meeteth hill."

With that he passed on sadly, and I knew
That these had met and missed in the dark night,
Blinded by blindness of the world untrue,
That hideth love and maketh wrong of right.
Then midst my pity for their lost delight,
Yet more with barren longing I grew weak,
Yet more I mourned that I had none to seek.

THE HALL AND THE WOOD

'Twas in the water-dwindling tide
When July days were done,
Sir Rafe of Greenhowes 'gan to ride
In the earliest of the sun.

He left the white-walled burg behind,
He rode amidst the wheat.
The westland-gotten wind blew kind
Across the acres sweet.

Then rose his heart and cleared his brow,
And slow he rode the way:
"As then it was, so is it now,
Not all hath worn away."

So came he to the long green lane
That leadeth to the ford,
And saw the sickle by the wain
Shine bright as any sword.

The brown carles stayed 'twixt draught and draught,
And murmuring, stood aloof,
But one spake out when he had laughed:
"God bless the Green-wood Roof!"

Then o'er the ford and up he fared:
And lo the happy hills!
And the mountain-dale by summer cleared,
That oft the winter fills.

Then forth he rode by Peter's gate,
And smiled and said aloud:
"No more a day doth the Prior wait;
White stands the tower and proud."

There leaned a knight on the gateway side
In armour white and wan,
And after the heels of the horse he cried,
"God keep the hunted man!"

Then quoth Sir Rafe, "Amen, amen!"
For he deemed the word was good;
But never a while he lingered then
Till he reached the Nether Wood.

He rode by ash, he rode by oak,
He rode the thicket round,
And heard no woodman strike a stroke,
No wandering wife he found.

He rode the wet, he rode the dry,
He rode the grassy glade:
At Wood-end yet the sun was high,
And his heart was unafraid.

There on the bent his rein he drew,
And looked o'er field and fold,
O'er all the merry meads he knew
Beneath the mountains old.

He gazed across to the good Green Howe
As he smelt the sun-warmed sward;
Then his face grew pale from chin to brow,
And he cried, "God save the sword!"

For there beyond the winding way,
Above the orchards green,
Stood up the ancient gables grey
With ne'er a roof between.

His naked blade in hand he had,
O'er rough and smooth he rode,
Till he stood where once his heart was glad
Amidst his old abode.

Across the hearth a tie-beam lay
Unmoved a weary while.
The flame that clomb the ashlar grey
Had burned it red as tile.

The sparrows bickering on the floor
Fled at his entering in;
The swift flew past the empty door
His winged meat to win.

Red apples from the tall old tree
O'er the wall's rent were shed.
Thence oft, a little lad, would he
Look down upon the lead.

There turned the cheeping chaffinch now
And feared no birding child;
Through the shot-window thrust a bough
Of garden-rose run wild.

He looked to right, he looked to left,
And down to the cold grey hearth,
Where lay an axe with half burned heft
Amidst the ashen dearth.

He caught it up and cast it wide
Against the gable wall;
Then to the daïs did he stride,
O'er beam and bench and all.

Amidst there yet the high-seat stood,
Where erst his sires had sat;
And the mighty board of oaken wood,
The fire had stayed thereat.

Then through the red wrath of his eyne
He saw a sheathed sword,
Laid thwart that wasted field of wine,
Amidmost of the board.

And by the hilts a slug-horn lay,
And therebeside a scroll,
He caught it up and turned away
From the lea-land of the bowl.

Then with the sobbing grief he strove,
For he saw his name thereon;

And the heart within his breast uphove
As the pen's tale now he won.

"O Rafe, my love of long ago!
Draw forth thy father's blade,
And blow the horn for friend and foe,
And the good green-wood to aid!"

He turned and took the slug-horn up,
And set it to his mouth,
And o'er that meadow of the cup
Blew east and west and south.

He drew the sword from out the sheath
And shook the fallow brand;
And there a while with bated breath,
And hearkening ear did stand.

Him-seemed the horn's voice he might hear—
Or the wind that blew o'er all.
Him-seemed that footsteps drew anear—
Or the boughs shook round the hall.

Him-seemed he heard a voice he knew—
Or a dream of while agone.
Him-seemed bright raiment towards him drew—
Or bright the sun-set shone.

She stood before him face to face,
With the sun-beam thwart her hand,
As on the gold of the Holy Place
The painted angels stand.

With many a kiss she closed his eyes;
She kissed him cheek and chin:
E'en so in the painted Paradise
Are Earth's folk welcomed in.

There in the door the green-coats stood,
O'er the bows went up the cry,
"O welcome, Rafe, to the free green-wood,
With us to live and die."

It was bill and bow by the high-seat stood,
And they cried above the bows,
"Now welcome, Rafe, to the good green-wood,
And welcome Kate the Rose!"

White, white in the moon is the woodland plash,
White is the woodland glade,
Forth wend those twain, from oak to ash,
With light hearts unafraid.

The summer moon high o'er the hill,
All silver-white is she,
And Sir Rafe's good men with bow and bill,
They go by two and three.

In the fair green-wood where lurks no fear,
Where the King's writ runneth not,
There dwell they, friends and fellows dear,
While summer days are hot.

And when the leaf from the oak-tree falls,

And winds blow rough and strong,
With the carles of the woodland thorps and halls
They dwell, and fear no wrong.

And there the merry yule they make,
And see the winter wane,
And fain are they for true-love's sake,
And the folk thereby are fain.

For the ploughing carle and the straying herd
Flee never for Sir Rafe:
No barefoot maiden wends afeard,
And she deems the thicket safe.

But sore adread do the chapmen ride;
Wide round the wood they go;
And the judge and the sergeants wander wide,
Lest they plead before the bow.

Well learned and wise is Sir Rafe's good sword,
And straight the arrows fly,
And they find the coat of many a lord,
And the crest that rideth high.

THE DAY OF DAYS

Each eve earth falleth down the dark,
As though its hope were o'er;
Yet lurks the sun when day is done
Behind to-morrow's door.

Grey grows the dawn while men-folk sleep,
Unseen spreads on the light,
Till the thrush sings to the coloured things,
And earth forgets the night.

No otherwise wends on our Hope:
E'en as a tale that's told
Are fair lives lost, and all the cost
Of wise and true and bold.

We've toiled and failed; we spake the word;
None hearkened; dumb we lie;
Our Hope is dead, the seed we spread
Fell o'er the earth to die.

What's this? For joy our hearts stand still,
And life is loved and dear,
The lost and found the Cause hath crowned,
The Day of Days is here.

TO THE MUSE OF THE NORTH

O muse that swayest the sad Northern Song,
Thy right hand full of smiting and of wrong,
Thy left hand holding pity; and thy breast
Heaving with hope of that so certain rest:
Thou, with the grey eyes kind and unafraid,
The soft lips trembling not, though they have said
The doom of the World and those that dwell therein.
The lips that smile not though thy children win
The fated Love that draws the fated Death.
O, borne adown the fresh stream of thy breath,
Let some word reach my ears and touch my heart,
That, if it may be, I may have a part
In that great sorrow of thy children dead
That vexed the brow, and bowed adown the head,
Whitened the hair, made life a wondrous dream,
And death the murmur of a restful stream,
But left no stain upon those souls of thine
Whose greatness through the tangled world doth shine.
O Mother, and Love and Sister all in one,
Come thou; for sure I am enough alone
That thou thine arms about my heart shouldst throw,
And wrap me in the grief of long ago.

OF THE THREE SEEKERS

There met three knights on the woodland,
And the first was clad in silk array:
The second was dight in iron and steel,
But the third was rags from head to heel.
"Lo, now is the year and the day come round
When we must tell what we have found."
The first said: "I have found a king
Who grudgeth no gift of anything."
The second said: "I have found a knight
Who hath never turned his back in fight."
But the third said: "I have found a love
That Time and the World shall never move."

Whither away to win good cheer?
"With me," said the first, "for my king is near."
So to the King they went their ways;
But there was a change of times and days.
"What men are ye," the great King said,
"That ye should eat my children's bread?
My waste has fed full many a store,
And mocking and grudge have I gained therefore.
Whatever waneth as days wax old.
Full worthy to win are goods and gold."

Whither away to win good cheer?
"With me," said the second, "my knight is near.
So to the knight they went their ways,
But there was a change of times and days.
He dwelt in castle sure and strong,
For fear lest aught should do him wrong.

Guards by gate and hall there were,
And folk went in and out in fear.
When he heard the mouse run in the wall,
"Hist!" he said, "what next shall befall?
Draw not near, speak under your breath,
For all new-comers tell of death.
Bring me no song nor minstrelsy,
Round death it babbleth still," said he.
"And what is fame and the praise of men,
When lost life cometh not again?"

Whither away to seek good cheer?
"Ah me!" said the third, "that my love were anear!
Were the world as little as it is wide,
In a happy house should ye abide.
Were the world as kind as it is hard,
Ye should behold a fair reward."

So far by high and low have they gone,
They have come to a waste was rock and stone.
But lo, from the waste, a company
Full well bedight came riding by;
And in the midst, a queen, so fair,
That God wrought well in making her.

The first and second knights abode
To gaze upon her as she rode,
Forth passed the third with head down bent,
And stumbling ever as he went.
His shoulder brushed her saddle-bow;
He trembled with his head hung low.
His hand brushed o'er her golden gown,

As on the waste he fell adown.
So swift to earth her feet she set,
It seemed that there her arms he met.
His lips that looked the stone to meet
Were on her trembling lips and sweet.
Softly she kissed him cheek and chin,
His mouth her many tears drank in.
"Where would'st thou wander, love," she said,
"Now I have drawn thee from the dead?"
"I go my ways," he said, "and thine
Have nought to do with grief and pine."
"All ways are one way now," she said,
"Since I have drawn thee from the dead."
Said he, "But I must seek again
Where first I met thee in thy pain:
I am not clad so fair," said he,
"But yet the old hurts thou may'st see.
And thou, but for thy gown of gold,
A piteous tale of thee were told."
"There is no pain on earth," she said,
"Since I have drawn thee from the dead."
"And parting waiteth for us there,"
Said he, "as it was yester-year."
"Yet first a space of love," she said,
"Since I have drawn thee from the dead."
He laughed; said he, "Hast thou a home
Where I and these my friends may come?"
Laughing, "The world's my home," she said,
"Now I have drawn thee from the dead.
Yet somewhere is a space thereof
Where I may dwell beside my love.
There clear the river grows for him

Till o'er its stones his keel shall swim.
There faint the thrushes in their song,
And deem he tarrieth overlong.
There summer-tide is waiting now
Until he bids the roses blow.
Come, tell my flowery fields," she said,
"How I have drawn thee from the dead."

Whither away to win good cheer?
"With me," he said, "for my love is here.
The wealth of my house it waneth not;
No gift it giveth is forgot.
No fear my house may enter in,
For nought is there that death may win.
Now life is little, and death is nought,
Since all is found that erst I sought."

LOVE'S GLEANING-TIDE

Draw not away thy hands, my love,
With wind alone the branches move,
And though the leaves be scant above
The Autumn shall not shame us.

Say; Let the world wax cold and drear,
What is the worst of all the year
But life, and what can hurt us, dear,
Or death, and who shall blame us?

Ah, when the summer comes again
How shall we say, we sowed in vain?
The root was joy, the stem was pain,
The ear a nameless blending.

The root is dead and gone, my love,
The stem's a rod our truth to prove;
The ear is stored for nought to move
Till heaven and earth have ending.

THE MESSAGE OF THE MARCH WIND

Fair now is the spring-tide, now earth lies beholding
With the eyes of a lover, the face of the sun;
Long lasteth the daylight, and hope is enfolding
The green-growing acres with increase begun.

Now sweet, sweet it is through the land to be straying
'Mid the birds and the blossoms and the beasts of the
field;
Love mingles with love, and no evil is weighing
On thy heart or mine, where all sorrow is healed.

From township to township, o'er down and by tillage
Fair, far have we wandered and long was the day;
But now cometh eve at the end of the village,
Where over the grey wall the church riseth grey.

There is wind in the twilight; in the white road before us
The straw from the ox-yard is blowing about;
The moon's rim is rising, a star glitters o'er us,
And the vane on the spire-top is swinging in doubt.

Down there dips the highway, toward the bridge crossing
over
The brook that runs on to the Thames and the sea.
Draw closer, my sweet, we are lover and lover;
This eve art thou given to gladness and me.

Shall we be glad always? Come closer and hearken:
Three fields further on, as they told me down there,
When the young moon has set, if the March sky should

darken,
>We might see from the hill-top the great city's glare.

Hark, the wind in the elm-boughs! from London it
bloweth,
>And telleth of gold, and of hope and unrest;
>Of power that helps not; of wisdom that knoweth,
>But teacheth not aught of the worst and the best.

Of the rich men it telleth, and strange is the story
>How they have, and they hanker, and grip far and wide;
>And they live and they die, and the earth and its glory
>Has been but a burden they scarce might abide.

Hark! the March wind again of a people is telling;
>Of the life that they live there, so haggard and grim,
>That if we and our love amidst them had been dwelling
>My fondness had faltered, thy beauty grown dim.

This land we have loved in our love and our leisure
>For them hangs in heaven, high out of their reach;
>The wide hills o'er the sea-plain for them have no plea-
sure,
>The grey homes of their fathers no story to teach.

The singers have sung and the builders have builded,
>The painters have fashioned their tales of delight;
>For what and for whom hath the world's book been gild-
ed,
>When all is for these but the blackness of night?

How long, and for what is their patience abiding?

How oft and how oft shall their story be told,
While the hope that none seeketh in darkness is hiding,
And in grief and in sorrow the world groweth old?

Come back to the inn, love, and the lights and the fire,
And the fiddler's old tune and the shuffling of feet;
For there in a while shall be rest and desire,
And there shall the morrow's uprising be sweet.

Yet, love, as we wend, the wind bloweth behind us,
And beareth the last tale it telleth to-night,
How here in the spring-tide the message shall find us;
For the hope that none seeketh is coming to light.

Like the seed of mid-winter, unheeded, unperished,
Like the autumn-sown wheat 'neath the snow lying
green,
Like the love that overtook us, unawares and uncher-
ished,
Like the babe 'neath thy girdle that groweth unseen;

So the hope of the people now buddeth and groweth,
Rest fadeth before it, and blindness and fear;
It biddeth us learn all the wisdom it knoweth;
It hath found us and held us, and biddeth us hear:

For it beareth the message: "Rise up on the morrow
And go on your ways toward the doubt and the strife;
Join hope to our hope and blend sorrow with sorrow.
And seek for men's love in the short days of life."

41

But lo, the old inn, and the lights, and the fire,
And the fiddler's old tune and the shuffling of feet;
Soon for us shall be quiet and rest and desire,
And to-morrow's uprising to deeds shall be sweet.

A DEATH SONG

What cometh here from west to east awending?
And who are these, the marchers stern and slow?
We bear the message that the rich are sending
Aback to those who bade them wake and know.
Not one, not one, nor thousands must they slay,
But one and all if they would dusk the day.

We asked them for a life of toilsome earning,
They bade us bide their leisure for our bread;
We craved to speak to tell our woeful learning:
We come back speechless, bearing back our dead.
Not one, not one, nor thousands must they slay,
But one and all if they would dusk the day.

They will not learn; they have no ears to hearken.
They turn their faces from the eyes of fate;
Their gay-lit halls shut out the skies that darken.
But, lo! this dead man knocking at the gate.
Not one, not one, nor thousands must they slay,
But one and all if they would dusk the day.

Here lies the sign that we shall break our prison;
Amidst the storm he won a prisoner's rest;
But in the cloudy dawn the sun arisen
Brings us our day of work to win the best.
Not one, not one, nor thousands must they slay,
But one and all if they would dusk the day.

ICELAND FIRST SEEN

Lo from our loitering ship
a new land at last to be seen;
Toothed rocks down the side of the firth
on the east guard a weary wide lea,
And black slope the hillsides above,
striped adown with their desolate green:
And a peak rises up on the west
from the meeting of cloud and of sea,
Foursquare from base unto point
like the building of Gods that have been,
The last of that waste of the mountains
all cloud-wreathed and snow-flecked and grey,
And bright with the dawn that began
just now at the ending of day.

Ah! what came we forth for to see
that our hearts are so hot with desire?
Is it enough for our rest,
the sight of this desolate strand,
And the mountain-waste voiceless as death
but for winds that may sleep not nor tire?
Why do we long to wend forth
through the length and breadth of a land,
Dreadful with grinding of ice,
and record of scarce hidden fire,
But that there 'mid the grey grassy dales
sore scarred by the ruining streams
Lives the tale of the Northland of old
and the undying glory of dreams?

O land, as some cave by the sea
where the treasures of old have been laid,
The sword it may be of a king
whose name was the turning of fight:
Or the staff of some wise of the world
that many things made and unmade.
Or the ring of a woman maybe
whose woe is grown wealth and delight.
No wheat and no wine grows above it,
no orchard for blossom and shade;
The few ships that sail by its blackness
but deem it the mouth of a grave;
Yet sure when the world shall awaken,
this too shall be mighty to save.

Or rather, O land, if a marvel
it seemeth that men ever sought
Thy wastes for a field and a garden
fulfilled of all wonder and doubt,
And feasted amidst of the winter
when the fight of the year had been fought,
Whose plunder all gathered together
was little to babble about;
Cry aloud from thy wastes, O thou land,
"Not for this nor for that was I wrought
Amid waning of realms and of riches
and death of things worshipped and sure,
I abide here the spouse of a God,
and I made and I make and endure."

O Queen of the grief without knowledge,
of the courage that may not avail,

Of the longing that may not attain,
of the love that shall never forget,
More joy than the gladness of laughter
thy voice hath amidst of its wail:
More hope than of pleasure fulfilled
amidst of thy blindness is set;
More glorious than gaining of all
thine unfaltering hand that shall fail:
For what is the mark on thy brow
but the brand that thy Brynhild doth bear?
Lone once, and loved and undone
by a love that no ages outwear.

Ah! when thy Balder comes back,
and bears from the heart of the Sun
Peace and the healing of pain,
and the wisdom that waiteth no more;
And the lilies are laid on thy brow
'mid the crown of the deeds thou hast done;
And the roses spring up by thy feet
that the rocks of the wilderness wore.
Ah! when thy Balder comes back
and we gather the gains he hath won,
Shall we not linger a little
to talk of thy sweetness of old,
Yea, turn back awhile to thy travail
whence the Gods stood aloof to behold?

THE RAVEN AND THE KING'S DAUGHTER

THE RAVEN

King's daughter sitting in tower so high,
Fair summer is on many a shield.
Why weepest thou as the clouds go by?
Fair sing the swans 'twixt firth and field.
Why weepest thou in the window-seat
Till the tears run through thy fingers sweet?

THE KING'S DAUGHTER

I weep because I sit alone
Betwixt these walls of lime and stone.
Fair folk are in my father's hall,
But for me he built this guarded wall.
And here the gold on the green I sew
Nor tidings of my true-love know.

THE RAVEN

King's daughter, sitting above the sea,
I shall tell thee a tale shall gladden thee.
Yestreen I saw a ship go forth
When the wind blew merry from the north.
And by the tiller Steingrim sat,
And O, but my heart was glad thereat!
For 'twixt ashen plank and dark blue sea
His sword sang sweet of deeds to be.

THE KING'S DAUGHTER

O barren sea, thou bitter bird,
And a barren tale my ears have heard.

THE RAVEN

Thy father's men were hard thereby
In byrny bright and helmet high.

THE KING'S DAUGHTER

O worser waxeth thy story far,
For these drew upon me bolt and bar.
Fly south, O fowl, to the field of death
For nothing sweet thy grey neb saith.

THE RAVEN

O, there was Olaf the lily-rose,
As fair as any oak that grows.

THE KING'S DAUGHTER

O sweet bird, what did he then
Among the spears of my father's men?

THE RAVEN

'Twixt ashen plank and dark blue sea,
He sang: My true love waiteth me.

THE KING'S DAUGHTER

As well as this dull floor knows my feet,
I am not weary yet, my sweet.

THE RAVEN

He sang: As once her hand I had,
Her lips at last shall make me glad.

THE KING'S DAUGHTER

As once our fingers met, O love,
So shall our lips be fain thereof.

THE RAVEN

He sang: Come wrack and iron and flame,
For what shall breach the wall but fame?

THE KING'S DAUGHTER

Be swift to rise and set, O Sun,
Lest life 'twixt hope and death be done.

THE RAVEN

King's daughter sitting in tower so high,
A gift for my tale ere forth I fly,
The gold from thy finger fair and fine,
Thou hadst it from no love of thine.

THE KING'S DAUGHTER

By my father's ring another there is,
I had it with my mother's kiss.
Fly forth, O fowl, across the sea
To win another gift of me.
Fly south to bring me tidings true,
Fair summer is on many a shield.
Of the eve grown red with the battle-dew,
Fair sing the swans 'twixt firth and field.

THE RAVEN

King's daughter sitting in tower so high,
Fair summer is on many a shield.
Tidings to hearken ere thou die,
Fair sing the swans 'twixt firth and field.
In the Frankish land the spear points met,
And wide about the field was wet.
And high ere the cold moon quenched the sun,
Blew Steingrim's horn for battle won.

THE KING'S DAUGHTER

Fair fall thee, fowl! Tell tidings true
Of deeds that men that day did do.

THE RAVEN

Steingrim before his banner went,
And helms were broke and byrnies rent.

THE KING'S DAUGHTER

A doughty man and good at need;
Tell men of any other's deed?

THE RAVEN

Where Steingrim through the battle bore
Still Olaf went a foot before.

THE KING'S DAUGHTER

O fair with deeds the world doth grow!
Where is my true-love gotten now?

THE RAVEN

Upon the deck beside the mast
He lieth now, and sleepeth fast.

THE KING'S DAUGHTER

Heard'st thou before his sleep began
That he spake word of any man?

THE RAVEN

Methought of thee he sang a song,
But nothing now he saith for long.

THE KING'S DAUGHTER

And wottest thou where he will wend
With the world before him from end to end?

THE RAVEN

Before the battle joined that day
Steingrim a word to him did say:
"If we bring the banner back in peace,
In the King's house much shall my fame increase;
Till there no guarded door shall be
But it shall open straight to me.
Then to the bower we twain shall go
Where thy love the golden seam doth sew.
I shall bring thee in and lay thine hand
About the neck of that lily-wand.
And let the King be lief or loth
One bed that night shall hold you both."
Now north belike runs Steingrim's prow,
And the rain and the wind from the south do blow.

THE KING'S DAUGHTER

Lo, fowl of death, my mother's ring,
But the bridal song I must learn to sing.
And fain were I for a space alone,
For O the wind, and the wind doth moan.
And I must array the bridal bed,
Fair summer is on many a shield.
For O the rain, and the rain drifts red!
Fair sing the swans 'twixt firth and field.

Before the day from the night was born,
Fair summer is on many a shield.
She heard the blast of Steingrim's horn,
Fair sing the swans 'twixt firth and field.
Before the day was waxen fair
Were Steingrim's feet upon the stair.
"O bolt and bar they fall away,
But heavy are Steingrim's feet to-day."
"O heavy the feet of one who bears
The longing of days and the grief of years!
Lie down, lie down, thou lily-wand
That on thy neck I may lay his hand.
Whether the King be lief or loth
To-day one bed shall hold you both.
O thou art still as he is still,
So sore as ye longed to talk your fill
And good it were that I depart,
Now heart is laid so close to heart.
For sure ye shall talk so left alone
Fair summer is on many a shield.
Of days to be below the stone."
Fair sing the swans 'twixt firth and field.

SPRING'S BEDFELLOW

Spring went about the woods to-day,
The soft-foot winter-thief,
And found where idle sorrow lay
'Twixt flower and faded leaf.

She looked on him, and found him fair
For all she had been told;
She knelt adown beside him there,
And sang of days of old.

His open eyes beheld her nought,
Yet 'gan his lips to move;
But life and deeds were in her thought,
And he would sing of love.

So sang they till their eyes did meet,
And faded fear and shame;
More bold he grew, and she more sweet,
Until they sang the same.

Until, say they who know the thing,
Their very lips did kiss,
And Sorrow laid abed with Spring
Begat an earthly bliss.

MEETING IN WINTER

Winter in the world it is,
Round about the unhoped kiss
Whose dream I long have sorrowed o'er;
Round about the longing sore,
That the touch of thee shall turn
Into joy too deep to burn.

Round thine eyes and round thy mouth
Passeth no murmur of the south,
When my lips a little while
Leave thy quivering tender smile,
As we twain, hand holding hand,
Once again together stand.

Sweet is that, as all is sweet;
For the white drift shalt thou meet,
Kind and cold-cheeked and mine own,
Wrapped about with deep-furred gown
In the broad-wheeled chariot:
Then the north shall spare us not;
The wide-reaching waste of snow
Wilder, lonelier yet shall grow
As the reddened sun falls down.
But the warders of the town,
When they flash the torches out
O'er the snow amid their doubt,
And their eyes at last behold
Thy red-litten hair of gold;
Shall they open, or in fear
Cry, "Alas! what cometh here?

Whence hath come this Heavenly One
To tell of all the world undone?"

They shall open, and we shall see
The long street litten scantily
By the long stream of light before
The guest-hall's half-open door;
And our horses' bells shall cease
As we reach the place of peace;
Thou shalt tremble, as at last
The worn threshold is o'er-past,
And the fire-light blindeth thee:
Trembling shalt thou cling to me
As the sleepy merchants stare
At thy cold hands slim and fair
Thy soft eyes and happy lips
Worth all lading of their ships.

O my love, how sweet and sweet
That first kissing of thy feet,
When the fire is sunk alow,
And the hall made empty now
Groweth solemn, dim and vast!
O my love, the night shall last
Longer than men tell thereof
Laden with our lonely love!

THE TWO SIDES OF THE RIVER

THE YOUTHS

O winter, O white winter, wert thou gone,
No more within the wilds were I alone,
Leaping with bent bow over stock and stone!

No more alone my love the lamp should burn,
Watching the weary spindle twist and turn,
Or o'er the web hold back her tears and yearn:
O winter, O white winter, wert thou gone!

THE MAIDENS

Sweet thoughts fly swiftlier than the drifting snow,
And with the twisting threads sweet longings grow,
And o'er the web sweet pictures come and go,
For no white winter are we long alone.

THE YOUTHS

O stream so changed, what hast thou done to me,
That I thy glittering ford no more can see
Wreathing with white her fair feet lovingly?

See, in the rain she stands, and, looking down
With frightened eyes upon thy whirlpools brown,
Drops to her feet again her girded gown.
O hurrying turbid stream, what hast thou done?

THE MAIDENS

The clouds lift, telling of a happier day
When through the thin stream I shall take my way,
Girt round with gold, and garlanded with may,
What rushing stream can keep us long alone?

THE YOUTHS

O burning Sun, O master of unrest,
Why must we, toiling, cast away the best,
Now, when the bird sleeps by her empty nest?

See, with my garland lying at her feet,
In lonely labour stands mine own, my sweet,
Above the quern half-filled with half-ground wheat.
O red taskmaster, that thy flames were done!

THE MAIDENS

O love, to-night across the half-shorn plain
Shall I not go to meet the yellow wain,
A look of love at end of toil to gain?
What flaming sun can keep us long alone?

THE YOUTHS

To-morrow, said I, is grape gathering o'er;
To-morrow, and our loves are twinned no more.
To-morrow came, to bring us woe and war.

What have I done, that I should stand with these

Hearkening the dread shouts borne upon the breeze,
While she, far off, sits weeping 'neath her trees?
Alas, O kings, what is it ye have done?

THE MAIDENS

Come, love, delay not; come, and slay my dread!
Already is the banquet table spread;
In the cool chamber flower-strewn is my bed:
Come, love, what king shall keep us long alone?

THE YOUTHS

O city, city, open thou thy gate!
See, with life snatched from out the hand of fate!
How on thy glittering triumph I must wait!

Are not her hands stretched out to me? Her eyes,
Grow they not weary as each new hope dies,
And lone before her still the long road lies?
O golden city, fain would I be gone!

THE MAIDENS

And thou art happy, amid shouts and songs,
And all that unto conquering men belongs.
Night hath no fear for me, and day no wrongs.
What brazen city gates can keep us, lone?

THE YOUTHS

O long, long road, how bare thou art, and grey!

Hill after hill thou climbest, and the day
Is ended now, O moonlit endless way!

And she is standing where the rushes grow,
And still with white hand shades her anxious brow,
Though 'neath the world the sun is fallen now,
O dreary road, when will thy leagues be done?

THE MAIDENS

O tremblest thou, grey road, or do my feet
Tremble with joy, thy flinty face to meet?
Because my love's eyes soon mine eyes shall greet?
No heart thou hast to keep us long alone.

THE YOUTHS

O wilt thou ne'er depart, thou heavy night?
When will thy slaying bring on the morning bright,
That leads my weary feet to my delight?

Why lingerest thou, filling with wandering fears
My lone love's tired heart; her eyes with tears
For thoughts like sorrow for the vanished years?
Weaver of ill thoughts, when wilt thou be gone?

THE MAIDENS

Love, to the east are thine eyes turned as mine,
In patient watching for the night's decline?
And hast thou noted this grey widening line?
Can any darkness keep us long alone?

THE YOUTHS

O day, O day, is it a little thing
That thou so long unto thy life must cling,
Because I gave thee such a welcoming?

I called thee king of all felicity,
I praised thee that thou broughtest joy so nigh;
Thine hours are turned to years, thou wilt not die;
O day so longed for, would that thou wert gone!

THE MAIDENS

The light fails, love; the long day soon shall be
Nought but a pensive happy memory
Blessed for the tales it told to thee and me.
How hard it was, O love, to be alone.

LOVE FULFILLED

Hast thou longed through weary days
For the sight of one loved face?
Hast thou cried aloud for rest,
Mid the pain of sundering hours;
Cried aloud for sleep and death,
Since the sweet unhoped for best
Was a shadow and a breath?
O, long now, for no fear lowers
O'er these faint feet-kissing flowers.
O, rest now; and yet in sleep
All thy longing shalt thou keep.

Thou shalt rest and have no fear
Of a dull awaking near,
Of a life for ever blind,
Uncontent and waste and wide.
Thou shalt wake and think it sweet
That thy love is near and kind.
Sweeter still for lips to meet;
Sweetest that thine heart doth hide
Longing all unsatisfied
With all longing's answering
Howsoever close ye cling.

Thou rememberest how of old
E'en thy very pain grew cold,
How thou might'st not measure bliss
E'en when eyes and hands drew nigh.
Thou rememberest all regret
For the scarce remembered kiss.

The lost dream of how they met,
Mouths once parched with misery.
Then seemed Love born but to die,
Now unrest, pain, bliss are one,
Love, unhidden and alone.

THE KING OF DENMARK'S SONS

In Denmark gone is many a year,
So fair upriseth the rim of the sun,
Two sons of Gorm the King there were,
So grey is the sea when day is done.

Both these were gotten in lawful bed
Of Thyrre Denmark's Surety-head.

Fair was Knut of face and limb
As the breast of the Queen that suckled him.

But Harald was hot of hand and heart
As lips of lovers ere they part.

Knut sat at home in all men's love,
But over the seas must Harald rove.

And for every deed by Harald won,
Gorm laid more love on Knut alone.

On a high-tide spake the King in hall,
"Old I grow as the leaves that fall.

"Knut shall reign when I am dead,
So shall the land have peace and aid.

"But many a ship shall Harald have,
For I deem the sea well wrought for his grave."

Then none spake save the King again,

"If Knut die all my days be vain.

"And whoso the tale of his death shall tell,
Hath spoken a word to gain him hell.

"Lo here a doom I will not break,"
So fair upriseth the rim of the sun.
"For life or death or any man's sake,"
So grey is the sea when day is done.

O merry days in the summer-tide!
So fair upriseth the rim of the sun.
When the ships sail fair and the young men ride,
So grey is the sea when day is done.

Now Harald has got him east away,
And each morrow of fight was a gainful day.

But Knut is to his fosterer gone
To deal in deeds of peace alone.

So wear the days, and well it is
Such lovely lords should dwell in bliss.

O merry in the winter-tide
When men to Yule-feast wend them wide.

And here lieth Knut in the Lima-firth
When the lift is low o'er the Danish earth.

"Tell me now, Shipmaster mine,
What are yon torches there that shine?"

"Lord, no torches may these be
But golden prows across the sea.

"For over there the sun shines now
And the gold worms gape from every prow."

The sun and the wind came down o'er the sea,
"Tell them over how many they be!"

"Ten I tell with shield-hung sides.
Nought but a fool his death abides."

"Ten thou tellest, and we be three,
Good need that we do manfully.

"Good fellows, grip the shield and spear
For Harald my brother draweth near.

"Well breakfast we when night is done,
And Valhall's cock crows up the sun."

Up spoke Harald in wrathful case:
"I would have word with this waxen face!

"What wilt thou pay, thou huckstered
That I let thee live another year?

"For oath that thou wilt never reign
Will I let thee live a year or twain."

"Kisses and love shalt thou have of me
If yet my liegeman thou wilt be.

"But stroke of sword, and dint of axe,
Or ere thou makest my face as wax."

As thick the arrows fell around
As fall sere leaves on autumn ground.

In many a cheek the red did wane
No maid might ever kiss again.

"Lay me aboard," Lord Harald said,
"The winter day will soon be dead!

"Lay me aboard the bastard's ship,
And see to it lest your grapnels slip!"

Then some they knelt and some they drowned,
And some lay dead Lord Knut around.

"Look here at the wax-white corpse of him,
As fair as the Queen in face and limb!

"Make now for the shore, for the moon is bright,
And I would be home ere the end of night.

"Two sons last night had Thyrre the Queen,
So fair upriseth the rim of the sun.
And both she may lack ere the woods wax green,"
So grey is the sea when day is done.

A little before the morning tide,
So fair upriseth the rim of the sun,
Queen Thyrre looked out of her window-side,
So grey is the sea when day is done.

"O men-at-arms, what men be ye?"
"Harald thy son come over the sea."

"Why is thy face so pale, my son?"
"It may be red or day is done."

"O evil words of an evil hour!
Come, sweet son, to thy mother's bower!"

None from the Queen's bower went that day
Till dark night over the meadows lay.

None thenceforth heard wail or cry
Till the King's feast was waxen high.

Then into the hall Lord Harald came
When the great wax lights were all aflame.

"What tidings, son, dost thou bear to me?
Speak out before I drink with thee."

"Tidings small for a seafarer.
Two falcons in the sea-cliffs were;

"And one was white and one was grey,
And they fell to battle on a day;

"They fought in the sun, they fought in the wind,
No boot the white fowl's wounds to bind.

"They fought in the wind, they fought in the sun,
And the white fowl died when the play was done."

"Small tidings these to bear o'er the sea!
Good hap that nothing worser they be!

"Small tidings for a travelled man!
Drink with me, son, whiles yet ye can!

"Drink with me ere thy day and mine,
So fair upriseth the rim of the sun,
Be nought but a tale told over the wine."
So grey is the sea when day is done.

Now fareth the King with his men to sleep,
So fair upriseth the rim of the sun,
And dim the maids from the Queen's bower creep,
So grey is the sea when day is done.

And in the hall is little light,
And there standeth the Queen with cheeks full white.

And soft the feet of women fall
From end to end of the King's great hall.

These bear the gold-wrought cloths away,

And in other wise the hall array;

Till all is black that hath been gold
So heavy a tale there must be told.

The morrow men looked on King Gorm and said,
"Hath he dreamed a dream or beheld the dead?

"Why is he sad who should be gay?
Why are the old man's lips so grey?"

Slow paced the King adown the hall,
Nor looked aside to either wall,

Till in high-seat there he sat him down,
And deadly old men deemed him grown.

"O Queen, what thrall's hands durst do this,
To strip my hall of mirth and bliss?"

"No thrall's hands in the hangings were,
No thrall's hands made the tenters bare.

"King's daughters' hands have done the deed,
The hands of Denmark's Surety-head."

"Nought betters the deed thy word unsaid.
Tell me that Knut my son is dead!"

She said: "The doom on thee, O King!
For thine own lips have said the thing."

Men looked to see the King arise,
The death of men within his eyes.

Men looked to see his bitter sword
That once cleared ships from board to board.

But in the hall no sword gleamed wide,
His hand fell down along his side.

No red there came into his cheek,
He fell aback as one made weak.

His wan cheek brushed the high-seat's side,
And in the noon of day he died.

So lieth King Gorm beneath the grass,
But from mouth to mouth this tale did pass.

And Harald reigned and went his way,
So fair upriseth the rim of the sun.
And still is the story told to-day,
So grey is the sea when day is done.

ON THE EDGE OF THE WILDERNESS

PUELLÆ

Whence comest thou, and whither goest thou?
Abide! abide! longer the shadows grow;
What hopest thou the dark to thee will show?

Abide! abide! for we are happy here.

AMANS

Why should I name the land across the sea
Wherein I first took hold on misery?
Why should I name the land that flees from me?

Let me depart, since ye are happy here.

PUELLÆ

What wilt thou do within the desert place
Whereto thou turnest now thy careful face?
Stay but a while to tell us of thy case.

Abide! abide! for we are happy here.

AMANS

What, nigh the journey's end shall I abide,
When in the waste mine own love wanders wide,
When from all men for me she still doth hide?

Let me depart, since ye are happy here.

PUELLÆ

Nay, nay; but rather she forgetteth thee,
To sit upon the shore of some warm sea,
Or in green gardens where sweet fountains be.

Abide! abide! for we are happy here.

AMANS

Will ye then keep me from the wilderness,
Where I at least, alone with my distress,
The quiet land of changing dreams may bless?

Let me depart, since ye are happy here.

PUELLÆ

Forget the false forgetter and be wise,
And 'mid these clinging hands and loving eyes,
Dream, not in vain, thou knowest paradise.

Abide! abide! for we are happy here.

AMANS

Ah! with your sweet eyes shorten not the day,
Nor let your gentle hands my journey stay!
Perchance love is not wholly cast away.

Let me depart, since ye are happy here.

PUELLÆ

Pluck love away as thou wouldst pluck a thorn
From out thy flesh; for why shouldst thou be born
To bear a life so wasted and forlorn?

Abide! abide! for we are happy here.

AMANS

Yea, why then was I born, since hope is pain,
And life a lingering death, and faith but vain,
And love the loss of all I seemed to gain?

Let me depart, since ye are happy here.

PUELLÆ

Dost thou believe that this shall ever be,
That in our land no face thou e'er shalt see,
No voice thou e'er shalt hear to gladden thee?

Abide! abide! for we are happy here.

AMANS

No longer do I know of good or bad,
I have forgotten that I once was glad;
I do but chase a dream that I have had.

Let me depart, since ye are happy here.

PUELLÆ

Stay! take one image for thy dreamful night;
Come, look at her, who in the world's despite
Weeps for delaying love and lost delight.

Abide! abide! for we are happy here.

AMANS

Mock me not till to-morrow. Mock the dead,
They will not heed it, or turn round the head,
To note who faithless are, and who are wed.

Let me depart, since ye are happy here.

PUELLÆ

We mock thee not. Hast thou not heard of those
Whose faithful love the loved heart holds so close,
That death must wait till one word lets it loose?

Abide! abide! for we are happy here.

AMANS

I hear you not: the wind from off the waste
Sighs like a song that bids me make good haste
The wave of sweet forgetfulness to taste.

Let me depart, since ye are happy here.

PUELLÆ

Come back! like such a singer is the wind,
As to a sad tune sings fair words and kind,
That he with happy tears all eyes may blind!

Abide! abide! for we are happy here.

AMANS

Did I not hear her sweet voice cry from far,
That o'er the lonely waste fair fields there are,
Fair days that know not any change or care?

Let me depart, since ye are happy here.

PUELLÆ

Oh, no! not far thou heardest her, but nigh;
Nigh, 'twixt the waste's edge and the darkling sky.
Turn back again, too soon it is to die.

Abide! a little while be happy here.

AMANS

How with the lapse of lone years could I strive,
And can I die now that thou biddest live?
What joy this space 'twixt birth and death can give.

Can we depart, who are so happy here?

A GARDEN BY THE SEA

I know a little garden-close,
Set thick with lily and red rose,
Where I would wander if I might
From dewy morn to dewy night,
And have one with me wandering.

And though within it no birds sing,
And though no pillared house is there,
And though the apple-boughs are bare
Of fruit and blossom, would to God
Her feet upon the green grass trod,
And I beheld them as before.

There comes a murmur from the shore,
And in the close two fair streams are,
Drawn from the purple hills afar,
Drawn down unto the restless sea:
Dark hills whose heath-bloom feeds no bee,
Dark shore no ship has ever seen,
Tormented by the billows green
Whose murmur comes unceasingly
Unto the place for which I cry.

For which I cry both day and night,
For which I let slip all delight,
Whereby I grow both deaf and blind,
Careless to win, unskilled to find,
And quick to lose what all men seek.

Yet tottering as I am and weak,

Still have I left a little breath
To seek within the jaws of death
An entrance to that happy place,
To seek the unforgotten face,
Once seen, once kissed, once reft from me
Anigh the murmuring of the sea.

MOTHER AND SON

Now sleeps the land of houses,
and dead night holds the street,
And there thou liest, my baby,
and sleepest soft and sweet;
My man is away for awhile,
but safe and alone we lie,
And none heareth thy breath but thy mother,
and the moon looking down from the sky
On the weary waste of the town,
as it looked on the grass-edged road
Still warm with yesterday's sun,
when I left my old abode;
Hand in hand with my love,
that night of all nights in the year;
When the river of love o'erflowed
and drowned all doubt and fear,
And we two were alone in the world,
and once if never again,
We knew of the secret of earth
and the tale of its labour and pain.

Lo amidst London I lift thee,
and how little and light thou art,
And thou without hope or fear
thou fear and hope of my heart!
Lo here thy body beginning,
O son, and thy soul and thy life;
But how will it be if thou livest,
and enterest into the strife,
And in love we dwell together

when the man is grown in thee,
When thy sweet speech I shall hearken,
and yet 'twixt thee and me
Shall rise that wall of distance,
that round each one doth grow,
And maketh it hard and bitter
each other's thought to know.

Now, therefore, while yet thou art little
and hast no thought of thine own,
I will tell thee a word of the world;
of the hope whence thou hast grown;
Of the love that once begat thee,
of the sorrow that hath made
Thy little heart of hunger,
and thy hands on my bosom laid.
Then mayst thou remember hereafter,
as whiles when people say
All this hath happened before
in the life of another day;
So mayst thou dimly remember
this tale of thy mother's voice,
As oft in the calm of dawning
I have heard the birds rejoice,
As oft I have heard the storm-wind
go moaning through the wood;
And I knew that earth was speaking,
and the mother's voice was good.

Now, to thee alone will I tell it
that thy mother's body is fair,
In the guise of the country maidens

Who play with the sun and the air;
Who have stood in the row of the reapers
in the August afternoon,
Who have sat by the frozen water
in the high day of the moon,
When the lights of the Christmas feasting
were dead in the house on the hill,
And the wild geese gone to the salt-marsh
had left the winter still.
Yea, I am fair, my firstling;
if thou couldst but remember me!
The hair that thy small hand clutcheth
is a goodly sight to see;
I am true, but my face is a snare;
soft and deep are my eyes,
And they seem for men's beguiling
fulfilled with the dreams of the wise.
Kind are my lips, and they look
as though my soul had learned
Deep things I have never heard of.
My face and my hands are burned
By the lovely sun of the acres;
three months of London town
And thy birth-bed have bleached them indeed,
"But lo, where the edge of the gown"
(So said thy father) "is parting
the wrist that is white as the curd
From the brown of the hand that I love,
bright as the wing of a bird."

Such is thy mother, O firstling,
yet strong as the maidens of old,

Whose spears and whose swords were the warders
of homestead, of field, and of fold.
Oft were my feet on the highway,
often they wearied the grass;
From dusk unto dusk of the summer
three times in a week would I pass
To the downs from the house on the river
through the waves of the blossoming corn.
Fair then I lay down in the even,
and fresh I arose on the morn,
And scarce in the noon was I weary.
Ah, son, in the days of thy strife,
If thy soul could but harbour a dream
of the blossom of my life!
It would be as the sunlit meadows
beheld from a tossing sea,
And thy soul should look on a vision
of the peace that is to be.

Yet, yet the tears on my cheek!
and what is this doth move
My heart to thy heart, beloved,
save the flood of yearning love?
For fair and fierce is thy father,
and soft and strange are his eyes
That look on the days that shall be
with the hope of the brave and the wise.
It was many a day that we laughed,
as over the meadows we walked,
And many a day I hearkened
and the pictures came as he talked;
It was many a day that we longed,

and we lingered late at eve
Ere speech from speech was sundered,
and my hand his hand could leave.
Then I wept when I was alone,
and I longed till the daylight came;
And down the stairs I stole,
and there was our housekeeping dame
(No mother of me, the foundling)
kindling the fire betimes
Ere the haymaking folk went forth
to the meadows down by the limes;
All things I saw at a glance;
the quickening fire-tongues leapt
Through the crackling heap of sticks,
and the sweet smoke up from it crept,
And close to the very hearth
the low sun flooded the floor,
And the cat and her kittens played
in the sun by the open door.
The garden was fair in the morning,
and there in the road he stood
Beyond the crimson daisies
and the bush of southernwood.
Then side by side together
through the grey-walled place we went,
And O the fear departed,
and the rest and sweet content!

Son, sorrow and wisdom he taught me,
and sore I grieved and learned
As we twain grew into one;
and the heart within me burned

With the very hopes of his heart.
Ah, son, it is piteous,
But never again in my life
shall I dare to speak to thee thus;
So may these lonely words
about thee creep and cling,
These words of the lonely night
in the days of our wayfaring.
Many a child of woman
to-night is born in the town,
The desert of folly and wrong;
and of what and whence are they grown?
Many and many an one
of wont and use is born;
For a husband is taken to bed
as a hat or a ribbon is worn.
Prudence begets her thousands;
"good is a housekeeper's life,
So shall I sell my body
that I may be matron and wife."
"And I shall endure foul wedlock
and bear the children of need."
Some are there born of hate,
many the children of greed.
"I, I too can be wedded,
though thou my love hast got."
"I am fair and hard of heart,
and riches shall be my lot."
And all these are the good and the happy,
on whom the world dawns fair.
O son, when wilt thou learn
of those that are born of despair,

As the fabled mud of the Nile
that quickens under the sun
With a growth of creeping things,
half dead when just begun?
E'en such is the care of Nature
that man should never die,
Though she breed of the fools of the earth,
and the dregs of the city sty.

But thou, O son, O son,
of very love wert born,
When our hope fulfilled bred hope,
and fear was a folly outworn.
On the eve of the toil and the battle
all sorrow and grief we weighed,
We hoped and we were not ashamed,
we knew and we were not afraid.

Now waneth the night and the moon;
ah, son, it is piteous
That never again in my life
shall I dare to speak to thee thus.
But sure from the wise and the simple
shall the mighty come to birth;
And fair were my fate, beloved,
if I be yet on the earth
When the world is awaken at last,
and from mouth to mouth they tell
Of thy love and thy deeds and thy valour,
and thy hope that nought can quell.

THUNDER IN THE GARDEN

When the boughs of the garden hang heavy with rain
And the blackbird reneweth his song,
And the thunder departing yet rolleth again,
I remember the ending of wrong.

When the day that was dusk while his death was aloof
Is ending wide-gleaming and strange
For the clearness of all things beneath the world's roof,
I call back the wild chance and the change.

For once we twain sat through the hot afternoon
While the rain held aloof for a while,
Till she, the soft-clad, for the glory of June
Changed all with the change of her smile.

For her smile was of longing, no longer of glee,
And her fingers, entwined with mine own,
With caresses unquiet sought kindness of me
For the gift that I never had known.

Then down rushed the rain, and the voice of the thunder
Smote dumb all the sound of the street,
And I to myself was grown nought but a wonder,
As she leaned down my kisses to meet.

That she craved for my lips that had craved her so often,
And the hand that had trembled to touch,
That the tears filled her eyes I had hoped not to soften
In this world was a marvel too much.

It was dusk 'mid the thunder, dusk e'en as the night,
When first brake out our love like the storm,
But no night-hour was it, and back came the light
While our hands with each other were warm.

And her smile killed with kisses, came back as at first
As she rose up and led me along,
And out to the garden, where nought was athirst,
And the blackbird renewing his song.

Earth's fragrance went with her, as in the wet grass,
Her feet little hidden were set;
She bent down her head, 'neath the roses to pass,
And her arm with the lily was wet.

In the garden we wandered while day waned apace
And the thunder was dying aloof;
Till the moon o'er the minster-wall lifted his face,
And grey gleamed out the lead of the roof.

Then we turned from the blossoms, and cold were they
grown:
In the trees the wind westering moved;
Till over the threshold back fluttered her gown,
And in the dark house was I loved.

THE GOD OF THE POOR

There was a lord that hight Maltete,
Among great lords he was right great,
On poor folk trod he like the dirt,
None but God might do him hurt.
Deus est Deus pauperum.

With a grace of prayers sung loud and late
Many a widow's house he ate;
Many a poor knight at his hands
Lost his house and narrow lands.
Deus est Deus pauperum.

He burnt the harvests many a time,
He made fair houses heaps of lime;
Whatso man loved wife or maid
Of Evil-head was sore afraid.
Deus est Deus pauperum.

He slew good men and spared the bad;
Too long a day the foul dog had,
E'en as all dogs will have their day;
But God is as strong as man, I say.
Deus est Deus pauperum.

For a valiant knight, men called Boncoeur,
Had hope he should not long endure,
And gathered to him much good folk,
Hardy hearts to break the yoke.
Deus est Deus pauperum.

But Boncoeur deemed it would be vain
To strive his guarded house to gain;
Therefore, within a little while,
He set himself to work by guile.
Deus est Deus pauperum.

He knew that Maltete loved right well
Red gold and heavy. If from hell
The Devil had cried, "Take this gold cup,"
Down had he gone to fetch it up.
Deus est Deus pauperum.

Twenty poor men's lives were nought
To him, beside a ring well wrought.
The pommel of his hunting-knife
Was worth ten times a poor man's life.
Deus est Deus pauperum.

A squire new-come from over-sea
Boncoeur called to him privily,
And when he knew his lord's intent,
Clad like a churl therefrom he went
Deus est Deus pauperum.

But when he came where dwelt Maltete,
With few words did he pass the gate,
For Maltete built him walls anew,
And, wageless, folk from field he drew.
Deus est Deus pauperum.

Now passed the squire through this and that,
Till he came to where Sir Maltete sat,

And over red wine wagged his beard:
Then spoke the squire as one afeard.
Deus est Deus pauperum.

"Lord, give me grace, for privily
I have a little word for thee."
"Speak out," said Maltete, "have no fear,
For how can thy life to thee be dear?"
Deus est Deus pauperum.

"Such an one I know," he said,
"Who hideth store of money red."
Maltete grinned at him cruelly:
"Thou florin-maker, come anigh."
Deus est Deus pauperum.

"E'en such as thou once preached of gold,
And showed me lies in books full old,
Nought gat I but evil brass,
Therefore came he to the worser pass."
Deus est Deus pauperum.

"Hast thou will to see his skin?
I keep my heaviest marks therein,
For since nought else of wealth had he,
I deemed full well he owed it me."
Deus est Deus pauperum.

"Nought know I of philosophy,"
The other said, "nor do I lie.
Before the moon begins to shine,
May all this heap of gold be thine."

Deus est Deus pauperum.

"Ten leagues from this a man there is,
Who seemeth to know but little bliss,
And yet full many a pound of gold
A dry well nigh his house doth hold."
Deus est Deus pauperum.

"John-a-Wood is he called, fair lord,
Nor know I whence he hath this hoard."
Then Maltete said, "As God made me,
A wizard over-bold is he!"
Deus est Deus pauperum.

"It were a good deed, as I am a knight,
To burn him in a fire bright;
This John-a-Wood shall surely die,
And his gold in my strong chest shall lie."
Deus est Deus pauperum.

"This very night, I make mine avow.
The truth of this mine eyes shall know."
Then spoke an old knight in the hall,
"Who knoweth what things may befall?"
Deus est Deus pauperum.

"I rede thee go with a great rout,
For thy foes they ride thick about."
"Thou and the devil may keep my foes,
Thou redest me this gold to lose."
Deus est Deus pauperum.

"I shall go with but some four or five,
So shall I take my thief alive.
For if a great rout he shall see,
Will he not hide his wealth from me?"
Deus est Deus pauperum.

The old knight muttered under his breath,
"Then mayhap ye shall but ride to death."
But Maltete turned him quickly round,
"Bind me this grey-beard under ground!"
Deus est Deus pauperum.

"Because ye are old, ye think to jape.
Take heed, ye shall not long escape.
When I come back safe, old carle, perdie,
Thine head shall brush the linden-tree."
Deus est Deus pauperum.

Therewith he rode with his five men,
And Boncoeur's spy, for good leagues ten,
Until they left the beaten way,
And dusk it grew at end of day.
Deus est Deus pauperum.

There, in a clearing of the wood,
Was John's house, neither fair nor good.
In a ragged plot his house anigh,
Thin coleworts grew but wretchedly.
Deus est Deus pauperum.

John-a-Wood in his doorway sat,
Turning over this and that,

And chiefly how he best might thrive,
For he had will enough to live.
Deus est Deus pauperum.

Green coleworts from a wooden bowl
He ate; but careful was his soul,
For if he saw another day,
Thenceforth was he in Boncoeur's pay.
Deus est Deus pauperum.

So when he saw how Maltete came,
He said, "Beginneth now the game!"
And in the doorway did he stand
Trembling, with hand joined fast to hand.
Deus est Deus pauperum.

When Maltete did this carle behold
Somewhat he doubted of his gold,
But cried out, "Where is now thy store
Thou hast through books of wicked lore?"
Deus est Deus pauperum.

Then said the poor man, right humbly,
"Fair lord, this was not made by me,
I found it in mine own dry well,
And had a mind thy grace to tell.
Deus est Deus pauperum.

"Therefrom, my lord, a cup I took
This day, that thou thereon mightst look,
And know me to be leal and true,"
And from his coat the cup he drew.

Deus est Deus pauperum.

Then Maltete took it in his hand,
Nor knew he aught that it used to stand
On Boncoeur's cupboard many a day.
"Go on," he said, "and show the way.
Deus est Deus pauperum.

"Give me thy gold, and thou shalt live,
Yea, in my house thou well mayst thrive."
John turned about and 'gan to go
Unto the wood with footsteps slow.
Deus est Deus pauperum.

But as they passed by John's woodstack,
Growled Maltete, "Nothing now doth lack
Wherewith to light a merry fire,
And give my wizard all his hire."
Deus est Deus pauperum.

The western sky was red as blood,
Darker grew the oaken-wood;
"Thief and carle, where are ye gone?
Why are we in the wood alone?
Deus est Deus pauperum.

"What is the sound of this mighty horn?
Ah, God! that ever I was born!
The basnets flash from tree to tree;
Show me, thou Christ, the way to flee!"

Deus est Deus pauperum.

Boncoeur it was with fifty men;
Maltete was but one to ten,
And his own folk prayed for grace,
With empty hands in that lone place.
Deus est Deus pauperum.

"Grace shall ye have," Boncoeur said,
"All of you but Evil-head."
Lowly could that great lord be,
Who could pray so well as he?
Deus est Deus pauperum.

Then could Maltete howl and cry,
Little will he had to die.
Soft was his speech, now it was late,
But who had will to save Maltete?
Deus est Deus pauperum.

They brought him to the house again,
And toward the road he looked in vain.
Lonely and bare was the great highway,
Under the gathering moonlight grey.
Deus est Deus pauperum.

They took off his gilt basnet,
That he should die there was no let;
They took off his coat of steel,
A damned man he well might feel.
Deus est Deus pauperum.

"Will ye all be rich as kings,
Lacking naught of all good things?"
"Nothing do we lack this eve;
When thou art dead, how can we grieve?"
Deus est Deus pauperum.

"Let me drink water ere I die,
None henceforth comes my lips anigh."
They brought it him in that bowl of wood.
He said, "This is but poor men's blood!"
Deus est Deus pauperum.

They brought it him in the cup of gold.
He said, "The women I have sold
Have wept it full of salt for me;
I shall die gaping thirstily."
Deus est Deus pauperum.

On the threshold of that poor homestead
They smote off his evil head;
They set it high on a great spear,
And rode away with merry cheer.
Deus est Deus pauperum.

At the dawn, in lordly state,
They rode to Maltete's castle-gate.
"Whoso willeth laud to win,
Make haste to let your masters in!"
Deus est Deus pauperum.

Forthwith opened they the gate,
No man was sorry for Maltete.

97

Boncoeur conquered all his lands,
A good knight was he of his hands.
Deus est Deus pauperum.

Good men he loved, and hated bad;
Joyful days and sweet he had;
Good deeds did he plenteously;
Beneath him folk lived frank and free.
Deus est Deus pauperum.

He lived long, with merry days;
None said aught of him but praise.
God on him have full mercy;
A good knight merciful was he.
Deus est Deus pauperum.

The great lord, called Maltete, is dead;
Grass grows above his feet and head,
And a holly-bush grows up between
His rib-bones gotten white and clean.
Deus est Deus pauperum.

A carle's sheep-dog certainly
Is a mightier thing than he.
Till London-bridge shall cross the Nen,
Take we heed of such-like men.
Deus est Deus pauperum.

LOVE'S REWARD

It was a knight of the southern land
Rode forth upon the way
When the birds sang sweet on either hand
About the middle of the May.

But when he came to the lily-close,
Thereby so fair a maiden stood,
That neither the lily nor the rose
Seemed any longer fair nor good.

"All hail, thou rose and lily-bough!
What dost thou weeping here,
For the days of May are sweet enow,
And the nights of May are dear?"

"Well may I weep and make my moan.
Who am bond and captive here;
Well may I weep who lie alone,
Though May be waxen dear."

"And is there none shall ransom thee?
Mayst thou no borrow find?"
"Nay, what man may my borrow be,
When all my wealth is left behind?"

"Perchance some ring is left with thee,
Some belt that did thy body bind?"
"Nay, no man may my borrow be,
My rings and belt are left behind."

"The shoes that the May-blooms kissed on thee
Might yet be things to some men's mind."
"Nay, no man may my borrow be,
My golden shoes are left behind."

"The milk-white sark that covered thee
A dear-bought token some should find."
"Nay, no man may my borrow be,
My silken sark is left behind."

"The kiss of thy mouth and the love of thee
Better than world's wealth should I find."
"Nay, thou mayst not my borrow be,
For all my love is left behind.

"A year agone come Midsummer-night
I woke by the Northern sea;
I lay and dreamed of my delight
Till love no more would let me be.

"Seaward I went by night and cloud
To hear the white swans sing;
But though they sang both clear and loud,
I hearkened a sweeter thing.

"O sweet and sweet as none may tell
Was the speech so close 'twixt lip and lip:
But fast, unseen, the black oars fell
That drave to shore the rover's ship.

"My love lay bloody on the strand
Ere stars were waxen wan:

Naught lacketh graves the Northern land
If to-day it lack a lovelier man.

"I sat and wept beside the mast
When the stars were gone away.
Naught lacketh the Northland joy gone past
If it lack the night and day."

"Is there no place in any land
Where thou wouldst rather be than here?"
"Yea, a lone grave on a cold sea-strand
My heart for a little holdeth dear."

"Of all the deeds that women do
Is there none shall bring thee some delight?"
"To lie down and die where lay we two
Upon Midsummer night."

"I will bring thee there where thou wouldst be,
A borrow shalt thou find."
"Wherewith shall I reward it thee
For wealth and good-hap left behind?"

"A kiss from lips that love not me,
A good-night somewhat kind;
A narrow house to share with thee
When we leave the world behind."

They have taken ship and sailed away
Across the Southland main;
They have sailed by hills were green and gay,
A land of goods and gain.

They have sailed by sea-cliffs stark and white
And hillsides fair enow;
They have sailed by lands of little night
Where great the groves did grow.

They have sailed by islands in the sea
That the clouds lay thick about;
And into a main where few ships be
Amidst of dread and doubt.

With broken mast and battered side
They drave amidst the tempest's heart;
But why should death to these betide
Whom love did hold so well apart?

The flood it drave them toward the strand,
The ebb it drew them fro;
The swallowing seas that tore the land
Cast them ashore and let them go.

"Is this the land? is this the land,
Where life and I must part a-twain?"
"Yea, this is e'en the sea-washed strand
That made me yoke-fellow of pain.

"The strand is this, the sea is this,
The grey bent and the mountains grey;

But no mound here his grave-mound is;
Where have they borne my love away?"

"What man is this with shield and spear
Comes riding down the bent to us?
A goodly man forsooth he were
But for his visage piteous."

"Ghost of my love, so kind of yore,
Art thou not somewhat gladder grown
To feel my feet upon this shore?
O love, thou shalt not long be lone."

"Ghost of my love, each day I come
To see where God first wrought us wrong:
Now kind thou com'st to call me home.
Be sure I shall not tarry long."

"Come here, my love; come here for rest,
So sore as my body longs for thee!
My heart shall beat against thy breast,
As arms of thine shall comfort me."

"Love, let thy lips depart no more
From those same eyes they once did kiss,
The very bosom wounded sore
When sorrow clave the heart of bliss!"

O was it day, or was it night,
As there they told their love again?

103

The high-tide of the sun's delight,
Or whirl of wind and drift of rain?

"Speak sweet, my love, of how it fell,
And how thou cam'st across the sea,
And what kind heart hath served thee well,
And who thy borrow there might be?"

Naught but the wind and sea made moan
As hastily she turned her round;
From light clouds wept the morn alone,
Not the dead corpse upon the ground.

"O look, my love, for here is he
Who once of all the world was kind,
And led my sad heart o'er the sea!
And now must he be left behind."

She kissed his lips that yet did smile,
She kissed his eyes that were not sad:
"O thou who sorrow didst beguile,
And now wouldst have me wholly glad!

"A little gift is this," she said,
"Thou once hadst deemed great gift enow;
Yet surely shalt thou rest thine head
Where I one day shall lie alow.

"There shalt thou wake to think of me,
And by thy face my face shall find;
And I shall then thy borrow be
When all the world is left behind."

THE FOLK-MOTE BY THE RIVER

It was up in the morn we rose betimes
From the hall-floor hard by the row of limes.

It was but John the Red and I,
And we were the brethren of Gregory;

And Gregory the Wright was one
Of the valiant men beneath the sun,

And what he bade us that we did
For ne'er he kept his counsel hid.

So out we went, and the clattering latch
Woke up the swallows under the thatch.

It was dark in the porch, but our scythes we felt,
And thrust the whetstone under the belt.

Through the cold garden boughs we went
Where the tumbling roses shed their scent.

Then out a-gates and away we strode
O'er the dewy straws on the dusty road,

And there was the mead by the town-reeve's close
Where the hedge was sweet with the wilding rose.

Then into the mowing grass we went
Ere the very last of the night was spent.

Young was the moon, and he was gone,
So we whet our scythes by the stars alone:

But or ever the long blades felt the hay
Afar in the East the dawn was grey.

Or ever we struck our earliest stroke
The thrush in the hawthorn-bush awoke.

While yet the bloom of the swathe was dim
The blackbird's bill had answered him.

Ere half of the road to the river was shorn
The sunbeam smote the twisted thorn.

Now wide was the way 'twixt the standing grass
For the townsfolk unto the mote to pass,

And so when all our work was done
We sat to breakfast in the sun,

While down in the stream the dragon-fly
'Twixt the quivering rushes flickered by;

And though our knives shone sharp and white
The swift bleak heeded not the sight.

So when the bread was done away
We looked along the new-shorn hay,

And heard the voice of the gathering-horn
Come over the garden and the corn;

For the wind was in the blossoming wheat
And drave the bees in the lime-boughs sweet.

Then loud was the horn's voice drawing near,
And it hid the talk of the prattling weir.

And now was the horn on the pathway wide
That we had shorn to the river-side.

So up we stood, and wide around
We sheared a space by the Elders' Mound;

And at the feet thereof it was
That highest grew the June-tide grass;

And over all the mound it grew
With clover blent, and dark of hue.

But never aught of the Elders' Hay
To rick or barn was borne away.

But it was bound and burned to ash
In the barren close by the reedy plash.

For 'neath that mound the valiant dead
Lay hearkening words of valiance said

When wise men stood on the Elders' Mound,
And the swords were shining bright around.

And now we saw the banners borne
On the first of the way that we had shorn;
So we laid the scythe upon the sward
And girt us to the battle-sword.

For after the banners well we knew
Were the Freemen wending two and two.

There then that highway of the scythe
With many a hue was brave and blythe.

And first below the Silver Chief
Upon the green was the golden sheaf.

And on the next that went by it
The White Hart in the Park did sit.

Then on the red the White Wings flew,
And on the White was the Cloud-fleck blue.

Last went the Anchor of the Wrights
Beside the Ship of the Faring-Knights.

Then thronged the folk the June-tide field
With naked sword and painted shield,

Till they came adown to the river-side,
And there by the mound did they abide.

Now when the swords stood thick and white

As the mace reeds stand in the streamless bight,

There rose a man on the mound alone
And over his head was the grey mail done.

When over the new-shorn place of the field
Was nought but the steel hood and the shield.

The face on the mound shone ruddy and hale,
But the hoar hair showed from the hoary mail.

And there rose a hand by the ruddy face
And shook a sword o'er the peopled place.

And there came a voice from the mound and said:
"O sons, the days of my youth are dead,

And gone are the faces I have known
In the street and the booths of the goodly town.

O sons, full many a flock have I seen
Feed down this water-girdled green.

Full many a herd of long-horned neat
Have I seen 'twixt water-side and wheat.

Here by this water-side full oft
Have I heaved the flowery hay aloft.

And oft this water-side anigh
Have I bowed adown the wheat-stalks high.

109

And yet meseems I live and learn
And lore of younglings yet must earn.

For tell me, children, whose are these
Fair meadows of the June's increase?

Whose are these flocks and whose the neat,
And whose the acres of the wheat?"

Scarce did we hear his latest word,
On the wide shield so rang the sword.

So rang the sword upon the shield
That the lark was hushed above the field.

Then sank the shouts and again we heard
The old voice come from the hoary beard:

"Yea, whose are yonder gables then,
And whose the holy hearths of men?
Whose are the prattling children there,
And whose the sunburnt maids and fair?

Whose thralls are ye, hereby that stand,
Bearing the freeman's sword in hand?"

As glitters the sun in the rain-washed grass,
So in the tossing swords it was;

As the thunder rattles along and adown
E'en so was the voice of the weaponed town.

And there was the steel of the old man's sword.
And there was his hollow voice, and his word:

"Many men, many minds, the old saw saith,
Though hereof ye be sure as death.

For what spake the herald yestermorn
But this, that ye were thrall-folk born;

That the lord that owneth all and some
Would send his men to fetch us home

Betwixt the haysel, and the tide
When they shear the corn in the country-side?

O children, Who was the lord? ye say,
What prayer to him did our fathers pray?

Did they hold out hands his gyves to bear?
Did their knees his high hall's pavement wear?

Is his house built up in heaven aloft?
Doth he make the sun rise oft and oft?

Doth he hold the rain in his hollow hand?
Hath he cleft this water through the land?

Or doth he stay the summer-tide,
And make the winter days abide?

O children, Who is the lord? ye say,
Have we heard his name before to-day?

O children, if his name I know,
He hight Earl Hugh of the Shivering Low:

For that herald bore on back and breast
The Black Burg under the Eagle's Nest."

As the voice of the winter wind that tears
At the eaves of the thatch and its emptied ears,

E'en so was the voice of laughter and scorn
By the water-side in the mead new-shorn;

And over the garden and the wheat
Went the voice of women shrilly-sweet.

But now by the hoary elder stood
A carle in raiment red as blood.

Red was his weed and his glaive was white,
And there stood Gregory the Wright.

So he spake in a voice was loud and strong:
"Young is the day though the road is long;

There is time if we tarry nought at all
For the kiss in the porch and the meat in the hall.

And safe shall our maidens sit at home
For the foe by the way we wend must come.

Through the three Lavers shall we go
And raise them all against the foe.

Then shall we wend the Downland ways,
And all the shepherd spearmen raise.

To Cheaping Raynes shall we come adown
And gather the bowmen of the town;

And Greenstead next we come unto
Wherein are all folk good and true.

When we come our ways to the Outer Wood
We shall be an host both great and good;

Yea when we come to the open field
There shall be a many under shield.

And maybe Earl Hugh shall lie alow
And yet to the house of Heaven shall go.

But we shall dwell in the land we love
And grudge no hallow Heaven above.

Come ye, who think the time o'er long
Till we have slain the word of wrong!

Come ye who deem the life of fear
On this last day hath drawn o'er near!

Come after me upon the road
That leadeth to the Erne's abode."

Down then he leapt from off the mound
And back drew they that were around

Till he was foremost of all those
Betwixt the river and the close.

And uprose shouts both glad and strong
As followed after all the throng;

And overhead the banners flapped,
As we went on our ways to all that happed.

The fields before the Shivering Low
Of many a grief of manfolk know;

There may the autumn acres tell
Of how men met, and what befell.

The Black Burg under the Eagle's nest
Shall tell the tale as it liketh best.

And sooth it is that the River-land
Lacks many an autumn-gathering hand.

And there are troth-plight maids unwed
Shall deem awhile that love is dead;

And babes there are to men shall grow
Nor ever the face of their fathers know.

And yet in the Land by the River-side
Doth never a thrall or an earl's man bide;

For Hugh the Earl of might and mirth
Hath left the merry days of Earth;

And we live on in the land we love,
And grudge no hallow Heaven above.

THE VOICE OF TOIL

I heard men saying, Leave hope and praying,
All days shall be as all have been;
To-day and to-morrow bring fear and sorrow,
The never-ending toil between.

When Earth was younger mid toil and hunger,
In hope we strove, and our hands were strong;
Then great men led us, with words they fed us,
And bade us right the earthly wrong.

Go read in story their deeds and glory,
Their names amidst the nameless dead;
Turn then from lying to us slow-dying
In that good world to which they led;

Where fast and faster our iron master,
The thing we made, for ever drives,
Bids us grind treasure and fashion pleasure
For other hopes and other lives.

Where home is a hovel and dull we grovel,
Forgetting that the world is fair;
Where no babe we cherish, lest its very soul perish;
Where mirth is crime, and love a snare.

Who now shall lead us, what god shall heed us
As we lie in the hell our hands have won?
For us are no rulers but fools and befoolers,
The great are fallen, the wise men gone.

I heard men saying, Leave tears and praying,
The sharp knife heedeth not the sheep;
Are we not stronger than the rich and the wronger,
When day breaks over dreams and sleep?

Come, shoulder to shoulder ere the world grows older!
Help lies in nought but thee and me;
Hope is before us, the long years that bore us
Bore leaders more than men may be.

Let dead hearts tarry and trade and marry,
And trembling nurse their dreams of mirth,
While we the living our lives are giving
To bring the bright new world to birth.

Come, shoulder to shoulder ere earth grows older!
The Cause spreads over land and sea;
Now the world shaketh, and fear awaketh,
And joy at last for thee and me.

GUNNAR'S HOWE ABOVE THE
HOUSE AT LITHEND

Ye who have come o'er the sea
to behold this grey minster of lands,
Whose floor is the tomb of time past,
and whose walls by the toil of dead hands
Show pictures amidst of the ruin
of deeds that have overpast death,
Stay by this tomb in a tomb
to ask of who lieth beneath.
Ah! the world changeth too soon,
that ye stand there with unbated breath,
As I name him that Gunnar of old,
who erst in the haymaking tide
Felt all the land fragrant and fresh,
as amidst of the edges he died.
Too swiftly fame fadeth away,
if ye tremble not lest once again
The grey mound should open and show him
glad-eyed without grudging or pain.
Little labour methinks to behold him
but the tale-teller laboured in vain.
Little labour for ears that may hearken
to hear his death-conquering song,
Till the heart swells to think of the gladness
undying that overcame wrong.
O young is the world yet meseemeth
and the hope of it flourishing green,
When the words of a man unremembered
so bridge all the days that have been,
As we look round about on the land

that these nine hundred years he hath seen.

Dusk is abroad on the grass
of this valley amidst of the hill:
Dusk that shall never be dark
till the dawn hard on midnight shall fill
The trench under Eyiafell's snow,
and the grey plain the sea meeteth grey.
White, high aloft hangs the moon
that no dark night shall brighten ere day,
For here day and night toileth the summer
lest deedless his time pass away.

THE DAY IS COMING

Come hither, lads, and hearken,
for a tale there is to tell,
Of the wonderful days a-coming, when all
shall be better than well.

And the tale shall be told of a country,
a land in the midst of the sea,
And folk shall call it England
in the days that are going to be.

There more than one in a thousand
in the days that are yet to come,
Shall have some hope of the morrow,
some joy of the ancient home.

For then, laugh not, but listen
to this strange tale of mine,
All folk that are in England
shall be better lodged than swine.

Then a man shall work and bethink him,
and rejoice in the deeds of his hand,
Nor yet come home in the even
too faint and weary to stand.

Men in that time a-coming
shall work and have no fear
For to-morrow's lack of earning
and the hunger-wolf anear.

I tell you this for a wonder,
that no man then shall be glad
Of his fellow's fall and mishap
to snatch at the work he had.

For that which the worker winneth
shall then be his indeed,
Nor shall half be reaped for nothing
by him that sowed no seed.

O strange new wonderful justice!
But for whom shall we gather the gain?
For ourselves and for each of our fellows,
and no hand shall labour in vain.

Then all Mine and all Thine shall be Ours,
and no more shall any man crave
For riches that serve for nothing
but to fetter a friend for a slave.

And what wealth then shall be left us
when none shall gather gold
To buy his friend in the market,
and pinch and pine the sold?

Nay, what save the lovely city,
and the little house on the hill,
And the wastes and the woodland beauty,
and the happy fields we till;

And the homes of ancient stories,
the tombs of the mighty dead;

And the wise men seeking out marvels,
and the poet's teeming head;

And the painter's hand of wonder;
and the marvellous fiddle-bow,
And the banded choirs of music:
all those that do and know.

For all these shall be ours and all men's,
nor shall any lack a share
Of the toil and the gain of living
in the days when the world grows fair.

Ah! such are the days that shall be!
But what are the deeds of to-day
In the days of the years we dwell in,
that wear our lives away?

Why, then, and for what are we waiting?
There are three words to speak;
WE WILL IT, and what is the foeman
but the dream-strong wakened and weak?

O why and for what are we waiting?
while our brothers droop and die,
And on every wind of the heavens
a wasted life goes by.

How long shall they reproach us
where crowd on crowd they dwell,
Poor ghosts of the wicked city,

the gold-crushed hungry hell?

Through squalid life they laboured,
in sordid grief they died,
Those sons of a mighty mother,
those props of England's pride.

They are gone; there is none can undo it,
nor save our souls from the curse;
But many a million cometh,
and shall they be better or worse?

It is we must answer and hasten,
and open wide the door
For the rich man's hurrying terror,
and the slow-foot hope of the poor.

Yea, the voiceless wrath of the wretched,
and their unlearned discontent,
We must give it voice and wisdom
till the waiting-tide be spent.

Come, then, since all things call us,
the living and the dead,
And o'er the weltering tangle
a glimmering light is shed.

Come, then, let us cast off fooling,
and put by ease and rest,
For the Cause alone is worthy
till the good days bring the best.

Come, join in the only battle
wherein no man can fail,
Where whoso fadeth and dieth,
yet his deed shall still prevail.

Ah! come, cast off all fooling,
for this, at least, we know:
That the Dawn and the Day is coming,
and forth the Banners go.

EARTH THE HEALER, EARTH THE KEEPER

So swift the hours are moving
Unto the time un-proved:
Farewell my love unloving,
Farewell my love beloved!

What! are we not glad-hearted?
Is there no deed to do?
Is not all fear departed
And Spring-tide blossomed new?

The sails swell out above us,
The sea-ridge lifts the keel;
For They have called who love us,
Who bear the gifts that heal:

A crown for him that winneth,
A bed for him that fails,
A glory that beginneth
In never-dying tales.

Yet now the pain is ended
And the glad hand grips the sword,
Look on thy life amended
And deal out due award.

Think of the thankless morning,
The gifts of noon unused;
Think of the eve of scorning,
The night of prayer refused.

And yet. The life before it,
Dost thou remember aught,
What terrors shivered o'er it
Born from the hell of thought?

And this that cometh after:
How dost thou live, and dare
To meet its empty laughter,
To face its friendless care?

In fear didst thou desire,
At peace dost thou regret,
The wasting of the fire,
The tangling of the net.

Love came and gat fair greeting;
Love went; and left no shame.
Shall both the twilights meeting
The summer sunlight blame?

What! cometh love and goeth
Like the dark night's empty wind,
Because thy folly soweth
The harvest of the blind?

Hast thou slain love with sorrow?
Have thy tears quenched the sun?
Nay even yet to-morrow
Shall many a deed be done.

This twilight sea thou sailest,
Has it grown dim and black

For that wherein thou failest,
And the story of thy lack?

Peace then! for thine old grieving
Was born of Earth the kind,
And the sad tale thou art leaving
Earth shall not leave behind.

Peace! for that joy abiding
Whereon thou layest hold
Earth keepeth for a tiding
For the day when this is old.

Thy soul and life shall perish,
And thy name as last night's wind;
But Earth the deed shall cherish
That thou to-day shalt find.

And all thy joy and sorrow
So great but yesterday,
So light a thing to-morrow,
Shall never pass away.

Lo! lo! the dawn-blink yonder,
The sunrise draweth nigh,
And men forget to wonder
That they were born to die.

Then praise the deed that wendeth
Through the daylight and the mirth!
The tale that never endeth
Whoso may dwell on earth.

ALL FOR THE CAUSE

Hear a word, a word in season,
for the day is drawing nigh,
When the Cause shall call upon us,
some to live, and some to die!

He that dies shall not die lonely,
many an one hath gone before;
He that lives shall bear no burden
heavier than the life they bore.

Nothing ancient is their story,
e'en but yesterday they bled,
Youngest they of earth's beloved,
last of all the valiant dead.

E'en the tidings we are telling
was the tale they had to tell,
E'en the hope that our hearts cherish,
was the hope for which they fell.

In the grave where tyrants thrust them,
lies their labour and their pain,
But undying from their sorrow
springeth up the hope again.

Mourn not therefore, nor lament it,
that the world outlives their life;
Voice and vision yet they give us,
making strong our hands for strife.

Some had name, and fame, and honour,
learn'd they were, and wise and strong;
Some were nameless, poor, unlettered,
weak in all but grief and wrong.

Named and nameless all live in us;
one and all they lead us yet
Every pain to count for nothing,
every sorrow to forget.

Hearken how they cry, "O happy,
happy ye that ye were born
In the sad slow night's departing,
in the rising of the morn.

"Fair the crown the Cause hath for you,
well to die or well to live
Through the battle, through the tangle,
peace to gain or peace to give."

Ah, it may be! Oft meseemeth,
in the days that yet shall be,
When no slave of gold abideth
'twixt the breadth of sea to sea,

Oft, when men and maids are merry,
ere the sunlight leaves the earth,
And they bless the day beloved,
all too short for all their mirth,

Some shall pause awhile and ponder

on the bitter days of old,
Ere the toil of strife and battle
overthrew the curse of gold;

Then 'twixt lips of loved and lover
solemn thoughts of us shall rise;
We who once were fools defeated,
then shall be the brave and wise.

There amidst the world new-builded
shall our earthly deeds abide,
Though our names be all forgotten,
and the tale of how we died.

Life or death then, who shall heed it,
what we gain or what we lose?
Fair flies life amid the struggle,
and the Cause for each shall choose.

Hear a word, a word in season,
for the day is drawing nigh,
When the Cause shall call upon us,
some to live, and some to die!

PAIN AND TIME STRIVE NOT

What part of the dread eternity
Are those strange minutes that I gain,
Mazed with the doubt of love and pain,
When I thy delicate face may see,
A little while before farewell?

What share of the world's yearning-tide
That flash, when new day bare and white
Blots out my half-dream's faint delight,
And there is nothing by my side,
And well remembered is farewell?

What drop in the grey flood of tears
That time, when the long day toiled through,
Worn out, shows nought for me to do,
And nothing worth my labour bears
The longing of that last farewell?

What pity from the heavens above,
What heed from out eternity,
What word from the swift world for me?
Speak, heed, and pity, O tender love,
Who knew'st the days before farewell!

DRAWING NEAR THE LIGHT

Lo, when we wade the tangled wood,
In haste and hurry to be there,
Nought seem its leaves and blossoms good,
For all that they be fashioned fair.

But looking up, at last we see
The glimmer of the open light,
From o'er the place where we would be:
Then grow the very brambles bright.

So now, amidst our day of strife,
With many a matter glad we play,
When once we see the light of life
Gleam through the tangle of to-day.

VERSES FOR PICTURES

DAY

I am Day; I bring again
Life and glory, Love and pain:
Awake, arise! from death to death
Through me the World's tale quickeneth.

SPRING

Spring am I, too soft of heart
Much to speak ere I depart:
Ask the Summer-tide to prove
The abundance of my love.

SUMMER

Summer looked for long am I;
Much shall change or e'er I die.
Prithee take it not amiss
Though I weary thee with bliss.

AUTUMN

Laden Autumn here I stand
Worn of heart, and weak of hand:
Nought but rest seems good to me,
Speak the word that sets me free.

WINTER

I am Winter, that do keep
Longing safe amidst of sleep:
Who shall say if I were dead
What should be remembered?

NIGHT

I am Night: I bring again
Hope of pleasure, rest from pain:
Thoughts unsaid 'twixt Life and Death
My fruitful silence quickeneth.

FOR THE BRIAR ROSE

THE BRIARWOOD

The fateful slumber floats and flows
About the tangle of the rose;
But lo! the fated hand and heart
To rend the slumberous curse apart!

THE COUNCIL ROOM

The threat of war, the hope of peace,
The Kingdom's peril and increase
Sleep on, and bide the latter day,
When Fate shall take her chain away.

THE GARDEN COURT

The maiden pleasance of the land
Knoweth no stir of voice or hand,
No cup the sleeping waters fill,
The restless shuttle lieth still.

THE ROSEBOWER

Here lies the hoarded love, the key
To all the treasure that shall be;
Come fated hand the gift to take,
And smite this sleeping world awake.

ANOTHER FOR THE BRIAR ROSE

O treacherous scent, O thorny sight,
O tangle of world's wrong and right,
What art thou 'gainst my armour's gleam
But dusky cobwebs of a dream?

Beat down, deep sunk from every gleam
Of hope, they lie and dully dream;
Men once, but men no more, that Love
Their waste defeated hearts should move.

Here sleeps the world that would not love!
Let it sleep on, but if He move
Their hearts in humble wise to wait
On his new-wakened fair estate.

O won at last is never late!
Thy silence was the voice of fate;
Thy still hands conquered in the strife;
Thine eyes were light; thy lips were life.

THE WOODPECKER

I once a King and chief
Now am the tree-bark's thief,
Ever 'twixt trunk and leaf
Chasing the prey.

THE LION

The Beasts that be
In wood and waste,
Now sit and see,
Nor ride nor haste.

THE FOREST

PEAR-TREE

By woodman's edge I faint and fail;
By craftsman's edge I tell the tale.

CHESTNUT-TREE

High in the wood, high o'er the hall,
Aloft I rise when low I fall.

OAK-TREE

Unmoved I stand what wind may blow.
Swift, swift before the wind I go.

POMONA

I am the ancient Apple-Queen,
As once I was so am I now.
For evermore a hope unseen,
Betwixt the blossom and the bough.

Ah, where's the river's hidden Gold!
And where the windy grave of Troy?
Yet come I as I came of old,
From out the heart of Summer's joy.

FLORA

I am the handmaid of the earth,
I broider fair her glorious gown,
And deck her on her days of mirth
With many a garland of renown.

And while Earth's little ones are fain
And play about the Mother's hem,
I scatter every gift I gain
From sun and wind to gladden them.

THE ORCHARD

Midst bitten mead and acre shorn,
The world without is waste and worn,

But here within our orchard-close,
The guerdon of its labour shows.

O valiant Earth, O happy year
That mocks the threat of winter near,

And hangs aloft from tree to tree
The banners of the Spring to be.

TAPESTRY TREES

OAK
I am the Roof-tree and the Keel;
I bridge the seas for woe and weal.

FIR
High o'er the lordly oak I stand,
And drive him on from land to land.

ASH
I heft my brother's iron bane;
I shaft the spear, and build the wain.

YEW
Dark down the windy dale I grow,
The father of the fateful Bow.

POPLAR
The war-shaft and the milking-bowl
I make, and keep the hay-wain whole.

OLIVE
The King I bless; the lamps I trim;
In my warm wave do fishes swim.

APPLE-TREE
I bowed my head to Adam's will;
The cups of toiling men I fill.

VINE
I draw the blood from out the earth;
I store the sun for winter mirth.

ORANGE-TREE
Amidst the greenness of my night,
My odorous lamps hang round and bright.

FIG-TREE
I who am little among trees
In honey-making mate the bees.

MULBERRY-TREE
Love's lack hath dyed my berries red:
For Love's attire my leaves are shed.

PEAR-TREE
High o'er the mead-flowers' hidden feet
I bear aloft my burden sweet.

BAY
Look on my leafy boughs, the Crown
Of living song and dead renown!

THE FLOWERING ORCHARD

SILK EMBROIDERY

Lo silken my garden,
and silken my sky,
And silken my apple-boughs
hanging on high;
All wrought by the Worm
in the peasant carle's cot
On the Mulberry leafage
when summer was hot!

THE END OF MAY

How the wind howls this morn
About the end of May,
And drives June on apace
To mock the world forlorn
And the world's joy passed away
And my unlonged-for face!
The world's joy passed away;
For no more may I deem
That any folk are glad
To see the dawn of day
Sunder the tangled dream
Wherein no grief they had.
Ah, through the tangled dream
Where others have no grief
Ever it fares with me
That fears and treasons stream
And dumb sleep slays belief
Whatso therein may be.
Sleep slayeth all belief
Until the hopeless light
Wakes at the birth of June
More lying tales to weave,
More love in woe's despite,
More hope to perish soon.

THE HALF OF LIFE GONE

The days have slain the days,
and the seasons have gone by
And brought me the summer again;
and here on the grass I lie
As erst I lay and was glad
ere I meddled with right and with wrong.
Wide lies the mead as of old,
and the river is creeping along
By the side of the elm-clad bank
that turns its weedy stream;
And grey o'er its hither lip
the quivering rashes gleam.
There is work in the mead as of old;
they are eager at winning the hay,
While every sun sets bright
and begets a fairer day.
The forks shine white in the sun
round the yellow red-wheeled wain,
Where the mountain of hay grows fast;
and now from out of the lane
Comes the ox-team drawing another,
comes the bailiff and the beer,
And thump, thump, goes the farmer's nag
o'er the narrow bridge of the weir.
High up and light are the clouds,
and though the swallows flit
So high o'er the sunlit earth,
they are well a part of it,
And so, though high over them,

are the wings of the wandering herne;
In measureless depths above him
doth the fair sky quiver and burn;
The dear sun floods the land
as the morning falls toward noon,
And a little wind is awake
in the best of the latter June.
They are busy winning the hay,
and the life and the picture they make
If I were as once I was,
I should deem it made for my sake;
For here if one need not work
is a place for happy rest,
While one's thought wends over the world
north, south, and east and west.

There are the men and the maids,
and the wives and the gaffers grey
Of the fields I know so well,
and but little changed are they
Since I was a lad amongst them;
and yet how great is the change!
Strange are they grown unto me;
yea I to myself am strange.
Their talk and their laughter mingling
with the music of the meads
Has now no meaning to me
to help or to hinder my needs,
So far from them have I drifted.
And yet amidst of them goes
A part of myself, my boy,
and of pleasure and pain he knows,

And deems it something strange,
when he is other than glad.
Lo now! the woman that stoops
and kisses the face of the lad,
And puts a rake in his hand
and laughs in his laughing face.
Whose is the voice that laughs
in the old familiar place?
Whose should it be but my love's,
if my love were yet on the earth?
Could she refrain from the fields
where my joy and her joy had birth,
When I was there and her child,
on the grass that knew her feet
'Mid the flowers that led her on
when the summer eve was sweet?

No, no, it is she no longer;
never again can she come
And behold the hay-wains creeping
o'er the meadows of her home;
No more can she kiss her son
or put the rake in his hand
That she handled a while agone
in the midst of the haymaking band.
Her laughter is gone and her life;
there is no such thing on the earth,
No share for me then in the stir,
no share in the hurry and mirth.
Nay, let me look and believe
that all these will vanish away,
At least when the night has fallen,

and that she will be there 'mid the hay,
Happy and weary with work,
waiting and longing for love.
There will she be, as of old,
when the great moon hung above,
And lightless and dead was the village,
and nought but the weir was awake;
There will she rise to meet me,
and my hands will she hasten to take,
And thence shall we wander away,
and over the ancient bridge
By many a rose-hung hedgerow,
till we reach the sun-burnt ridge
And the great trench digged by the Romans:
there then awhile shall we stand,
To watch the dawn come creeping
o'er the fragrant lovely land,
Till all the world awaketh,
and draws us down, we twain,
To the deeds of the field and the fold
and the merry summer's gain.

Ah thus, only thus shall I see her,
in dreams of the day or the night,
When my soul is beguiled of its sorrow
to remember past delight.
She is gone. She was and she is not;
there is no such thing on the earth
But e'en as a picture painted;
and for me there is void and dearth
That I cannot name or measure.
Yet for me and all these she died,

E'en as she lived for awhile,
that the better day might betide.
Therefore I live, and I shall live
till the last day's work shall fail.
Have patience now but a little
and I will tell you the tale
Of how and why she died,
And why I am weak and worn,
And have wandered away to the meadows
and the place where I was born;
But here and to-day I cannot;
for ever my thought will stray
To that hope fulfilled for a little
and the bliss of the earlier day.
Of the great world's hope and anguish
to-day I scarce can think;
Like a ghost, from the lives of the living
and their earthly deeds I shrink.
I will go adown by the water
and over the ancient bridge,
And wend in our footsteps of old
till I come to the sun-burnt ridge,
And the great trench digged by the Romans;
and thence awhile will I gaze,
And see three teeming counties
stretch out till they fade in the haze;
And in all the dwellings of man
that thence mine eyes shall see,
What man as hapless as I am
beneath the sun shall be?

O fool, what words are these?

Thou hast a sorrow to nurse,
And thou hast been bold and happy;
but these, if they utter a curse,
No sting it has and no meaning,
it is empty sound on the air.
Thy life is full of mourning,
and theirs so empty and bare,
That they have no words of complaining;
nor so happy have they been
That they may measure sorrow
or tell what grief may mean.
And thou; thou hast deeds to do,
and toil to meet thee soon;
Depart and ponder on these
through the sun-worn afternoon.

MINE AND THINE

FROM A FLEMISH POEM OF THE FOUR-TEENTH CENTURY

Two words about the world we see,
And nought but Mine and Thine they be.
Ah! might we drive them forth and wide
With us should rest and peace abide;
All free, nought owned of goods and gear,
By men and women though it were.
Common to all all wheat and wine
Over the seas and up the Rhine.
No manslayer then the wide world o'er
When Mine and Thine are known no more.
Yea, God, well counselled for our health,
Gave all this fleeting earthly wealth
A common heritage to all,
That men might feed them therewithal,
And clothe their limbs and shoe their feet
And live a simple life and sweet.
But now so rageth greediness
That each desireth nothing less
Than all the world, and all his own;
And all for him and him alone.

THE LAY OF CHRISTINE

TRANSLATED FROM THE ICELANDIC

Of silk my gear was shapen,
Scarlet they did on me,
Then to the sea-strand was I borne
And laid in a bark of the sea.
O well were I from the World away.

Befell it there I might not drown,
For God to me was good;
The billows bare me up a-land
Where grew the fair green-wood.
O well were I from the World away.

There came a Knight a-riding
With three swains along the way,
And he took me up, the little-one,
On the sea-sand as I lay.
O well were I from the World away.

He took me up, and bare me home
To the house that was his own,
And there bode I so long with him
That I was his love alone.
O well were I from the World away.

But the very first night we lay abed
Befell his sorrow and harm,
That thither came the King's ill men,
And slew him on mine arm.

O well were I from the World away.

There slew they Adalbright the King,
Two of his swains slew they,
But the third sailed swiftly from the land
Sithence I saw him never a day.
O well were I from the World away.

O wavering hope of this world's bliss,
How shall men trow in thee?
My Grove of Gems is gone away
For mine eyes no more to see!
O well were I from the World away.

Each hour the while my life shall last
Remembereth him alone,
Such heavy sorrow have I got
From our meeting long agone.
O well were I from the World away.

O, early in the morning-tide
Men cry: "Christine the fair,
Art thou well content with that true love
Thou sittest loving there?"
O well were I from the World away.

"Ah, yea, so well I love him,
And so dear my love shall be,
That the very God of Heaven aloft
Worshippeth him and me.
O well were I from the World away.

"Ah, all the red gold I have got
Well would I give to-day,
Only for this and nothing else
From the world to win away."
O well were I from the World away.

"Nay, midst all folk upon the earth
Keep thou thy ruddy gold,
And love withal the mighty lord
That wedded thee of old."
O well were I from the World away.

HILDEBRAND AND HELLELIL

TRANSLATED FROM THE DANISH

Hellelil sitteth in bower there,
None knows my grief but God alone,
And seweth at the seam so fair,
I never wail my sorrow to any other one.

But there whereas the gold should be
With silk upon the cloth sewed she.

Where she should sew with silken thread
The gold upon the cloth she laid.

So to the Queen the word came in
That Hellelil wild work doth win.

Then did the Queen do furs on her
And went to Hellelil the fair.

"O swiftly sewest thou, Hellelil,
Yet nought but mad is thy sewing still!"

"Well may my sewing be but mad
Such evil hap as I have had.

My father was good king and lord,
Knights fifteen served before his board.

He taught me sewing royally,
Twelve knights had watch and ward of me.

Well served eleven day by day,
To folly the twelfth did me bewray.

And this same was hight Hildebrand,
The King's son of the English Land.

But in bower were we no sooner laid
Than the truth thereof to my father was said.

Then loud he cried o'er garth and hall:
'Stand up, my men, and arm ye all!

'Yea draw on mail and dally not,
Hard neck lord Hildebrand hath got!'

They stood by the door with glaive and spear;
'Hildebrand rise and hasten here!'

Lord Hildebrand stroked my white white cheek:
'O love, forbear my name to speak.

'Yea even if my blood thou see,
Name me not, lest my death thou be.'

Out from the door lord Hildebrand leapt,
And round about his good sword swept.

The first of all that he slew there
Were my seven brethren with golden hair.

Then before him stood the youngest one,

And dear he was in the days agone.

Then I cried out: 'O Hildebrand,
In the name of God now stay thine hand.

'O let my youngest brother live
Tidings hereof to my mother to give!'

No sooner was the word gone forth
Than with eight wounds fell my love to earth.

My brother took me by the golden hair,
And bound me to the saddle there.

There met me then no littlest root,
But it tore off somewhat of my foot.

No littlest brake the wild-wood bore,
But somewhat from my legs it tore.

No deepest dam we came unto
But my brother's horse he swam it through

But when to the castle gate we came,
There stood my mother in sorrow and shame.

My brother let raise a tower high,
Bestrewn with sharp thorns inwardly.

He took me in my silk shirt bare
And cast me into that tower there.

And wheresoe'er my legs I laid
Torment of the thorns I had.

Wheresoe'er on feet I stood
The prickles sharp drew forth my blood.

My youngest brother me would slay,
But my mother would have me sold away.

A great new bell my price did buy
In Mary's Church to hang on high.

But the first stroke that ever it strake
My mother's heart asunder brake."

So soon as her sorrow and woe was said,
None knows my grief but God alone,
In the arm of the Queen she sat there dead,
I never tell my sorrow to any other one.

THE SON'S SORROW

FROM THE ICELANDIC

The King has asked of his son so good,
"Why art thou hushed and heavy of mood?
O fair it is to ride abroad.
Thou playest not, and thou laughest not;
All thy good game is clean forgot."

"Sit thou beside me, father dear,
And the tale of my sorrow shalt thou hear.

Thou sendedst me unto a far-off land,
And gavest me into a good Earl's hand.

Now had this good Earl daughters seven,
The fairest of maidens under heaven.

One brought me my meat when I should dine,
One cut and sewed my raiment fine.

One washed and combed my yellow hair,
And one I fell to loving there.

Befell it on so fair a day,
We minded us to sport and play.

Down in a dale my horse bound I,
Bound on my saddle speedily.

Bright red she was as the flickering flame

When to my saddle-bow she came.

Beside my saddle-bow she stood,
'To flee with thee to my heart were good.'

Kind was my horse and good to aid,
My love upon his back I laid.

We gat us from the garth away,
And none was ware of us that day.

But as we rode along the sand
Behold a barge lay by the land.

So in that boat did we depart,
And rowed away right glad at heart.

When we came to the dark wood and the shade
To raise the tent my true-love bade.

Three sons my true-love bore me there,
And syne she died who was so dear.

A grave I wrought her with my sword,
With my fair shield the mould I poured.

First in the mould I laid my love,
Then all my sons her breast above.

And I without must lie alone;
So from the place I gat me gone."

No man now shall stand on his feet
To love that love, to woo that sweet:
O fair it is to ride abroad.

AGNES AND THE HILL-MAN

TRANSLATED FROM THE DANISH

Agnes went through the meadows a-weeping,
Fowl are a-singing.
There stood the hill-man heed thereof keeping.
Agnes, fair Agnes!
"Come to the hill, fair Agnes, with me,
The reddest of gold will I give unto thee!"

Twice went Agnes the hill round about,
Then wended within, left the fair world without.

In the hillside bode Agnes, three years thrice told o'er,
For the green earth sithence fell she longing full sore.

There she sat, and lullaby sang in her singing,
And she heard how the bells of England were ringing.

Agnes before her true-love did stand:
"May I wend to the church of the English Land?"

"To England's Church well mayst thou be gone,
So that no hand thou lay the red gold upon.

"So that when thou art come the churchyard anear,
Thou cast not abroad thy golden hair.

"So that when thou standest the church within,
To thy mother on bench thou never win.

"So that when thou hearest the high God's name,
No knee unto earth thou bow to the same."

Hand she laid on all gold that was there,
And cast abroad her golden hair.

And when the church she stood within,
To her mother on bench straight did she win.

And when she heard the high God's name,
Knee unto earth she bowed to the same.

When all the mass was sung to its end,
Home with her mother dear did she wend.

"Come, Agnes, into the hillside to me,
For thy seven small sons greet sorely for thee!"

"Let them greet, let them greet, as they have will to do;
For never again will I hearken thereto!"

Weird laid he on her, sore sickness he wrought,
Fowl are a-singing.
That self-same hour to death was she brought.
Agnes, fair Agnes!

KNIGHT AAGEN AND MAIDEN ELSE

TRANSLATED FROM THE DANISH

It was the fair knight Aagen
To an isle he went his way,
And plighted troth to Else,
Who was so fair a may.

He plighted troth to Else
All with the ruddy gold,
But or ere that day's moon came again
Low he lay in the black, black mould.

It was the maiden Else,
She was fulfilled of woe
When she heard how the fair knight Aagen
In the black mould lay alow.

Uprose the fair knight Aagen,
Coffin on back took he,
And he's away to her bower,
Sore hard as the work might be.

With that same chest on door he smote,
For the lack of flesh and skin;
"O hearken, maiden Else,
And let thy true-love in!"

Then answered maiden Else,
"Never open I my door,
But and if thou namest Jesu's name

As thou hadst might before."

"O hearken, maiden Else,
And open thou thy door,
For Jesu's name I well may name
As I had might before!"

Then uprose maiden Else,
O'er her cheek the salt tears ran,
Nor spared she into her very bower
To welcome that dead man.

O, she's taken up her comb of gold
And combed adown her hair,
And for every hair she combed adown
There fell a weary tear.

"Hearken thou, knight Aagen,
Hearken, true-love, and tell,
If down-adown in the black, black earth
Thou farest ever well?"

"O whenso thou art joyous,
And the heart is glad in thee,
Then fares it with my coffin
That red roses are with me.

"But whenso thou art sorrowful
And weary is thy mood,
Then all within my coffin
Is it dreadful with dark blood.

"Now is the red cock a-crowing,
To the earth adown must I;
Down to the earth wend all dead folk,
And I wend in company.

"Now is the black cock a-crowing,
To the earth must I adown,
For the gates of Heaven are opening now,
Thereto must I begone."

Uprose the fair knight Aagen,
Coffin on back took he,
And he's away to the churchyard now,
Sore hard as the work might be.

But so wrought maiden Else,
Because of her weary mood,
That she followed after own true love
All through the mirk wild wood.

But when the wood was well passed through,
And in the churchyard they were,
Then was the fair knight Aagen
Waxen wan of his golden hair.

And when therefrom they wended
And were the church within,
Then was the fair knight Aagen
Waxen wan of cheek and chin.

"Hearken thou, maiden Else,
Hearken, true-love, to me,

Weep no more for thine own troth-plight,
However it shall be!

"Look thou up to the heavens aloft,
To the little stars and bright,
And thou shalt see how sweetly
It fareth with the night!"

She looked up to the heavens aloft,
To the little stars bright above.
The dead man sank into his grave,
Ne'er again she saw her love.

Home then went maiden Else,
Mid sorrow manifold,
And ere that night's moon came again
She lay alow in the mould.

HAFBUR AND SIGNY

TRANSLATED FROM THE DANISH.

King Hafbur and King Siward
They needs must stir up strife,
All about the sweetling Signy
Who was so fair a wife.
O wilt thou win me then,
or as fair a maid as I be?

It was the King's son Hafbur
Woke up amid the night,
And 'gan to tell of a wondrous dream
In swift words nowise light.

"Me-dreamed I was in heaven
Amid that fair abode,
And my true-love lay upon mine arm
And we fell from cloud to cloud."

As there they sat, the dames and maids
Of his words they took no keep,
Only his mother well-beloved
Heeded his dreamful sleep.

"Go get thee gone to the mountain,
And make no long delay;
To the elve's eldest daughter
For thy dream's areding pray."

So the King's son, even Hafbur,

Took his sword in his left hand,
And he's away to the mountain
To get speech of that Lily-wand.

He beat thereon with hand all bare,
With fingers small and fine,
And there she lay, the elve's daughter,
And well wotted of that sign.

"Bide hail, Elve's sweetest daughter,
As on skins thou liest fair,
I pray thee by the God of Heaven
My dream arede thou clear.

"Me-dreamed I was in heaven,
Yea amid that fair abode,
And my true-love lay upon mine arm
And we fell from cloud to cloud."

"Whereas thou dreamed'st thou wert in heaven,
So shalt thou win that may;
Dreamed'st thou of falling through the clouds,
So falls for her thy life away."

"And if it lieth in my luck
To win to me that may,
In no sorrow's stead it standeth me
For her to cast my life away."

Lord Hafbur lets his hair wax long,
And will have the gear of mays,
And he rideth to King Siward's house

And will well learn weaving ways.

Lord Hafbur all his clothes let shape
In such wise as maidens do,
And thus he rideth over the land
King Siward's daughter to woo.

Now out amid the castle-garth
He cast his cloak aside,
And goeth forth to the high-bower
Where the dames and damsels abide.

Hail, sit ye there, dames and damsels,
Maids and queens kind and fair,
And chiefest of all to the Dane-King's daughter
If she abideth here!

"Hail, sittest thou, sweet King's daughter,
A-spinning the silken twine,
It is King Hafbur sends me hither
To learn the sewing fine."

Hath Hafbur sent thee here to me?
Then art thou a welcome guest,
And all the sewing that I can
Shall I learn thee at my best.

"And all the sewing that I can
I shall learn thee lovingly,
Out of one bowl shalt thou eat with me,

And by my nurse shalt thou lie."

"King's children have I eaten with,
And lain down by their side:
Must I lie abed now with a very nurse?
Then woe is me this tide!"

"Nay, let it pass, fair maiden!
Of me gettest thou no harm,
Out of one bowl shalt thou eat with me
And sleep soft upon mine arm."

There sat they, all the damsels,
And sewed full craftily;
But ever the King's son Hafbur
With nail in mouth sat he.

They sewed the hart, they sewed the hind,
As they run through the wild-wood green,
Never gat Hafbur so big a bowl
But the bottom soon was seen.

In there came the evil nurse
In the worst tide that might be:
"Never saw I fair maiden
Who could sew less craftily.

"Never saw I fair maiden
Seam worse the linen fine,
Never saw I noble maiden
Who better drank the wine."

This withal spake the evil nurse,
The nighest that she durst:
"Never saw I yet fair maiden
Of drink so sore athirst.

"So little a seam as ever she sews
Goes the needle into her mouth,
As big a bowl as ever she gets
Out is it drunk forsooth.

"Ne'er saw I yet in maiden's head
Two eyes so bright and bold,
And those two hands of her withal
Are hard as the iron cold."

"Hearken, sweet nurse, whereso thou art,
Why wilt thou mock me still?
Never cast I one word at thee,
Went thy sewing well or ill.

"Still wilt thou mock, still wilt thou spy;
Nought such thou hast of me,
Whether mine eyes look out or look in
Nought do they deal with thee."

O it was Hafbur the King's son
Began to sew at last;
He sowed the hart, and he sewed the hind,
As they flee from the hound so fast.

He sewed the lily, and he sewed the rose,
And the little fowls of the air;

Then fell the damsels a-marvelling,
For nought had they missed him there.

Day long they sewed till the evening,
And till the long night was deep,
Then up stood dames and maidens
And were fain in their beds to sleep.

So fell on them the evening-tide,
O'er the meads the dew drave down,
And fain was Signy, that sweet thing,
With her folk to bed to be gone.

Therewith asked the King's son Hafbur,
"And whatten a bed for me?"
"O thou shalt sleep in the bower aloft,
And blue shall thy bolster be."

She went before, sweet Signy,
O'er the high-bower's bridge aright,
And after her went Hafbur
Laughing from heart grown light.

Then kindled folk the waxlights,
That were so closely twined,
And after them the ill nurse went
With an ill thought in her mind.

The lights were quenched, the nurse went forth,
They deemed they were alone:
Lord Hafbur drew off his kirtle red,
Then first his sword outshone.

Lord Hafbur mid his longing sore
Down on the bed he sat:
I tell you of my soothfastness,
His byrny clashed thereat.

Then spake the darling Signy,
Out of her heart she said,
"Never saw I so rough a shirt
Upon so fair a maid."

She laid her hand on Hafbur's breast
With the red gold all a-blaze:
"Why wax thy breasts in no such wise
As they wax in other mays?"

"The wont it is in my father's land
For maids to ride to the Thing,
Therefore my breasts are little of growth
Beneath the byrny-ring."

And there they lay through the night so long,
The King's son and the may,
In talk full sweet, but little of sleep,
So much on their minds there lay.

"Hearken, sweet maiden Signy,
As here alone we lie,
Who is thy dearest in the world,
And lieth thine heart most nigh?"

175

"O there is none in all the world
Who lieth so near to my heart
As doth the bold King Hafbur:
Ne'er in him shall I have a part.

"As doth the bold King Hafbur
That mine eyes shall never know:
Nought but the sound of his gold-wrought horn
As he rides to the Thing and fro."

"O, is it Hafbur the King's son
That thy loved heart holdeth dear?
Turn hither, O my well-beloved,
To thy side I lie so near."

"If thou art the King's son Hafbur,
Why wilt thou shame me, love,
Why ridest thou not to my father's garth
With hound, and with hawk upon glove?"

"Once was I in thy father's garth,
With hound and hawk and all;
And with many mocks he said me nay,
In such wise did our meeting fall."

All the while they talked together
They deemed alone they were,
But the false nurse ever stood close without,
And nought thereof she failed to hear.

O shame befall that evil nurse,
Ill tidings down she drew,
She stole away his goodly sword,
But and his byrny new.

She took to her his goodly sword,
His byrny blue she had away,
And she went her ways to the high bower
Whereas King Siward lay.

"Wake up, wake up, King Siward!
Over long thou sleepest there,
The while the King's son Hafbur
Lies abed by Signy the fair."

"No Hafbur is here, and no King's son,
That thou shouldst speak this word;
He is far away in the east-countries,
Warring with knight and lord.

"Hold thou thy peace, thou evil nurse,
And lay on her no lie,
Or else tomorn ere the sun is up
In the bale-fire shall ye die."

"O hearken to this, my lord and king,
And trow me nought but true;
Look here upon his bright white sword,
But and his byrny blue!"

Then mad of mind waxed Siward,

Over all the house 'gan he cry,
"Rise up, O mighty men of mine,
For a hardy knight is anigh:

"Take ye sword and shield in hand,
And look that they be true;
For Hafbur the King hath guested with us;
Stiffnecked he is, great deeds to do."

So there anigh the high-bower door
They stood with spear and glaive
"Rise up, rise up, Young Hafbur,
Out here we would thee have!"

That heard the goodly Signy,
And she wrang her hands full sore:
"Hearken and heed, O Hafbur,
Who stand without by the door!"

Thank and praise to the King's son Hafbur,
Manly he played and stout!
None might lay hand upon him
While the bed-post yet held out.

But they took him, the King's son Hafbur,
And set him in bolts new wrought;
Then lightly he rent them asunder,
As though they were leaden and nought.

Out and spake the ancient nurse,
And she gave a rede of ill;
"Bind ye him but in Signy's hair.

178

So shall hand and foot lie still.

"Take ye but one of Signy's hairs
Hafbur's hands to bind,
Ne'er shall he rend them asunder,
His heart to her is so kind."

Then took they two of Signy's hairs
Bonds for his hands to be,
Nor might he rive them asunder,
So dear to his heart was she.

Then spake the sweetling Signy
As the tears fast down her cheek did fall:
"O rend it asunder, Hafbur,
That gift to thee I give withal."

Now sat the-King's son Hafbur
Amidst the castle-hall,
And thronged to behold him man and maid,
But the damsels chiefest of all.

They took him, the King's son Hafbur,
Laid bolts upon him in that place,
And ever went Signy to and fro,
The weary tears fell down apace.

She speaketh to him in sorrowful mood:
"This will I, Hafbur, for thee,
Piteous prayer for thee shall make

My mother's sisters three.

"For my father's mind stands fast in this,
To do thee to hang upon the bough
On the topmost oak in the morning-tide
While the sun is yet but low."

But answered thereto young Hafbur
Out of a wrathful mind:
"Of all heeds I heeded, this was the last,
To be prayed for by womankind.

"But hearken, true-love Signy,
Good heart to my asking turn,
When thou seest me swing on oaken-bough
Then let thy high-bower burn."

Then answered the noble Signy,
So sore as she must moan,
"God to aid, King's son Hafbur,
Well will I grant thy boon."

They followed him, King Hafbur,
Thick thronging from the castle-bent:
And all who saw him needs must greet
And in full piteous wise they went.

But when they came to the fair green mead
Where Hafbur was to die,
He prayed them hold a little while:

For his true-love would he try.

"O hang me up my cloak of red,
That sight or my ending let me see.
Perchance yet may King Siward rue
My hanging on the gallows tree."

Now of the cloak was Signy ware
And sorely sorrow her heart did rive,
She thought: "The ill tale all is told,
No longer is there need to live."

Straightway her damsels did she call
As weary as she was of mind:
"Come, let us go to the bower aloft
Game and glee for a while to find."

Yea and withal spake Signy,
She spake a word of price:
"To-day shall I do myself to death
And meet Hafbur in Paradise.

"And whoso there be in this our house
Lord Hafbur's death that wrought,
Good reward I give them now
To red embers to be brought.

"So many there are in the King's garth
Of Hafbur's death shall be glad;
Good reward for them to lose
The trothplight mays they had."

She set alight to the bower aloft
And it burned up speedily,
And her good love and her great heart
Might all with eyen see.

It was the King's son Hafbur
O'er his shoulder cast his eye,
And beheld how Signy's house of maids
On a red low stood on high.

"Now take ye down my cloak of red.
Let it lie on the earth a-cold;
Had I ten lives of the world for one,
Nought of them all would I hold."

King Siward looked out of his window fair
In fearful mood enow,
For he saw Hafbur hanging on oak
And Signy's bower on a low.

Out then spake a little page
Was clad in kirtle red:
"Sweet Signy burns in her bower aloft,
With all her mays unwed."

Therewithal spake King Siward
From rueful heart unfain;
"Ne'er saw I two King's children erst
Such piteous ending gain.

"But had I wist or heard it told
That love so strong should be,
Ne'er had I held those twain apart
For all Denmark given me.

"O hasten and run to Signy's bower
For the life of that sweet thing;
Hasten and run to the gallows high,
No thief is Hafbur the King."

But when they came to Signy's bower
Low it lay in embers red;
And when they came to the gallows tree,
Hafbur was stark and dead.

They took him the King's son Hafbur,
Swathed him in linen white,
And laid him in the earth of Christ
By Signy his delight.
O wilt thou win me then,
or as fair a maid as I be?

GOLDILOCKS AND GOLDILOCKS

It was Goldilocks woke up in the morn
At the first of the shearing of the corn.

There stood his mother on the hearth
And of new-leased wheat was little dearth.

There stood his sisters by the quern,
For the high-noon cakes they needs must earn.

"O tell me Goldilocks my son,
Why hast thou coloured raiment on?"

"Why should I wear the hodden grey
When I am light of heart to-day?"

"O tell us, brother, why ye wear
In reaping-tide the scarlet gear?

Why hangeth the sharp sword at thy side
When through the land 'tis the hook goes wide?"

"Gay-clad am I that men may know
The freeman's son where'er I go.

The grinded sword at side I bear
Lest I the dastard's word should hear."

"O tell me Goldilocks my son,
Of whither away thou wilt be gone?"

"The morn is fair and the world is wide,
And here no more will I abide."

"O Brother, when wilt thou come again?"
"The autumn drought, and the winter rain,

The frost and the snow, and St. David's wind,
All these that were time out of mind,

All these a many times shall be
Ere the Upland Town again I see."

"O Goldilocks my son, farewell,
As thou wendest the world 'twixt home and hell!"

"O brother Goldilocks, farewell,
Come back with a tale for men to tell!"

So 'tis wellaway for Goldilocks,
As he left the land of the wheaten shocks.

He's gotten him far from the Upland Town,
And he's gone by Dale and he's gone by Down.

He's come to the wild-wood dark and drear,
Where never the bird's song doth he hear.

He has slept in the moonless wood and dim
With never a voice to comfort him.

He has risen up under the little light

Where the noon is as dark as the summer night.

Six days therein has he walked alone
Till his scrip was bare and his meat was done.

On the seventh morn in the mirk, mirk wood,
He saw sight that he deemed was good.

It was as one sees a flower a-bloom
In the dusky heat of a shuttered room.

He deemed the fair thing far aloof,
And would go and put it to the proof.

But the very first step he made from the place
He met a maiden face to face.

Face to face, and so close was she
That their lips met soft and lovingly.

Sweet-mouthed she was, and fair he wist;
And again in the darksome wood they kissed.

Then first in the wood her voice he heard,
As sweet as the song of the summer bird.

"O thou fair man with the golden head.
What is the name of thee?" she said.

"My name is Goldilocks," said he;
"O sweet-breathed, what is the name of thee?"

"O Goldilocks the Swain," she said,
"My name is Goldilocks the Maid."

He spake, "Love me as I love thee,
And Goldilocks one flesh shall be."

She said, "Fair man, I wot not how
Thou lovest, but I love thee now.

But come a little hence away,
That I may see thee in the day.

For hereby is a wood-lawn clear
And good for awhile for us it were."

Therewith she took him by the hand
And led him into the lighter land.

There on the grass they sat adown.
Clad she was in a kirtle brown.

In all the world was never maid
So fair, so evilly arrayed.

No shoes upon her feet she had,
And scantly were her shoulders clad;

Through her brown kirtle's rents full wide
Shone out the sleekness of her side.

An old scrip hung about her neck,
Nought of her raiment did she reck.

No shame of all her rents had she;
She gazed upon him eagerly.

She leaned across the grassy space
And put her hands about his face.

She said: "O hunger-pale art thou,
Yet shalt thou eat though I hunger now."

She took him apples from her scrip,
She kissed him, cheek and chin and lip.

She took him cakes of woodland bread:
"Whiles am I hunger-pinched," she said.

She had a gourd and a pilgrim shell;
She took him water from the well.

She stroked his breast and his scarlet gear;
She spake, "How brave thou art and dear!"

Her arms about him did she wind;
He felt her body dear and kind.

"O love," she said, "now two are one,
And whither hence shall we be gone?"

"Shall we fare further than this wood,"
Quoth he, "I deem it dear and good?"

She shook her head, and laughed, and spake;

"Rise up! For thee, not me, I quake.

Had she been minded me to slay
Sure she had done it ere to-day.

But thou: this hour the crone shall know
That thou art come, her very foe.

No minute more on tidings wait,
Lest e'en this minute be too late."

She led him from the sunlit green,
Going sweet-stately as a queen.

There in the dusky wood, and dim,
As forth they went, she spake to him:

"Fair man, few people have I seen
Amidst this world of woodland green:

But I would have thee tell me now
If there be many such as thou."

"Betwixt the mountains and the sea,
O Sweet, be many such," said he.

Athwart the glimmering air and dim
With wistful eyes she looked on him.

"But ne'er an one so shapely made
Mine eyes have looked upon," she said.

He kissed her face, and cried in mirth:
"Where hast thou dwelt then on the earth?"

"Ever," she said, "I dwell alone
With a hard-handed cruel crone.

And of this crone am I the thrall
To serve her still in bower and hall;

And fetch and carry in the wood,
And do whate'er she deemeth good.

But whiles a sort of folk there come
And seek my mistress at her home;

But such-like are they to behold
As make my very blood run cold.

Oft have I thought, if there be none
On earth save these, would all were done!

Forsooth, I knew it was not so,
But that fairer folk on earth did grow.

But fain and full is the heart in me
To know that folk are like to thee."

Then hand in hand they stood awhile
Till her tears rose up beneath his smile.

And he must fold her to his breast
To give her heart a while of rest.

Till sundered she and gazed about,
And bent her brows as one in doubt.

She spake: "The wood is growing thin,
Into the full light soon shall we win.

Now crouch we that we be not seen,
Under yon bramble-bushes green."

Under the bramble-bush they lay
Betwixt the dusk and the open day.

"O Goldilocks my love, look forth
And let me know what thou seest of worth."

He said: "I see a house of stone,
A castle excellently done."

"Yea," quoth she, "There doth the mistress dwell.
What next thou seest shalt thou tell."

"What lookest thou to see come forth?"
"Maybe a white bear of the North."

"Then shall my sharp sword lock his mouth."
"Nay," she said, "or a worm of the South."

"Then shall my sword his hot blood cool."
"Nay, or a whelming poison-pool."

"The trees its swelling flood shall stay,
And thrust its venomed lip away."

"Nay, it may be a wild-fire flash
To burn thy lovely limbs to ash."

"On mine own hallows shall I call,
And dead its flickering flame shall fall."

"O Goldilocks my love, I fear
That ugly death shall seek us here.

Look forth, O Goldilocks my love.
That I thine hardy heart may prove.

What cometh down the stone-wrought stair
That leadeth up to the castle fair?"

"Adown the doorward stair of stone
There cometh a woman all alone."

"Yea, that forsooth shall my mistress be:
O Goldilocks, what like is she?"

"O fair she is of her array,
As hitherward she wends her way."

"Unlike her wont is that indeed:
Is she not foul beneath her weed?"

"O nay, nay! But most wondrous fair
Of all the women earth doth bear."

"O Goldilocks, my heart, my heart!
Woe, woe! for now we drift apart."

But up he sprang from the bramble-side,
And "O thou fairest one!" he cried:

And forth he ran that Queen to meet,
And fell before her gold-clad feet.

About his neck her arms she cast,
And into the fair-built house they passed.

And under the bramble-bushes lay
Unholpen, Goldilocks the may.

Thenceforth a while of time there wore,
And Goldilocks came forth no more.

Throughout that house he wandered wide,
Both up and down, from side to side.

But never he saw an evil crone,
But a full fair Queen on a golden throne.

Never a barefoot maid did he see,
But a gay and gallant company.

He sat upon the golden throne,
And beside him sat the Queen alone.

Kind she was, as she loved him well,

And many a merry tale did tell.

But nought he laughed, nor spake again,
For all his life was waste and vain.

Cold was his heart, and all afraid
To think on Goldilocks the Maid.

Withal now was the wedding dight
When he should wed that lady bright.

The night was gone, and the day was up
When they should drink the bridal cup.

And he sat at the board beside the Queen,
Amidst of a guest-folk well beseen.

But scarce was midmorn on the hall,
When down did the mirk of midnight fall.

Then up and down from the board they ran,
And man laid angry hand on man.

There was the cry, and the laughter shrill,
And every manner word of ill.

Whoso of men had hearkened it,
Had deemed he had woke up over the Pit.

Then spake the Queen o'er all the crowd,
And grim was her speech, and harsh, and loud:

"Hold now your peace, ye routing swine,
While I sit with mine own love over the wine!

For this dusk is the very deed of a foe,
Or under the sun no man I know."

And hard she spake, and loud she cried
Till the noise of the bickering guests had died.

Then again she spake amidst of the mirk,
In a voice like an unoiled wheel at work:

"Whoso would have a goodly gift,
Let him bring aback the sun to the lift.

Let him bring aback the light and the day,
And rich and in peace he shall go his way."

Out spake a voice was clean and clear:
"Lo, I am she to dight your gear;

But I for the deed a gift shall gain,
To sit by Goldilocks the Swain.

I shall sit at the board by the bridegroom's side,
And be betwixt him and the bride.

I shall eat of his dish, and drink of his cup,
Until for the bride-bed ye rise up."

Then was the Queen's word wailing-wild:
"E'en so must it be, thou Angel's child.

Thou shalt sit by my groom till the dawn of night,
And then shalt thou wend thy ways aright."

Said the voice, "Yet shalt thou swear an oath
That free I shall go though ye be loth."

"How shall I swear?" the false Queen spake:
"Wherewith the sure oath shall I make?"

"Thou shalt swear by the one eye left in thine head,
And the throng of the ghosts of the evil dead."

She swore the oath, and then she spake:
"Now let the second dawn awake."

And e'en therewith the thing was done;
There was peace in the hall, and the light of the sun.

And again the Queen was calm and fair,
And courteous sat the guest-folk there.

Yet unto Goldilocks it seemed
As if amidst the night he dreamed;

As if he sat in a grassy place,
While slim hands framed his hungry face;

As if in the clearing of the wood
One gave him bread and apples good;

And nought he saw of the guest-folk gay,

And nought of all the Queen's array.

Yet saw he betwixt board and door,
A slim maid tread the chequered floor.

Her gown of green so fair was wrought,
That clad her body seemed with nought

But blossoms of the summer-tide,
That wreathed her, limbs and breast and side.

And, stepping towards him daintily,
A basket in her hand had she.

And as she went, from head to feet,
Surely was she most dainty-sweet.

Love floated round her, and her eyes
Gazed from her fairness glad and wise;

But babbling-loud the guests were grown;
Unnoted was she and unknown.

Now Goldilocks she sat beside,
But nothing changed was the Queenly bride;

Yea too, and Goldilocks the Swain
Was grown but dull and dazed again.

The Queen smiled o'er the guest-rich board,
Although his wine the Maiden poured;

Though from his dish the Maiden ate,
The Queen sat happy and sedate.

But now the Maiden fell to speak
From lips that well-nigh touched his cheek:

"O Goldilocks, dost thou forget?
Or mindest thou the mirk-wood yet?

Forgettest thou the hunger-pain
And all thy young life made but vain?

How there was nought to help or aid,
But for poor Goldilocks the Maid?"

She murmured, "Each to each we two,
Our faces from the wood-mirk grew.

Hast thou forgot the grassy place,
And love betwixt us face to face?

Hast thou forgot how fair I deemed
Thy face? How fair thy garment seemed?

Thy kisses on my shoulders bare,
Through rents of the poor raiment there?

My arms that loved thee nought unkissed
All o'er from shoulder unto wrist?

Hast thou forgot how brave thou wert,
Thou with thy fathers' weapon girt;

When underneath the bramble-bush
I quaked like river-shaken rash,

Wondering what new-wrought shape of death
Should quench my new love-quickened breath?

Or else: forget'st thou, Goldilocks,
Thine own land of the wheaten shocks?

Thy mother and thy sisters dear,
Thou said'st would bide thy true-love there?

Hast thou forgot? Hast thou forgot?
O love, my love, I move thee not."

Silent the fair Queen sat and smiled,
And heeded nought the Angel's child,

For like an image fashioned fair
Still sat the Swain with empty stare.

These words seemed spoken not, but writ
As foolish tales through night-dreams flit.

Vague pictures passed before his sight,
As in the first dream of the night.

But the Maiden opened her basket fair,
And set two doves on the table there.

And soft they cooed, and sweet they billed

Like man and maid with love fulfilled.

Therewith the Maiden reached a hand
To a dish that on the board did stand;

And she crumbled a share of the spice-loaf brown,
And the Swain upon her hand looked down;

Then unto the fowl his eyes he turned;
And as in a dream his bowels yearned

For somewhat that he could not name;
And into his heart a hope there came.

And still he looked on the hands of the Maid,
As before the fowl the crumbs she laid.

And he murmured low, "O Goldilocks!
Were we but amid the wheaten shocks!"

Then the false Queen knit her brows and laid
A fair white hand by the hand of the Maid.

He turned his eyes away thereat,
And closer to the Maiden sat.

But the queen-bird now the carle-bird fed
Till all was gone of the sugared bread.

Then with wheedling voice for more he craved,
And the Maid a share from the spice-loaf shaved;

And the crumbs within her hollow hand
She held where the creeping doves did stand.

But Goldilocks, he looked and longed,
And saw how the carle the queen-bird wronged.

For when she came to the hand to eat
The hungry queen-bird thence he beat.

Then Goldilocks the Swain spake low:
"Foul fall thee, bird, thou doest now

As I to Goldilocks, my sweet,
Who gave my hungry mouth to eat."

He felt her hand as he did speak,
He felt her face against his cheek.

He turned and stood in the evil hall,
And swept her up in arms withal.

Then was there hubbub wild and strange,
And swiftly all things there 'gan change.

The fair Queen into a troll was grown,
A one-eyed, bow-backed, haggard crone.

And though the hall was yet full fair,
And bright the sunshine streamed in there,

On evil shapes it fell forsooth:
Swine-heads; small red eyes void of ruth;

And bare-boned bodies of vile things,
And evil-feathered bat-felled wings.

And all these mopped and mowed and grinned,
And sent strange noises down the wind.

There stood those twain unchanged alone
To face the horror of the crone;

She crouched against them by the board;
And cried the Maid: "Thy sword, thy sword!

Thy sword, O Goldilocks! For see
She will not keep her oath to me."

Out flashed the blade therewith. He saw
The foul thing sidelong toward them draw,

Holding within her hand a cup
Wherein some dreadful drink seethed up.

Then Goldilocks cried out and smote,
And the sharp blade sheared the evil throat.

The head fell noseling to the floor;
The liquor from the cup did pour,

And ran along a sparkling flame
That nigh unto their footsoles came.

Then empty straightway was the hall,

Save for those twain, and she withal.

So fled away the Maid and Man,
And down the stony stairway ran.

Fast fled they o'er the sunny grass,
Yet but a little way did pass

Ere cried the Maid: "Now cometh forth
The snow-white ice-bear of the North;

Turn, Goldilocks, and heave up sword!"
Then fast he stood upon the sward,

And faced the beast, that whined and cried,
And shook his head from side to side.

But round him the Swain danced and leaped,
And soon the grisly head he reaped.

And then the ancient blade he sheathed,
And ran unto his love sweet-breathed;

And caught her in his arms and ran
Fast from that house, the bane of man.

Yet therewithal he spake her soft
And kissed her over oft and oft,

Until from kissed and trembling mouth
She cried: "The Dragon of the South!"

He set her down and turned about,
And drew the eager edges out.

And therewith scaly coil on coil
Reared 'gainst his face the mouth aboil:

The gaping jaw and teeth of dread
Was dark 'twixt heaven and his head.

But with no fear, no thought, no word,
He thrust the thin-edged ancient sword.

And the hot blood ran from the hairy throat,
And set the summer grass afloat.

Then back he turned and caught her hand,
And never a minute did they stand.

But as they ran on toward the wood,
He deemed her swift feet fair and good.

She looked back o'er her shoulder fair:
"The whelming poison-pool is here;

And now availeth nought the blade:
O if my cherished trees might aid!

But now my feet fail. Leave me then!
And hold my memory dear of men."

He caught her in his arms again;
Of her dear side was he full fain.

Her body in his arms was dear:
"Sweet art thou, though we perish here!"

Like quicksilver came on the flood:
But lo, the borders of the wood!

She slid from out his arms and stayed;
Round a great oak her arms she laid.

"If e'er I saved thee, lovely tree,
From axe and saw, now succour me:

Look how the venom creeps anigh,
Help! lest thou see me writhe and die."

She crouched beside the upheaved root,
The bubbling venom touched her foot;

Then with a sucking gasping sound
It ebbed back o'er the blighted ground.

Up then she rose and took his hand
And never a moment did they stand.

"Come, love," she cried, "the ways I know,
How thick soe'er the thickets grow.

O love, I love thee! O thine heart!
How mighty and how kind thou art!"

Therewith they saw the tree-dusk lit,

Bright grey the great boles gleamed on it.

"O flee," she said, "the sword is nought
Against the flickering fire-flaught."

"But this availeth yet," said he,
"That Hallows All our love may see."

He turned about and faced the glare:
"O Mother, help us, kind and fair!

Now help me, true St. Nicholas,
If ever truly thine I was!"

Therewith the wild-fire waned and paled,
And in the wood the light nigh failed;

And all about 'twas as the night.
He said: "Now won is all our fight,

And now meseems all were but good
If thou mightst bring us from the wood."

She fawned upon him, face and breast;
She said: "It hangs 'twixt worst and best.

And yet, O love, if thou be true,
One thing alone thou hast to do."

Sweetly he kissed her, cheek and chin:
"What work thou biddest will I win."

"O love, my love, I needs must sleep;
Wilt thou my slumbering body keep,

And, toiling sorely, still bear on
The love thou seemest to have won?"

"O easy toil," he said, "to bless
Mine arms with all thy loveliness."

She smiled; "Yea, easy it may seem,
But harder is it than ye deem.

For hearken! Whatso thou mayst see,
Piteous as it may seem to thee,

Heed not nor hearken! bear me forth,
As though nought else were aught of worth.

For all earth's wealth that may be found
Lay me not sleeping on the ground,

To help, to hinder, or to save!
Or there for me thou diggest a grave."

He took her body on his arm,
Her slumbering head lay on his barm.

Then glad he bore her on the way,
And the wood grew lighter with the day.

All still it was, till suddenly
He heard a bitter wail near by.

Poems By The Way

Yet on he went until he heard
The cry become a shapen word:

"Help me, O help, thou passer by!
Turn from the path, let me not die!

I am a woman; bound and left
To perish; of all help bereft."

Then died the voice out in a moan;
He looked upon his love, his own,

And minding all she spake to him
Strode onward through the wild-wood dim.

But lighter grew the woodland green
Till clear the shapes of things were seen.

And therewith wild halloos he heard,
And shrieks, and cries of one afeard.

Nigher it grew and yet more nigh
Till burst from out a brake near by

A woman bare of breast and limb,
Who turned a piteous face to him

E'en as she ran: for hard at heel
Followed a man with brandished steel,

And yelling mouth. Then the Swain stood

One moment in the glimmering wood

Trembling, ashamed: Yet now grown wise
Deemed all a snare for ears and eyes.

So onward swiftlier still he strode
And cast all thought on his fair load.

And yet in but a little space
Back came the yelling shrieking chase,

And well-nigh gripped now by the man,
Straight unto him the woman ran;

And underneath the gleaming steel
E'en at his very feet did kneel.

She looked up; sobs were all her speech,
Yet sorely did her face beseech.

While o'er her head the chaser stared,
Shaking aloft the edges bared.

Doubted the Swain, and a while did stand
As she took his coat-lap in her hand.

Upon his hand he felt her breath
Hot with the dread of present death.

Sleek was her arm on his scarlet coat,
The sobbing passion rose in his throat.

But e'en therewith he looked aside
And saw the face of the sleeping bride.

Then he tore his coat from the woman's hand,
And never a moment there did stand.

But swiftly thence away he strode
Along the dusky forest road.

And there rose behind him laughter shrill,
And then was the windless wood all still,

He looked around o'er all the place,
But saw no image of the chase.

And as he looked the night-mirk now
O'er all the tangled wood 'gan flow.

Then stirred the sweetling that he bore,
And she slid adown from his arms once more.

Nought might he see her well-loved face;
But he felt her lips in the mirky place.

"'Tis night," she said, "and the false day's gone,
And we twain in the wild-wood all alone.

Night o'er the earth; so rest we here
Until to-morrow's sun is clear.

For overcome is every foe
And home to-morrow shall we go."

So 'neath the trees they lay, those twain,
And to them the darksome night was gain.

But when the morrow's dawn was grey
They woke and kissed whereas they lay.

And when on their feet they came to stand
Swain Goldilocks stretched out his hand.

And he spake: "O love, my love indeed,
Where now is gone thy goodly weed?

For again thy naked feet I see,
And thy sweet sleek arms so kind to me.

Through thy rent kirtle once again
Thy shining shoulder showeth plain."

She blushed as red as the sun-sweet rose:
"My garments gay were e'en of those

That the false Queen dight to slay my heart;
And sore indeed was their fleshly smart.

Yet must I bear them, well-beloved,
Until thy truth and troth was proved

And this tattered coat is now for a sign
That thou hast won me to be thine.

Now wilt thou lead along thy maid

To meet thy kindred unafraid."

As stoops the falcon on the dove
He cast himself about her love.

He kissed her over, cheek and chin,
He kissed the sweetness of her skin.

Then hand in hand they went their way
Till the wood grew light with the outer day.

At last behind them lies the wood,
And before are the Upland Acres good.

On the hill's brow awhile they stay
At midmorn of the merry day.

He sheareth a deal from his kirtle meet,
To make her sandals for her feet.

He windeth a wreath of the beechen tree,
Lest men her shining shoulders see.

And a wreath of woodbine sweet, to hide
The rended raiment of her side;

And a crown of poppies red as wine,
Lest on her head the hot sun shine.

She kissed her love withal and smiled:
"Lead forth, O love, the Woodland Child!

Most meet and right meseems it now
That I am clad with the woodland bough.

For betwixt the oak-tree and the thorn
Meseemeth erewhile was I born.

And if my mother aught I knew,
It was of the woodland folk she grew.

And O that thou art well at ease
To wed the daughter of the trees!"

Now Goldilocks and Goldilocks
Go down amidst the wheaten shocks,

But when anigh to the town they come,
Lo there is the wain a-wending home,

And many a man and maid beside,
Who tossed the sickles up, and cried:

"O Goldilocks, now whither away?
And what wilt thou with the woodland may?"

"O this is Goldilocks my bride,
And we come adown from the wild-wood side,

And unto the Fathers' House we wend
To dwell therein till life shall end."

"Up then on the wain, that ye may see
From afar how thy mother bideth thee.

That ye may see how kith and kin
Abide thee, bridal brave to win."

So Goldilocks and Goldilocks
Sit high aloft on the wheaten shocks,

And fair maids sing before the wain,
For all of Goldilocks are fain.

But when they came to the Fathers' door,
There stood his mother old and hoar.

Yet was her hair with grey but blent,
When forth from the Upland Town he went.

There by the door his sisters stood:
Full fair they were and fresh of blood;

Little they were when he went away;
Now each is meet for a young man's may.

"O tell me, Goldilocks, my son,
What are the deeds that thou hast done?"

"I have wooed me a wife in the forest wild,
And home I bring the Woodland Child."

"A little deed to do, O son,
So long a while as thou wert gone."

"O mother, yet is the summer here

Now I bring aback my true-love dear.

And therewith an Evil Thing have I slain;
Yet I come with the first-come harvest-wain."

"O Goldilocks, my son, my son!
How good is the deed that thou hast done?

But how long the time that is worn away!
Lo! white is my hair that was but grey.

And lo these sisters here, thine own,
How tall, how meet for men-folk grown!

Come, see thy kin in the feasting-hall,
And tell me if thou knowest them all!

O son, O son, we are blithe and fain;
But the autumn drought, and the winter rain,

The frost and the snow, and St. David's wind,
All these that were, time out of mind,

All these a many times have been
Since thou the Upland Town hast seen."

Then never a word spake Goldilocks
Till they came adown from the wheaten shocks.

And there beside his love he stood
And he saw her body sweet and good.

Then round her love his arms he cast:
"The years are as a tale gone past.

But many the years that yet shall be
Of the merry tale of thee and me.

Come, love, and look on the Fathers' Hall,
And the folk of the kindred one and all!

For now the Fathers' House is kind,
And all the ill is left behind.

And Goldilocks and Goldilocks
Shall dwell in the land of the Wheaten Shocks."

Poems By The Way

LOVE IS ENOUGH
OR
THE FREEING OF PHARAMOND

DRAMATIS PERSONAE

GILES,
JOAN, his Wife,
Peasant-folk.

THE EMPEROR.
THE EMPRESS.
THE MAYOR.

A COUNCILLOR.
MASTER OLIVER, King Pharamond's Foster-father.
A NORTHERN LORD.
KING PHARAMOND.
AZALAIS, his Love.
KING THEOBALD.
HONORIUS, the Councillor.

LOVE.

LOVE IS ENOUGH

ARGUMENT

This story, which is told by way of a morality set before an Emperor and Empress newly wedded, showeth of a King whom nothing but Love might satisfy, who left all to seek Love, and, having found it, found this also, that he had enough, though he lacked all else.

In the streets of a great town where the people are gathered together thronging to see the Emperor and Empress pass.

GILES
Look long, Joan, while I hold you so,
For the silver trumpets come arow.

JOAN
O the sweet sound! the glorious sight!
O Giles, Giles, see this glittering Knight!

GILES
Nay 'tis the Marshalls'-sergeant, sweet—
—Hold, neighbour, let me keep my feet!—
There, now your head is up again;
Thus held up have you aught of pain?

JOAN
Nay, clear I see, and well at ease!
God's body! what fair Kings be these?

GILES
The Emperor's chamberlains, behold
Their silver shoes and staves of gold.
Look, look! how like some heaven come down
The maidens go with girded gown!

JOAN
Yea, yea, and this last row of them
Draw up their kirtles by the hem,
And scatter roses e'en like those
About my father's garden-close.

GILES
Ah! have I hurt you? See the girls
Whose slim hands scatter very pearls.

JOAN
Hold me fast, Giles! here comes one
Whose raiment flashes down the sun.

GILES
O sweet mouth! O fair lids cast down!
O white brow! O the crown, the crown!

JOAN
How near! if nigher I might stand
By one ell, I could touch his hand.

GILES
Look, Joan! if on this side she were
Almost my hand might touch her hair.

JOAN
Ah me! what is she thinking on?

GILES
Is he content now all is won?

JOAN
And does she think as I thought, when
Betwixt the dancing maids and men,
Twixt the porch rose-boughs blossomed red
I saw the roses on my bed?

GILES
Hath he such fear within his heart
As I had, when the wind did part
The jasmine-leaves, and there within
The new-lit taper glimmered thin?

THE MUSIC
(As the EMPEROR and EMPRESS enter.)
LOVE IS ENOUGH; though the World be a-waning
And the woods have no voice but the voice of complain-
ing,
  Though the sky be too dark for dim eyes to discover
  The gold-cups and daisies fair blooming thereunder;
  Though the hills be held shadows, and the sea a dark
wonder,
  And this day draw a veil over all deeds passed over,
  Yet their hands shall not tremble, their feet shall not fal-
ter,
  The void shall not weary, the fear shall not alter

These lips and these eyes of the loved and the lover.

THE EMPEROR

The spears flashed by me, and the swords swept round,
And in war's hopeless tangle was I bound,
But straw and stubble were the cold points found,
For still thy hands led down the weary way.

THE EMPRESS

Through hall and street they led me as a queen,
They looked to see me proud and cold of mien,
I heeded not though all my tears were seen,
For still I dreamed of thee throughout the day.

THE EMPEROR

Wild over bow and bulwark swept the sea
Unto the iron coast upon our lee,
Like painted cloth its fury was to me,
For still thy hands led down the weary way.

THE EMPRESS

They spoke to me of war within the land,
They bade me sign defiance and command;
I heeded not though thy name left my hand,
For still I dreamed of thee throughout the day.

THE EMPEROR

But now that I am come, and side by side
We go, and men cry gladly on the bride
And tremble at the image of my pride,
Where is thy hand to lead me down the way?

THE EMPRESS
But now that thou art come, and heaven and earth
Are laughing in the fulness of their mirth,
A shame I knew not in my heart has birth—
—Draw me through dreams unto the end of day!

THE EMPEROR
Behold, behold, how weak my heart is grown
Now all the heat of its desire is known!
Pearl beyond price I fear to call mine own,
Where is thy hand to lead me down the way?

THE EMPRESS
Behold, behold, how little I may move!
Think in thy heart how terrible is Love,
O thou who know'st my soul as God above—
—Draw me through dreams unto the end of day!

The stage for the play in another part of the street, and
the people thronging all about.

GILES
Here, Joan, this is so good a place
'Tis worth the scramble and the race!
There is the Empress just sat down,
Her white hands on her golden gown,
While yet the Emperor stands to hear
The welcome of the bald-head Mayor
Unto the show; and you shall see
The player-folk come in presently.
The king of whom is e'en that one,

Who wandering but a while agone
Stumbled upon our harvest-home
That August when you might not come.
Betwixt the stubble and the grass
Great mirth indeed he brought to pass.
But liefer were I to have seen
Your nimble feet tread down the green
In threesome dance to pipe and fife.

JOAN
Thou art a dear thing to my life,
And nought good have I far to seek—
But hearken! for the Mayor will speak.

THE MAYOR
Since your grace bids me speak without stint or sparing
A thing little splendid I pray you to see:
Early is the day yet, for we near the dawning
Drew on chains dear-bought, and gowns done with gold;
So may ye high ones hearken an hour
A tale that our hearts hold worthy and good,
Of Pharamond the Freed, who, a king feared and hon-
oured,
Fled away to find love from his crown and his folk.
E'en as I tell of it somewhat I tremble
Lest we, fearful of treason to the love that fulfils you,
Should seem to make little of the love that ye give us,
Of your lives full of glory, of the deeds that your lifetime
Shall gleam with for ever when we are forgotten.
Forgive it for the greatness of that Love who compels
us.—
Hark! in the minster-tower minish the joy-bells,

And all men are hushed now these marvels to hear.

THE EMPEROR (to the MAYOR)
We thank your love, that sees our love indeed
Toward you, toward Love, toward life of toil and need:
We shall not falter though your poet sings
Of all defeat, strewing the crowns of kings
About the thorny ways where Love doth wend,
Because we know us faithful to the end
Toward you, toward Love, toward life of war and deed,
And well we deem your tale shall help our need.

(To the EMPRESS)
So many hours to pass before the sun
Shall blush ere sleeping, and the day be done!
How thinkest thou, my sweet, shall such a tale
For lengthening or for shortening them avail?

THE EMPRESS
Nay, dreamland has no clocks the wise ones say,
And while our hands move at the break of day
We dream of years: and I am dreaming still
And need no change my cup of joy to fill:
Let them say on, and I shall hear thy voice
Telling the tale, and in its love rejoice.

THE MUSIC
(As the singers enter and stand before the curtain, the
player-king and player-maiden in the midst.)
   LOVE IS ENOUGH: have no thought for to-morrow
If ye lie down this even in rest from your pain,
Ye who have paid for your bliss with great sorrow:

For as it was once so it shall be again.
Ye shall cry out for death as ye stretch forth in vain.

Feeble hands to the hands that would help but they may
not,
    Cry out to deaf ears that would hear if they could;
    Till again shall the change come, and words your lips say
not
    Your hearts make all plain in the best wise they would
    And the world ye thought waning is glorious and good:

And no morning now mocks you and no nightfall is
weary,
    The plains are not empty of song and of deed:
    The sea strayeth not, nor the mountains are dreary;
    The wind is not helpless for any man's need,
    Nor falleth the rain but for thistle and weed.

O surely this morning all sorrow is hidden,
All battle is hushed for this even at least;
And no one this noontide may hunger, unbidden
To the flowers and the singing and the joy of your feast
Where silent ye sit midst the world's tale increased.

Lo, the lovers unloved that draw nigh for your blessing!
For your tale makes the dreaming whereby yet they live
The dreams of the day with their hopes of redressing,
The dreams of the night with the kisses they give,
The dreams of the dawn wherein death and hope strive.

Ah, what shall we say then, but that earth threatened
often

Shall live on for ever that such things may be,
That the dry seed shall quicken, the hard earth shall soft-
en,
   And the spring-bearing birds flutter north o'er the sea,
   That earth's garden may bloom round my love's feet and
me?

THE EMPEROR

Lo you, my sweet, fair folk are one and all
And with good grace their broidered robes do fall,
And sweet they sing indeed: but he, the King,
Look but a little how his fingers cling
To her's, his love that shall be in the play—
His love that hath been surely ere to-day:
And see, her wide soft eyes cast down at whiles
Are opened not to note the people's smiles
But her love's lips, and dreamily they stare
As though they sought the happy country, where
They two shall be alone, and the world dead.

THE EMPRESS

Most faithful eyes indeed look from the head
The sun has burnt, and wind and rain has beat,
Well may he find her slim brown fingers sweet.
And he—methinks he trembles, lest he find
That song of his not wholly to her mind.
Note how his grey eyes look askance to see
Her bosom heaving with the melody
His heart loves well: rough with the wind and rain
His cheek is, hollow with some ancient pain;
The sun has burned and blanched his crispy hair,

And over him hath swept a world of care
And left him careless, rugged, and her own;
Still fresh desired, still strange and new, though known.

THE EMPEROR
His eyes seem dreaming of the mysteries
Deep in the depths of her familiar eyes,
Tormenting and alluring; does he dream,
As I ofttime this morn, how they would seem
Loved but unloving?—Nay the world's too sweet
That we the ghost of such a pain should meet—
Behold, she goes, and he too, turning round,
Remembers that his love must yet be found,
That he is King and loveless in this story
Wrought long ago for some dead poet's glory.
[Exeunt players behind the curtain.

Enter before the curtain LOVE crowned as a King.

LOVE
All hail, my servants! tremble ye, my foes!
A hope for these I have, a fear for those
Hid in this tale of Pharamond the Freed.
To-day, my Faithful, nought shall be your need
Of tears compassionate:—although full oft
The crown of love laid on my bosom soft
Be woven of bitter death and deathless fame,
Bethorned with woe, and fruited thick with shame.
—This for the mighty of my courts I keep,
Lest through the world there should be none to weep
Except for sordid loss; and not to gain
But satiate pleasure making mock of pain.

—Yea, in the heaven from whence my dreams go forth
Are stored the signs that make the world of worth:
There is the wavering wall of mighty Troy
About my Helen's hope and Paris' joy:
There lying neath the fresh dyed mulberry-tree
The sword and cloth of Pyramus I see:
There is the number of the joyless days
Wherein Medea won no love nor praise:
There is the sand my Ariadne pressed;
The footprints of the feet that knew no rest
While o'er the sea forth went the fatal sign:
The asp of Egypt, the Numidian wine,
My Sigurd's sword, my Brynhild's fiery bed,
The tale of years of Gudrun's drearihead,
And Tristram's glaive, and Iseult's shriek are here,
And cloister-gown of joyless Guenevere.

Save you, my Faithful! how your loving eyes
Grow soft and gleam with all these memories!
But on this day my crown is not of death:
My fire-tipped arrows, and my kindling breath
Are all the weapons I shall need to-day.
Nor shall my tale in measured cadence play
About the golden lyre of Gods long gone,
Nor dim and doubtful 'twixt the ocean's moan
Wail out about the Northern fiddle-bow,
Stammering with pride or quivering shrill with woe.
Rather caught up at hazard is the pipe
That mixed with scent of roses over ripe,
And murmur of the summer afternoon,
May charm you somewhat with its wavering tune
'Twixt joy and sadness: whatsoe'er it saith,

I know at least there breathes through it my breath

OF PHARAMOND THE FREED
Scene: In the Kings Chamber of Audience.
MASTER OLIVER and many LORDS and COUN-
CILLORS.

A COUNCILLOR
Fair Master Oliver, thou who at all times
Mayst open thy heart to our lord and master,
Tell us what tidings thou hast to deliver;
For our hearts are grown heavy, and where shall we turn
to
If thus the king's glory, our gain and salvation,
Must go down the wind amid gloom and despairing?

MASTER OLIVER
Little may be looked for, fair lords, in my story,
To lighten your hearts of the load lying on them.
For nine days the king hath slept not an hour,
And taketh no heed of soft words or beseeching.
Yea, look you, my lords, if a body late dead
In the lips and the cheeks should gain some little colour,
And arise and wend forth with no change in the eyes,
And wander about as if seeking its soul—
Lo, e'en so sad is my lord and my master;
Yea, e'en so far hath his soul drifted from us.

A COUNCILLOR
What say the leeches? Is all their skill left them?

MASTER OLIVER

Nay, they bade lead him to hunt and to tilting,
To set him on high in the throne of his honour
To judge heavy deeds: bade him handle the tiller,
And drive through the sea with the wind at its wildest;
All things he was wont to hold kingly and good.
So we led out his steed and he straight leapt upon him
With no word, and no looking to right nor to left,
And into the forest we fared as aforetime:
Fast on the king followed, and cheered without stinting
The hounds to the strife till the bear stood at bay;
Then there he alone by the beech-trees alighted;
Barehanded, unarmoured, he handled the spear-shaft,
And blew up the death on the horn of his father;
Yet still in his eyes was no look of rejoicing,
And no life in his lips; but I likened him rather
To King Nimrod carved fair on the back of the high-seat
When the candles are dying, and the high moon is
streaming
Through window and luffer white on the lone pavement
Whence the guests are departed in the hall of the pal-
ace.—
—Rode we home heavily, he with his rein loose,
Feet hanging free from the stirrups, and staring
At a clot of the bear's blood that stained his green kir-
tle;—
Unkingly, unhappy, he rode his ways homeward.

A COUNCILLOR
Was this all ye tried, or have ye more tidings?
For the wall tottereth not at first stroke of the ram.

MASTER OLIVER

231

Nay, we brought him a-board the Great Dragon one
dawning,
When the cold bay was flecked with the crests of white
billows
And the clouds lay alow on the earth and the sea;
He looked not aloft as they hoisted the sail,
But with hand on the tiller hallooed to the shipmen
In a voice grown so strange, that it scarce had seemed
stranger
If from the ship Argo, in seemly wise woven
On the guard-chamber hangings, some early grey dawn-
ing
Great Jason had cried, and his golden locks wavered.
Then e'en as the oars ran outboard, and dashed
In the wind-scattered foam and the sails bellied out,
His hand dropped from the tiller, and with feet all un-
certain
And dull eye he wended him down to the midship,
And gazing about for the place of the gangway
Made for the gate of the bulwark half open,
And stood there and stared at the swallowing sea,
Then turned, and uncertain went wandering back stern-
ward,
And sat down on the deck by the side of the helmsman,
Wrapt in dreams of despair; so I bade them turn shore-
ward,
And slowly he rose as the side grated stoutly
'Gainst the stones of the quay and they cast forth the
hawser.—
Unkingly, unhappy, he went his ways homeward.

A COUNCILLOR

But by other ways yet had thy wisdom to travel;
How else did ye work for the winning him peace?

MASTER OLIVER
We bade gather the knights for the goodliest tilting,
There the ladies went lightly in glorious array;
In the old arms we armed him whose dints well he knew
That the night dew had dulled and the sea salt had sul-
lied:
On the old roan yet sturdy we set him astride;
So he stretched forth his hand to lay hold of the spear
Neither laughing nor frowning, as lightly his wont was
When the knights are awaiting the voice of the trumpet.
It awoke, and back beaten from barrier to barrier
Was caught up by knights' cries, by the cry of the king.—
—Such a cry as red Mars in the Council-room window
May awake with some noon when the last horn is wind-
ed,
And the bones of the world are dashed grinding together.
So it seemed to my heart, and a horror came o'er me,
As the spears met, and splinters flew high o'er the field,
And I saw the king stay when his course was at swiftest,
His horse straining hard on the bit, and he standing
Stiff and stark in his stirrups, his spear held by the mid-
most,
His helm cast a-back, his teeth set hard together;
E'en as one might, who, riding to heaven, feels round him
The devils unseen: then he raised up the spear
As to cast it away, but therewith failed his fury,
He dropped it, and faintly sank back in the saddle,
And, turning his horse from the press and the turmoil,
Came sighing to me, and sore grieving I took him

And led him away, while the lists were fallen silent
As a fight in a dream that the light breaketh through.—
To the tune of the clinking of his fight-honoured armour
Unkingly, unhappy, he went his ways homeward.

A COUNCILLOR
What thing worse than the worst in the budget yet lieth?

MASTER OLIVER
To the high court we brought him, and bade him to hearken
The pleading of his people, and pass sentence on evil.
His face changed with great pain, and his brow grew all furrowed,
As a grim tale was told there of the griefs of the lowly;
Till he took up the word, mid the trembling of tyrants,
As his calm voice and cold wrought death on ill doers—
—E'en so might King Minos in marble there carven
Mid old dreaming of Crete give doom on the dead,
When the world and its deeds are dead too and buried.—
But lo, as I looked, his clenched hands were loosened,
His lips grew all soft, and his eyes were beholding
Strange things we beheld not about and above him.
So he sat for a while, and then swept his robe round him
And arose and departed, not heeding his people,
The strange looks, the peering, the rustle and whisper;
But or ever he gained the gate that gave streetward,
Dull were his eyes grown, his feet were grown heavy,
His lips crooned complaining, as onward he stumbled;—
Unhappy, unkingly, he went his ways homeward.

A COUNCILLOR

Is all striving over then, fair Master Oliver?

MASTER OLIVER

All mine, lords, for ever! help who may help henceforth
I am but helpless: too surely meseemeth
He seeth me not, and knoweth no more
Me that have loved him. Woe worth the while, Phara-
mond,
    That men should love aught, love always as I loved!
Mother and sister and the sweetling that scorned me,
The wind of the autumn-tide over them sweepeth,
All are departed, but this one, the dear one—
I should die or he died and be no more alone,
But God's hatred hangs round me, and the life and the
glory
    That grew with my waning life fade now before it,
And leaving no pity depart through the void.

A COUNCILLOR

This is a sight full sorry to see
These tears of an elder! But soft now, one cometh.

MASTER OLIVER

The feet of the king: will ye speak or begone?

A NORTHERN LORD

I will speak at the least, whoever keeps silence,
For well it may be that the voice of a stranger
Shall break through his dreaming better than thine;
And lo now a word in my mouth is a-coming,
    That the king well may hearken: how sayst thou, fair
master,

Whose name now I mind not, wilt thou have me essay it?

MASTER OLIVER

Try whatso thou wilt, things may not be worser. [Enter
KING.

Behold, how he cometh weighed down by his woe!
(To the KING)
All hail, lord and master! wilt thou hearken a little
These lords high in honour whose hearts are full heavy
Because thy heart sickeneth and knoweth no joy?—
(To the COUNCILLORS)
Ah, see you! all silent, his eyes set and dreary,
His lips moving a little—how may I behold it?

THE NORTHERN LORD

May I speak, king? dost hearken? many matters I have
To deal with or death. I have honoured thee duly
Down in the north there; a great name I have held thee;
Rough hand in the field, ready righter of wrong,
Reckless of danger, but recking of pity.
But now—is it false what the chapmen have told us,
And are thy fair robes all thou hast of a king?
Is it bragging and lies, that thou beardless and tender
Weptst not when they brought thy slain father before
thee,
Trembledst not when the leaguer that lay round thy city
Made a light for these windows, a noise for thy pillow?
Is it lies what men told us of thy singing and laughter
As thou layst in thy lair fled away from lost battle?
Is it lies how ye met in the depths of the mountains,
And a handful rushed down and made nought of an
army?

236

Those tales of your luck, like the tide at its turning,
Trusty and sure howso slowly it cometh,
Are they lies? Is it lies of wide lands in the world,
How they sent thee great men to lie low at thy footstool
In five years thenceforward, and thou still a youth?
Are they lies, these fair tidings, or what see thy lords
here—
Some love-sick girl's brother caught up by that sickness,
As one street beggar catches the pest from his neigh-
bour?

KING PHARAMOND
What words are these of lies and love-sickness?
Why am I lonely among all this brawling?
O foster-father, is all faith departed
That this hateful face should be staring upon me?

THE NORTHERN LORD
Lo, now thou awakest; so tell me in what wise
I shall wend back again: set a word in my mouth
To meet the folks' murmur, and give heart to the heavy;
For there man speaks to man that thy measure is full,
And thy five-years-old kingdom is falling asunder.
[KING draws his sword.
Yea, yea, a fair token thy sword were to send them;
Thou dost well to draw it; (KING brandishes his sword
over the
lord's head, as if to strike him): soft sound is its whistle;
Strike then, O king, for my wars are well over,
And dull is the way my feet tread to the grave!

KING PHARAMOND (sheathing his sword)

Man, if ye have waked me, I bid you be wary
Lest my sword yet should reach you; ye wot in your
northland
What hatred he winneth who waketh the shipman
From the sweet rest of death mid the welter of waves;
So with us may it fare; though I know thee full faithful,
Bold in field and in council, most fit for a king.
—Bear with me. I pray you that to none may be meted
Such a measure of pain as my soul is oppressed with.
Depart all for a little, till my spirit grows lighter,
Then come ye with tidings, and hold we fair council,
That my countries may know they have yet got a king.
[Exeunt all but OLIVER and KING.
Come, my foster-father, ere thy visage fade from me,
Come with me mid the flowers some opening to find
In the clouds that cling round me; if thou canst remem-
ber
Thine old lovingkindness when I was a king.

THE MUSIC
LOVE IS ENOUGH; it grew up without heeding
In the days when ye knew not its name nor its measure
And its leaflets untrodden by the light feet of pleasure
Had no boast of the blossom, no sign of the seeding,
As the morning and evening passed over its treasure.

And what do ye say then?—that Spring long departed
Has brought forth no child to the softness and showers;
—That we slept and we dreamed through the Summer
of flowers;
We dreamed of the Winter, and waking dead-hearted
Found Winter upon us and waste of dull hours.

238

Nay, Spring was o'er happy and knew not the reason,
And Summer dreamed sadly, for she thought all was
ended
In her fulness of wealth that might not be amended;
But this is the harvest and the garnering season,
And the leaf and the blossom in the ripe fruit are blend-
ed.

It sprang without sowing, it grew without heeding,
Ye knew not its name and ye knew not its measure,
Ye noted it not mid your hope and your pleasure;
There was pain in its blossom, despair in its seeding,
But daylong your bosom now nurseth its treasure.

Enter before the curtain LOVE clad as an image-maker.

LOVE
How mighty and how fierce a king is here
The stayer of falling folks, the bane of fear!
Fair life he liveth, ruling passing well,
Disdaining praise of Heaven and hate of Hell;
And yet how goodly to us Great in Heaven
Are such as he, the waning world that leaven!
How well it were that such should never die!
How well it were at least that memory
Of such should live, as live their glorious deeds!
—But which of all the Gods think ye it needs
To shape the mist of Rumour's wavering breath
Into a golden dream that fears no death?
Red Mars belike?—since through his field is thrust

The polished plough-share o'er the helmets' rust!—
Apollo's beauty?—surely eld shall spare
Smooth skin, and flashing eyes, and crispy hair!—
Nay, Jove himself?—the pride that holds the low
Apart, despised, to mighty tales must grow!—
Or Pallas?—for the world that knoweth nought,
By that great wisdom to the wicket brought,
Clear through the tangle evermore shall see!
—O Faithful, O Beloved, turn to ME!
I am the Ancient of the Days that were
I am the Newborn that To-day brings here,
I am the Life of all that dieth not;
Through me alone is sorrow unforgot.

My Faithful, knowing that this man should live,
I from the cradle gifts to him did give
Unmeet belike for rulers of the earth;
As sorrowful yearning in the midst of mirth,
Pity midst anger, hope midst scorn and hate.
Languor midst labour, lest the day wax late,
And all be wrong, and all be to begin.
Through these indeed the eager life did win
That was the very body to my soul;
Yet, as the tide of battle back did roll
Before his patience: as he toiled and grieved
O'er fools and folly, was he not deceived,
But ever knew the change was drawing nigh,
And in my mirror gazed with steadfast eye.
Still, O my Faithful, seemed his life so fair
That all Olympus might have left him there
Until to bitter strength that life was grown,
And then have smiled to see him die alone,

Had I not been.—— Ye know me; I have sent
A pain to pierce his last coat of content:
Now must he tear the armour from his breast
And cast aside all things that men deem best,
And single-hearted for his longing strive
That he at last may save his soul alive.
How say ye then, Beloved? Ye have known
The blossom of the seed these hands have sown;
Shall this man starve in sorrow's thorny brake?
Shall Love the faithful of his heart forsake?

In the King's Garden.
KING PHARAMOND, MASTER OLIVER.

MASTER OLIVER
In this quiet place canst thou speak, O my King,
Where nought but the lilies may hearken our counsel?

KING PHARAMOND
What wouldst thou have of me? why came we hither?

MASTER OLIVER
Dear lord, thou wouldst speak of the woe that weighs on
thee.

KING PHARAMOND
Wouldst thou bear me aback to the strife and the battle?
Nay, hang up my banner: 'tis all passed and over!

MASTER OLIVER
Speak but a little, lord! have I not loved thee?

KING PHARAMOND
Yea,—thou art Oliver: I saw thee a-lying
A long time ago with the blood on thy face,
When my father wept o'er thee for thy faith and thy
valour.

MASTER OLIVER
Years have passed over, but my faith hath not failed me;
Spent is my might, but my love not departed.
Shall not love help—yea, look long in my eyes!
There is no more to see if thou sawest my heart.

KING PHARAMOND
Yea, thou art Oliver, full of all kindness!
Have patience, for now is the cloud passing over—
Have patience and hearken—yet shalt thou be shamed.

MASTER OLIVER
Thou shalt shine through thy shame as the sun through
the haze
When the world waiteth gladly the warm day a-coming:
As great as thou seem'st now, I know thee for greater
Than thy deeds done and told of: one day I shall know
thee:
Lying dead in my tomb I shall hear the world praising.

KING PHARAMOND
Stay thy praise—let me speak, lest all speech depart from
me.
    —There is a place in the world, a great valley
That seems a green plain from the brow of the moun-

tains,

But hath knolls and fair dales when adown there thou
goest:

There are homesteads therein with gardens about them,

And fair herds of kine and grey sheep a-feeding,

And willow-hung streams wend through deep grassy
meadows,

And a highway winds through them from the outer
world coming:

Girthed about is the vale by a grey wall of mountains,

Rent apart in three places and tumbled together

In old times of the world when the earth-fires flowed
forth:

And as you wend up these away from the valley

You think of the sea and the great world it washes;

But through two you may pass not, the shattered rocks
shut them.

And up through the third there windeth a highway,

And its gorge is fulfilled by a black wood of yew-trees.

And I know that beyond, though mine eyes have not
seen it,

A city of merchants beside the sea lieth.——

I adjure thee, my fosterer, by the hand of my father,

By thy faith without stain, by the days unforgotten,

When I dwelt in thy house ere the troubles' beginning,

By thy fair wife long dead and thy sword-smitten chil-
dren,

By thy life without blame and thy love without blemish,

Tell me how, tell me when, that fair land I may come to!

Hide it not for my help, for my honour, but tell me,

Lest my time and thy time be lost days and confusion!

MASTER OLIVER

O many such lands!—O my master, what ails thee?
Tell me again, for I may not remember.
—I prayed God give thee speech, and lo God hath given
it—
May God give me death! if I dream not this evil.

KING PHARAMOND

Said I not when thou knew'st it, all courage should fail
thee?
But me—my heart fails not, I am Pharamond as ever.
I shall seek and shall find—come help me, my fosterer!
—Yet if thou shouldst ask for a sign from that country
What have I to show thee—I plucked a blue milk-wort
From amidst of the field where she wandered fair-foot-
ed—
It was gone when I wakened—and once in my wallet
I set some grey stones from the way through the forest—
These were gone when I wakened—and once as I wan-
dered
A lock of white wool from a thorn-bush I gathered;
It was gone when I wakened—the name of that coun-
try—
Nay, how should I know it?—but ever meseemeth
'Twas not in the southlands, for sharp in the sunset
And sunrise the air is, and whiles I have seen it
Amid white drift of snow—ah, look up, foster-father!

MASTER OLIVER

O woe, woe is me that I may not awaken!
Or else, art thou verily Pharamond my fosterling,
The Freed and the Freer, the Wise, the World's Wonder?

KING PHARAMOND

Why fainteth thy great heart? nay, Oliver, hearken,
E'en such as I am now these five years I have been.
Through five years of striving this dreamer and dotard
Has reaped glory from ruin, drawn peace from destruc-
tion.

MASTER OLIVER

Woe's me! wit hath failed me, and all the wise counsel
I was treasuring up down the wind is a-drifting—
Yet what wouldst thou have there if ever thou find it?
Are the gates of heaven there? is Death bound there and
helpless?

KING PHARAMOND

Nay, thou askest me this not as one without knowledge,
For thou know'st that my love in that land is abiding.

MASTER OLIVER

Yea—woe worth the while—and all wisdom hath failed
me:
Yet if thou wouldst tell me of her, I will hearken
Without mocking or mourning, if that may avail thee.

KING PHARAMOND

Lo, thy face is grown kind—Thou rememberest the even
When I first wore the crown after sore strife and mourn-
ing?

MASTER OLIVER

Who shall ever forget it? the dead face of thy father,

245

And thou in thy fight-battered armour above it,
Mid the passion of tears long held back by the battle;
And thy rent banner o'er thee and the ring of men mail-
clad,
Victorious to-day, since their ruin but a spear-length
Was thrust away from them.—Son, think of thy glory
And e'en in such wise break the throng of these devils!

KING PHARAMOND

Five years are passed over since in the fresh dawning
On the field of that fight I lay wearied and sleepless
Till slumber came o'er me in the first of the sunrise;
Then as there lay my body rapt away was my spirit,
And a cold and thick mist for a while was about me,
And when that cleared away, lo, the mountain-walled
country
'Neath the first of the sunrise in e'en such a spring-tide
As the spring-tide our horse-hoofs that yestereve tram-
pled:
By the withy-wrought gate of a garden I found me
'Neath the goodly green boughs of the apple full-blos-
somed;
And fulfilled of great pleasure I was as I entered
The fair place of flowers, and wherefore I knew not.
Then lo, mid the birds' song a woman's voice singing.
Five years passed away, in the first of the sunrise.
[He is silent, brooding.

MASTER OLIVER

God help us if God is!—for this man, I deemed him
More a glory of God made man for our helping
Than a man that should die: all the deeds he did surely,

246

Too great for a man's life, have undone the doer.

KING PHARAMOND (rousing himself)
Thou art waiting, my fosterer, till I tell of her singing
And the words that she sang there: time was when I
knew them;
But too much of strife is about us this morning,
And whiles I forget and whiles I remember.
[Falls a-musing again.

MASTER OLIVER
But a night's dream undid him, and he died, and his
kingdom
By unheard-of deeds fashioned, was tumbled together,
By false men and fools to be fought for and ruined.
Such words shall my ghost see the chronicler writing
In the days that shall be:—ah—what wouldst thou, my
fosterling?
Knowest thou not how words fail us awaking
That we seemed to hear plain amid sleep and its sweet-
ness?
Nay, strive not, my son, rest awhile and be silent;
Or sleep while I watch thee: full fair is the garden,
Perchance mid the flowers thy sweet dream may find
thee,
And thou shalt have pleasure and peace for a little.—
(Aside) And my soul shall depart ere thou wak'st perad-
venture.

KING PHARAMOND
Yea, thou deemest me mad: a dream thou mayst call it,
But not such a dream as thou know'st of: nay, hearken!

For what manner of dream then is this that remembers
The words that she sang on that morning of glory;—
O love, set a word in my mouth for our meeting;
Cast thy sweet arms about me to stay my hearts beating!
Ah, thy silence, thy silence! nought shines on the dark-
ness!
—O close-serried throng of the days that I see not!
[Falls a-musing again.

MASTER OLIVER
Thus the worse that shall be, the bad that is, bettereth.
—Once more he is speechless mid evil dreams sunken.

KING PHARAMOND (speaking very low).
Hold silence, love, speak not of the sweet day departed;
Cling close to me, love, lest I waken sad-hearted!
[Louder to OLIVER.
Thou starest, my fosterer: what strange thing beholdst
thou?
A great king, a strong man, that thou knewest a child
once:
Pharamond the fair babe: Pharamond the warrior;
Pharamond the king, and which hast thou feared yet?
And why wilt thou fear then this Pharamond the lover?
Shall I fail of my love who failed not of my fame?
Nay, nay, I shall live for the last gain and greatest.

MASTER OLIVER
I know not—all counsel and wit is departed,
I wait for thy will; I will do it, my master.

KING PHARAMOND

248

Through the boughs of the garden I followed the singing
To a smooth space of sward: there the unknown desire
Of my soul I beheld,—wrought in shape of a woman.

MASTER OLIVER

O ye warders of Troy-walls, join hands through the dark-
ness,
Tell us tales of the Downfall, for we too are with you!

KING PHARAMOND

As my twin sister, young of years was she and slender,
Yellow blossoms of spring-tide her hands had been gath-
ering,
But the gown-lap that held them had fallen adown
And had lain round her feet with the first of the singing;
Now her singing had ceased, though yet heaved her bo-
som
As with lips lightly parted and eyes of one seeking
She stood face to face with the Love that she knew not,
The love that she longed for and waited unwitting;
She moved not, I breathed not—till lo, a horn winded,
And she started, and o'er her came trouble and wonder,
Came pallor and trembling; came a strain at my heart-
strings
As bodiless there I stretched hands toward her beauty,
And voiceless cried out, as the cold mist swept o'er me.
Then again clash of arms, and the morning watch calling,
And the long leaves and great twisted trunks of the
chesnuts,
As I sprang to my feet and turned round to the trumpets
And gathering of spears and unfolding of banners
That first morn of my reign and my glory's beginning.

MASTER OLIVER

O well were we that tide though the world was against us.

KING PHARAMOND

Hearken yet!—through that whirlwind of danger and battle,

Beaten back, struggling forward, we fought without blemish

On my banner spear-rent in the days of my father,
On my love of the land and the longing I cherished
For a tale to be told when I, laid in the minster,
Might hear it no more; was it easy of winning,
Our bread of those days? Yet as wild as the work was,
Unforgotten and sweet in my heart was that vision,
And her eyes and her lips and her fair body's fashion
Blest all times of rest, rent the battle asunder,
Turned ruin to laughter and death unto dreaming;
And again and thrice over again did I go there
Ere spring was grown winter: in the meadows I met her,
By the sheaves of the corn, by the down-falling apples,
Kind and calm, yea and glad, yet with eyes of one seeking.
—Ah the mouth of one waiting, ere all shall be over!—
But at last in the winter-tide mid the dark forest

Side by side did we wend down the pass: the wind tangled

Mid the trunks and black boughs made wild music about us,

But her feet on the scant snow and the sound of her breathing

Made music much better: the wood thinned, and I saw

her,
  As we came to the brow of the pass; for the moon gleamed
  Bitter cold in the cloudless black sky of the winter.
  Then the world drew me back from my love, and depart-
ing
  I saw her sweet serious look pass into terror
  And her arms cast abroad—and lo, clashing of armour,
  And a sword in my hand, and my mouth crying loud,
  And the moon and cold steel in the doorway burst open
  And thy doughty spear thrust through the throat of the
foeman
  My dazed eyes scarce saw—thou rememberest, my fos-
terer?

MASTER OLIVER
  Yea, Theobald the Constable had watched but unduly;
  We were taken unwares, and wild fleeing there was
  O'er black rock and white snow—shall such times come
again, son?

KING PHARAMOND
  Yea, full surely they shall; have thou courage, my foster-
er!—
  Day came thronging on day, month thrust month aside,
  Amid battle and strife and the murder of glory,
  And still oft and oft to that land was I led
  And still through all longing I young in Love's dealings,
  Never called it a pain: though, the battle passed over,
  The council determined, back again came my craving:
  I knew not the pain, but I knew all the pleasure,
  When now, as the clouds o'er my fortune were parting,
  I felt myself waxing in might and in wisdom;

And no city welcomed the Freed and the Freer,
And no mighty army fell back before rumour
Of Pharamond's coming, but her heart bid me thither,
And the blithest and kindest of kingfolk ye knew me.
Then came the high tide of deliverance upon us,
When surely if we in the red field had fallen
The stocks and the stones would have risen to avenge us.
—Then waned my sweet vision midst glory's fulfilment,
And still with its waning, hot waxed my desire:
And did ye not note then that the glad-hearted Phara-
mond
Was grown a stern man, a fierce king, it may be?
Did ye deem it the growth of my manhood, the harden-
ing
Of battle and murder and treason about me?
Nay, nay, it was love's pain, first named and first noted
When a long time went past, and I might not behold her.
—Thou rememberest a year agone now, when the legate
Of the Lord of the Waters brought here a broad letter
Full of prayers for good peace and our friendship thence-
forward—
—He who erst set a price on the lost head of Phara-
mond—
How I bade him stand up on his feet and be merry,
Eat his meat by my side and drink out of my beaker,
In memory of days when my meat was but little
And my drink drunk in haste between saddle and straw.
But lo! midst of my triumph, as I noted the feigning
Of the last foeman humbled, and the hall fell a murmur-
ing,
And blithely the horns blew, Be glad, spring prevaileth,
—As I sat there and changed not, my soul saw a vision:

All folk faded away, and my love that I long for
Came with raiment a-rustling along the hall pavement,
Drawing near to the high-seat, with hands held out a
little,
Till her hallowed eyes drew me a space into heaven,
And her lips moved to whisper, 'Come, love, for I weary!'
Then she turned and went from me, and I heard her feet
falling
On the floor of the hall, e'en as though it were empty
Of all folk but us twain in the hush of the dawning.
Then again, all was gone, and I sat there a smiling
On the faint-smiling legate, as the hall windows quivered
With the rain of the early night sweeping across them.
Nought slept I that night, yet I saw her without sleep-
ing:—
Betwixt midnight and morn of that summer-tide was I
Amidst of the lilies by her house-door to hearken
If perchance in her chamber she turned amid sleeping:
When lo, as the East 'gan to change, and stars faded
Were her feet on the stairs, and the door opened softly,
And she stood on the threshold with the eyes of one
seeking,
And there, gathering the folds of her gown to her girdle,
Went forth through the garden and followed the high-
way,
All along the green valley, and I ever beside her,
Till the light of the low sun just risen was falling
On her feet in the first of the pass—and all faded.
Yet from her unto me had gone forth her intent,
And I saw her face set to the heart of that city,
And the quays where the ships of the outlanders come to,
And I said: She is seeking, and shall I not seek?

The sea is her prison wall; where is my prison?
—Yet I said: Here men praise me, perchance men may
love me
If I live long enough for my justice and mercy
To make them just and merciful—one who is master
Of many poor folk, a man pity moveth
Love hath dealt with in this wise, no minstrel nor dream-
er.
The deeds that my hand might find for the doing
Did desire undo them these four years of fight?
And now time and fair peace in my heart have begotten
More desire and more pain, is the day of deeds done
with?
Lo here for my part my bonds and my prison!—
Then with hands holding praise, yet with fierce heart be-
like
Did I turn to the people that I had delivered—
And the deeds of this year passed shall live peradventure!
But now came no solace of dreams in the night-tide
From that day thenceforward; yet oft in the council,
Mid the hearkening folk craving for justice or mercy,
Mid the righting of wrongs and the staying of ruin,
Mid the ruling a dull folk, who deemed all my kingship
A thing due and easy as the dawning and sunset
To the day that God made once to deal with no further—
—Mid all these a fair face, a sad face, could I fashion,
And I said, She is seeking, and shall I not seek?
—Tell over the days of the year of hope's waning;
Tell over the hours of the weary days wearing:
Tell over the minutes of the hours of thy waking,
Then wonder he liveth who fails of his longing!

MASTER OLIVER
What wouldst thou have, son, wherein I might help thee?

KING PHARAMOND
Hearken yet:—for a long time no more I beheld her
Till a month agone now at the ending of Maytide;
And then in the first of the morning I found me
Fulfilled of all joy at the edge of the yew-wood;
Then lo, her gown's flutter in the fresh breeze of morning,
And slower and statelier than her wont was aforetime
And fairer of form toward the yew-wood she wended.
But woe's me! as she came and at last was beside me
With sobbing scarce ended her bosom was heaving,
Stained with tears was her face, and her mouth was yet
quivering
With torment of weeping held back for a season.
Then swiftly my spirit to the King's bed was wafted
While still toward the sea were her weary feet wending.
—Ah surely that day of all wrongs that I hearkened
Mine own wrongs seemed heaviest and hardest to bear—
Mine own wrongs and hers—till that past year of ruling
Seemed a crime and a folly. Night came, and I saw her
Stealing barefoot, bareheaded amidst of the tulips
Made grey by the moonlight: and a long time Love gave
me
To gaze on her weeping—morn came, and I wakened—
I wakened and said: Through the World will I wander,
Till either I find her, or find the World empty.

MASTER OLIVER
Yea, son, wilt thou go? Ah thou knowest from of old time
My words might not stay thee from aught thou wert

willing;
    And e'en so it must be now. And yet hast thou asked me
    To go with thee, son, if aught I might help thee?—
    Ah me, if thy face might gladden a little
    I should meet the world better and mock at its mocking:
    If thou goest to find her, why then hath there fallen
    This heaviness on thee? is thy heart waxen feeble?

KING PHARAMOND

    O friend, I have seen her no more, and her mourning
    Is alone and unhelped—yet to-night or to-morrow
    Somewhat nigher will I be to her love and her longing.
    Lo, to thee, friend, alone of all folk on the earth
    These things have I told: for a true man I deem thee
    Beyond all men call true; yea, a wise man moreover
    And hardy and helpful; and I know thy heart surely
    That thou holdest the world nought without me thy fos-
terling.
    Come, leave all awhile! it may be as time weareth
    With new life in our hands we shall wend us back hither.

MASTER OLIVER

    Yea; triumph turns trouble, and all the world changeth,
    Yet a good world it is since we twain are together.

KING PHARAMOND

    Lo, have I not said it?—thou art kinder than all men.
    Cast about then, I pray thee, to find us a keel
    Sailing who recketh whither, since the world is so wide.
    Sure the northlands shall know of the blessings she brin-
geth,
    And the southlands be singing of the tales that foretold

her.

MASTER OLIVER

Well I wot of all chapmen—and to-night weighs a dro-
mond
    Sailing west away first, and then to the southlands.
    Since in such things I deal oft they know me, but know
not
    King Pharamond the Freed, since now first they sail
hither.
    So make me thy messenger in a fair-writ broad letter
    And thyself make my scrivener, and this very night sail
we.—
    O surely thy face now is brightening and blesseth me!
    Peer through these boughs toward the bay and the haven,
    And high masts thou shalt see, and white sails hanging
ready.
    [Exit OLIVER.

KING PHARAMOND

Dost thou weep now, my darling, and are thy feet wan-
dering
    On the ways ever empty of what thou desirest?
    Nay, nay, for thou know'st me, and many a night-tide
    Hath Love led thee forth to a city unknown:
    Thou hast paced through this palace from chamber to
chamber
    Till in dawn and stars' paling I have passed forth before
thee:
    Thou hast seen thine own dwelling nor known how to
name it:
    Thine own dwelling that shall be when love is victorious.

Thou hast seen my sword glimmer amidst of the moon-
light,
As we rode with hoofs muffled through waylaying mur-
der.
Through the field of the dead hast thou fared to behold
me,
Seen me waking and longing by the watch-fires' flicker;
Thou hast followed my banner amidst of the battle
And seen my face change to the man that they fear,
Yet found me not fearful nor turned from beholding:
Thou hast been at my triumphs, and heard the tale's end-
ing
Of my wars, and my winning through days evil and wea-
ry:
For this eve hast thou waited, and wilt be peradventure
By the sea-strand to-night, for thou wottest full surely
That the word is gone forth, and the world is a-moving.
—Abide me, beloved! to-day and to-morrow
Shall be little words in the tale of our loving,
When the last morn ariseth, and thou and I meeting
From lips laid together tell tales of these marvels.

THE MUSIC
LOVE IS ENOUGH: draw near and behold me
Ye who pass by the way to your rest and your laughter,
And are full of the hope of the dawn coming after;
For the strong of the world have bought me and sold me
And my house is all wasted from threshold to rafter.
—Pass by me, and hearken, and think of me not!

Cry out and come near; for my ears may not hearken,
And my eyes are grown dim as the eyes of the dying.

Is this the grey rack o'er the sun's face a-flying?
Or is it your faces his brightness that darken?
Comes a wind from the sea, or is it your sighing?
—Pass by me, and hearken, and pity me not!

Ye know not how void is your hope and your living:
Depart with your helping lest yet ye undo me!
Ye know not that at nightfall she draweth near to me,
There is soft speech between us and words of forgiving
Till in dead of the midnight her kisses thrill through me.
—Pass by me, and hearken, and waken me not!

Wherewith will ye buy it, ye rich who behold me?
Draw out from your coffers your rest and your laughter,
And the fair gilded hope of the dawn coming after!
Nay this I sell not,—though ye bought me and sold
me,—
For your house stored with such things from threshold
to rafter.
—Pass by me, I hearken, and think of you not!

Enter before the curtain LOVE clad as a maker of Pic-
tured Cloths.

LOVE
That double life my faithful king has led
My hand has untwined, and old days are dead
As in the moon the sails run up the mast.
Yea, let this present mingle with the past,
And when ye see him next think a long tide
Of days are gone by; for the world is wide,

And if at last these hands, these lips shall meet,
What matter thorny ways and weary feet?
A faithful king, and now grown wise in love:
Yet from of old in many ways I move
The hearts that shall be mine: him by the hand
Have I led forth, and shown his eyes the land
Where dwells his love, and shown him what she is:
He has beheld the lips that he shall kiss,
The eyes his eyes shall soften, and the cheek
His voice shall change, the limbs he maketh weak:
—All this he hath as in a picture wrought—
But lo you, 'tis the seeker and the sought:
For her no marvels of the night I make,
Nor keep my dream-smiths' drowsy heads awake;
Only about her have I shed a glory
Whereby she waiteth trembling for a story
That she shall play in,—and 'tis not begun:
Therefore from rising sun to setting sun
There flit before her half-formed images
Of what I am, and in all things she sees
Something of mine: so single is her heart
Filled with the worship of one set apart
To be my priestess through all joy and sorrow;
So sad and sweet she waits the certain morrow.
—And yet sometimes, although her heart be strong,
You may well think I tarry over-long:
The lonely sweetness of desire grows pain,
The reverent life of longing void and vain:
Then are my dream-smiths mindful of my lore:
They weave a web of sighs and weeping sore,
Of languor, and of very helplessness,
Of restless wandering, lonely dumb distress,

Till like a live thing there she stands and goes,
Gazing at Pharamond through all her woes.
Then forth they fly, and spread the picture out
Before his eyes, and how then may he doubt
She knows his life, his deeds, and his desire?
How shall he tremble lest her heart should tire?
—It is not so; his danger and his war,
His days of triumph, and his years of care,
She knows them not—yet shall she know some day
The love that in his lonely longing lay.
What, Faithful—do I lie, that overshot
My dream-web is with that which happeneth not?
Nay, nay, believe it not!—love lies alone
In loving hearts like fire within the stone:
Then strikes my hand, and lo, the flax ablaze!
—Those tales of empty striving, and lost days
Folk tell of sometimes—never lit my fire
Such ruin as this; but Pride and Vain-desire,
My counterfeits and foes, have done the deed.
Beware, beloved! for they sow the weed
Where I the wheat: they meddle where I leave,
Take what I scorn, cast by what I receive,
Sunder my yoke, yoke that I would dissever,
Pull down the house my hands would build for ever.

Scene: In a Forest among the Hills of a Foreign Land.
KING PHARAMOND, MASTER OLIVER.

KING PHARAMOND
Stretch forth thine hand, foster-father, I know thee,
And fain would be sure I am yet in the world:
Where am I now, and what things have befallen?

Why am I so weary, and yet have wrought nothing?

MASTER OLIVER
Thou hast been sick, lord, but thy sickness abateth.

KING PHARAMOND
Thou art sad unto weeping: sorry rags are thy raiment,
For I see thee a little now: where am I lying?

MASTER OLIVER
On the sere leaves thou liest, lord, deep in the wild wood

KING PHARAMOND
What meaneth all this? was I not Pharamond,
A worker of great deeds after my father,
Freer of my land from murder and wrong,
Fain of folks' love, and no blencher in battle?

MASTER OLIVER
Yea, thou wert king and the kindest under heaven.

KING PHARAMOND
Was there not coming a Queen long desired,
From a land over sea, my life to fulfil?

MASTER OLIVER
Belike it was so—but thou leftst it untold of.

KING PHARAMOND
Why weepest thou more yet? O me, which are dreams,
Which are deeds of my life mid the things I remember?

MASTER OLIVER
Dost thou remember the great council chamber,
O my king, and the lords there gathered together
With drawn anxious faces one fair morning of summer,
And myself in their midst, who would move thee to
speech?

KING PHARAMOND
A brawl I remember, some wordy debating,
Whether my love should be brought to behold me.
Sick was I at heart, little patience I had.

MASTER OLIVER
Hast thou memory yet left thee, how an hour thereafter
We twain lay together in the midst of the pleasance
'Neath the lime-trees, nigh the pear-tree, beholding the
conduit?

KING PHARAMOND
Fair things I remember of a long time thereafter—
Of thy love and thy faith and our gladness together

MASTER OLIVER
And the thing that we talked of, wilt thou tell me about
it?

KING PHARAMOND
We twain were to wend through the wide world together
Seeking my love—O my heart! is she living?

MASTER OLIVER
God wot that she liveth as she hath lived ever.

KING PHARAMOND

Then soon was it midnight, and moonset, as we wended
Down to the ship, and the merchant-folks' babble.
The oily green waves in the harbour mouth glistened,
Windless midnight it was, but the great sweeps were run
out,
As the cable came rattling mid rich bales on the deck,
And slow moved the black side that the ripple was lap-
ping,
And I looked and beheld a great city behind us
By the last of the moon as the stars were a-brightening,
And Pharamond the Freed grew a tale of a singer,
With the land of his fathers and the fame he had toiled
for.
Yet sweet was the scent of the sea-breeze arising;
And I felt a chain broken, a sickness put from me
As the sails drew, and merchant-folk, gathered together
On the poop or the prow, 'gan to move and begone,
Till at last 'neath the far-gazing eyes of the steersman
By the loitering watch thou and I were left lonely,
And we saw by the moon the white horses arising
Where beyond the last headland the ocean abode us,
Then came the fresh breeze and the sweep of the spray,
And the beating of ropes, and the empty sails' thunder,
As we shifted our course toward the west in the dawning;
Then I slept and I dreamed in the dark I was lying,
And I heard her sweet breath and her feet falling near
me,
And the rustle of her raiment as she sought through the
darkness,
Sought, I knew not for what, till her arms clung about

264

me
With a cry that was hers, that was mine as I wakened.

MASTER OLIVER
Yea, a sweet dream it was, as thy dreams were aforetime.

KING PHARAMOND
Nay not so, my fosterer: thy hope yet shall fail thee
If thou lookest to see me turned back from my folly,
Lamenting and mocking the life of my longing.
Many such have I had, dear dreams and deceitful,
When the soul slept a little from all but its search,
And lied to the body of bliss beyond telling;
Yea, waking had lied still but for life and its torment.
Not so were those dreams of the days of my kingship,
Slept my body—or died—but my soul was not sleeping,
It knew that she touched not this body that trembled
At the thought of her body sore trembling to see me;
It lied of no bliss as desire swept it onward,
Who knows through what sundering space of its prison;
It saw, and it heard, and it hoped, and was lonely,
Had no doubt and no joy, but the hope that endureth.
—Woe's me I am weary: wend we forward to-morrow?

MASTER OLIVER
Yea, well it may be if thou wilt but be patient,
And rest thee a little, while time creepeth onward.

KING PHARAMOND
But tell me, has the fourth year gone far mid my sickness?

MASTER OLIVER

Nay, for seven days only didst thou lie here a-dying,
As full often I deemed: God be thanked it is over!
But rest thee a little, lord; gather strength for the striving.

KING PHARAMOND
Yea, for once again sleep meseems cometh to struggle
With the memory of times past: come tell thou, my fos-
terer,
Of the days we have fared through, that dimly before me
Are floating, as I look on thy face and its trouble.

MASTER OLIVER
Rememberest thou aught of the lands where we wended?

KING PHARAMOND
Yea, many a thing—as the moonlit warm evening
When we stayed by the trees in the Gold-bearing Land,
Nigh the gate of the city, where a minstrel was singing
That tale of the King and his fate, o'er the cradle
Foretold by the wise of the world; that a woman
Should win him to love and to woe, and despairing
In the last of his youth, the first days of his manhood.

MASTER OLIVER
I remember the evening; but clean gone is the story:
Amid deeds great and dreadful, should songs abide by
me?

KING PHARAMOND
They shut the young king in a castle, the tale saith,
Where never came woman, and never should come,
And sadly he grew up and stored with all wisdom,

Not wishing for aught in his heart that he had not,
Till the time was come round to his twentieth birthday.
Then many fair gifts brought his people unto him,
Gold and gems, and rich cloths, and rare things and
dear-bought,
And a book fairly written brought a wise man among
them,
Called the Praising of Prudence; wherein there was
painted
The image of Prudence:—and that, what but a woman,
E'en she forsooth that the painter found fairest;—
Now surely thou mindest what needs must come after?

MASTER OLIVER
Yea, somewhat indeed I remember the misery
Told in that tale, but all mingled it is
With the manifold trouble that met us full often,
E'en we ourselves. Of nought else hast thou memory?

KING PHARAMOND
Of many such tales that the Southland folk told us,
Of many a dream by the sunlight and moonlight;
Of music that moved me, of hopes that my heart had;
The high days when my love and I held feast together.
—But what land is this, and how came we hither?

MASTER OLIVER
Nay, hast thou no memory of our troubles that were
many?
How thou criedst out for Death and how near Death
came to thee?
How thou needs must dread war, thou the dreadful in

267

battle?

Of the pest in the place where that tale was told to us;
And how we fled thence o'er the desert of horror?
How weary we wandered when we came to the moun-
tains,
All dead but one man of those who went with us?
How we came to the sea of the west, and the city,
Whose Queen would have kept thee her slave and her
lover,
And how we escaped by the fair woman's kindness,
Who loved thee, and cast her life by for thy welfare?
Of the waste of thy life when we sailed from the South-
lands,
And the sea-thieves fell on us and sold us for servants
To that land of hard gems, where thy life's purchase
seemed
Little better than mine, and we found to our sorrow
Whence came the crown's glitter, thy sign once of glory:
Then naked a king toiled in sharp rocky crannies,
And thy world's fear was grown but the task-master's
whip,
And thy world's hope the dream in the short dead of
night?
And hast thou forgotten how again we fled from it,
And that fight of despair in the boat on the river,
And the sea-strand again and white bellying sails;
And the sore drought and famine that on ship-board fell
on us,
Ere the sea was o'erpast, and we came scarcely living
To those keepers of sheep, the poor folk and the kind?
Dost thou mind not the merchants who brought us
thence northward,

And this land that we made in the twilight of dawning?
And the city herein where all kindness forsook us,
And our bitter bread sought we from house-door to
house-door.

KING PHARAMOND

As the shadow of clouds o'er the summer sea sailing
Is the memory of all now, and whiles I remember
And whiles I forget; and nought it availeth
Remembering, forgetting; for a sleep is upon me
That shall last a long while:—there thou liest, my fosterer,
As thou lay'st a while since ere that twilight of dawning;
And I woke and looked forth, and the dark sea, long
changeless,
Was now at last barred by a dim wall that swallowed
The red shapeless moon, and the whole sea was rolling,
Unresting, unvaried, as grey as the void is,
Toward that wall 'gainst the heavens as though rest were
behind it.
Still onward we fared and the moon was forgotten,
And colder the sea grew and colder the heavens,
And blacker the wall grew, and grey, green-besprinkled,
And the sky seemed to breach it; and lo at the last
Many islands of mountains, and a city amongst them.
White clouds of the dawn, not moving yet waning,
Wreathed the high peaks about; and the sea beat for ever
'Gainst the green sloping hills and the black rocks and
beachless.
—Is this the same land that I saw in that dawning?
For sure if it is thou at least shalt hear tidings,
Though I die ere the dark: but for thee, O my fosterer,
Lying there by my side, I had deemed the old vision

Had drawn forth the soul from my body to see her.
And with joy and fear blended leapt the heart in my bo-
som,
And I cried, "The last land, love; O hast thou abided?"
But since then hath been turmoil, and sickness, and
slumber,
And my soul hath been troubled with dreams that I
knew not.
And such tangle is round me life fails me to rend it,
And the cold cloud of death rolleth onward to hide me.—
—O well am I hidden, who might not be happy!
I see not, I hear not, my head groweth heavy.
[Falls back as if sleeping.

MASTER OLIVER
—O Son, is it sleep that upon thee is fallen?
Not death, O my dear one!—speak yet but a little!

KING PHARAMOND (raising himself again)
O be glad, foster-father! and those troubles past over,—
Be thou thereby when once more I remember
And sit with my maiden and tell her the story,
And we pity our past selves as a poet may pity
The poor folk he tells of amid plentiful weeping.
Hush now! as faint noise of bells over water
A sweet sound floats towards me, and blesses my slum-
ber:
If I wake never more I shall dream and shall see her.
[Sleeps.

MASTER OLIVER
Is it swooning or sleeping? in what wise shall he waken?

—Nay, no sound I hear save the forest wind wailing.
Who shall help us to-day save our yoke-fellow Death?
Yet fain would I die mid the sun and the flowers;
For a tomb seems this yew-wood ere yet we are dead.
And its wailing wind chilleth my yearning for time past,
And my love groweth cold in this dusk of the daytime.
What will be? is worse than death drawing anear us?
Flit past, dreary day! come, night-tide and resting!
Come, to-morrow's uprising with light and new tidings!
—Lo, Lord, I have borne all with no bright love before me;
   Wilt thou break all I had and then give me no blessing?

THE MUSIC

LOVE IS ENOUGH: through the trouble and tangle
   From yesterdays dawning to yesterday's night
I sought through the vales where the prisoned winds wrangle,
   Till, wearied and bleeding, at end of the light
   I met him, and we wrestled, and great was my might.

O great was my joy, though no rest was around me,
   Though mid wastes of the world were we twain all alone,
For methought that I conquered and he knelt and he crowned me,
   And the driving rain ceased, and the wind ceased to moan,
   And through clefts of the clouds her planet outshone.

O through clefts of the clouds 'gan the world to awaken,
   And the bitter wind piped, and down drifted the rain,
   And I was alone—and yet not forsaken,

271

For the grass was untrodden except by my pain:
With a Shadow of the Night had I wrestled in vain.

And the Shadow of the Night and not Love was depart-
ed;
I was sore, I was weary, yet Love lived to seek;
So I scaled the dark mountains, and wandered sad-heart-
ed
Over wearier wastes, where e'en sunlight was bleak,
With no rest of the night for my soul waxen weak.

With no rest of the night; for I waked mid a story
Of a land wherein Love is the light and the lord,
Where my tale shall be heard, and my wounds gain a
glory,
And my tears be a treasure to add to the hoard
Of pleasure laid up for his people's reward.

Ah, pleasure laid up! haste thou onward and listen,
For the wind of the waste has no music like this,
And not thus do the rocks of the wilderness glisten:
With the host of his faithful through sorrow and bliss
My Lord goeth forth now, and knows me for his.

Enter before the curtain LOVE, with a cup of bitter
drink and his hands bloody.

LOVE
O Pharamond, I knew thee brave and strong,
And yet how might'st thou live to bear this wrong?
—A wandering-tide of three long bitter years,

Solaced at whiles by languor of soft tears,
By dreams self-wrought of night and sleep and sorrow,
Holpen by hope of tears to be to-morrow:
Yet all, alas, but wavering memories;
No vision of her hands, her lips, her eyes,
Has blessed him since he seemed to see her weep,
No wandering feet of hers beset his sleep.
Woe's me then! am I cruel, or am I grown
The scourge of Fate, lest men forget to moan?
What!—is there blood upon these hands of mine?
Is venomed anguish mingled with my wine?
—Blood there may be, and venom in the cup;
But see, Beloved, how the tears well up
From my grieved heart my blinded eyes to grieve,
And in the kindness of old days believe!
So after all then we must weep to-day—
—We, who behold at ending of the way,
These lovers tread a bower they may not miss
Whose door my servant keepeth, Earthly Bliss:
There in a little while shall they abide,
Nor each from each their wounds of wandering hide,
But kiss them, each on each, and find it sweet,
That wounded so the world they may not meet.
—Ah, truly mine! since this your tears may move,
The very sweetness of rewarded love!
Ah, truly mine, that tremble as ye hear
The speech of loving lips grown close and dear;
—Lest other sounds from other doors ye hearken,
Doors that the wings of Earthly Anguish darken.

Scene: On a Highway in a Valley near the last, with a
Mist over all things.

KING PHARAMOND, MASTER OLIVER.

KING PHARAMOND
Hold a while, Oliver! my limbs are grown weaker
Than when in the wood I first rose to my feet.
There was hope in my heart then, and now nought but
sickness;
There was sight in my eyes then, and now nought but
blindness.
Good art thou, hope, while the life yet tormenteth,
But a better help now have I gained than thy goading.
Farewell, O life, wherein once I was merry!
O dream of the world, I depart now, and leave thee
A little tale added to thy long-drawn-out story.
Cruel wert thou, O Love, yet have thou and I conquered.
—Come nearer, O fosterer, come nearer and kiss me,
Bid farewell to thy fosterling while the life yet is in me,
For this farewell to thee is my last word meseemeth.
[He lies down and sleeps.

MASTER OLIVER
O my king, O my son! Ah, woe's me for my kindness,
For the day when thou drew'st me and I let thee be drawn
Into toils I knew deadly, into death thou desiredst!
And woe's me that I die not! for my body made hardy
By the battles of old days to bear every anguish!
—Speak a word and forgive me, for who knows how long
yet
Are the days of my life, and the hours of my loathing!
He speaks not, he moves not; yet he draweth breath soft-
ly:
I have seen men a-dying, and not thus did the end come.

Surely God who made all forgets not love's rewarding,
Forgets not the faithful, the guileless who fear not.
Oh, might there be help yet, and some new life's begin-
ning!
 —Lo, lighter the mist grows: there come sounds through
its dulness,
The lowing of kine, or the whoop of a shepherd,
The bell-wether's tinkle, or clatter of horse-hoofs.
A homestead is nigh us: I will fare down the highway
And seek for some helping: folk said simple people
Abode in this valley, and these may avail us—
If aught it avail us to live for a little.
 —Yea, give it us, God!—all the fame and the glory
We fought for and gained once; the life of well-doing,
Fair deed thrusting on deed, and no day forgotten;
And due worship of folk that his great heart had hol-
pen;—
All I prayed for him once now no longer I pray for.
Let it all pass away as my warm breath now passeth
In the chill of the morning mist wherewith thou hidest
Fair vale and grey mountain of the land we are come to!
Let it all pass away! but some peace and some pleasure
I pray for him yet, and that I may behold it.
A prayer little and lowly,—and we in the old time
When the world lay before us, were we hard to the lowly?
Thou know'st we were kind, howso hard to be beaten;
Wilt thou help us this last time? or what hast thou hid-
den
We know not, we name not, some crown for our striving?
 —O body and soul of my son, may God keep thee!
For, as lone as thou liest in a land that we see not
When the world loseth thee, what is left for its losing?

[Exit OLIVER.

THE MUSIC
LOVE IS ENOUGH: cherish life that abideth,
Lest ye die ere ye know him, and curse and misname
him;
For who knows in what ruin of all hope he hideth,
On what wings of the terror of darkness he rideth?
And what is the joy of man's life that ye blame him
For his bliss grown a sword, and his rest grown a fire?

Ye who tremble for death, or the death of desire,
Pass about the cold winter-tide garden and ponder
On the rose in his glory amidst of June's fire,
On the languor of noontide that gathered the thunder,
On the morn and its freshness, the eve and its wonder;
Ye may wake it no more—shall Spring come to awaken?

Live on, for Love liveth, and earth shall be shaken
By the wind of his wings on the triumphing morning,
When the dead, and their deeds that die not shall awak-
en,
And the world's tale shall sound in your trumpet of
warning,
And the sun smite the banner called Scorn of the Scorn-
ing,
And dead pain ye shall trample, dead fruitless desire,
As ye wend to pluck out the new world from the fire.

Enter before the curtain, LOVE clad as a Pilgrim.

LOVE

Alone, afar from home doth Pharamond lie,
Drawn near to death, ye deem—or what draws nigh?
Afar from home—and have ye any deeming
How far may be that country of his dreaming?
Is it not time, is it not time, say ye,
That we the day-star in the sky should see?
Patience, Beloved; these may come to live
A life fulfilled of all I have to give,
But bare of strife and story; and ye know well
How wild a tale of him might be to tell
Had I not snatched away the sword and crown;
Yea, and she too was made for world's renown,
And should have won it, had my bow not been;
These that I love were very king and queen;
I have discrowned them, shall I not crown too?
Ye know, Beloved, what sharp bitter dew,
What parching torment of unresting day
Falls on the garden of my deathless bay:
Hands that have gathered it and feet that came
Beneath its shadow have known flint and flame;
Therefore I love them; and they love no less
Each furlong of the road of past distress.
—Ah, Faithful, tell me for what rest and peace,
What length of happy days and world's increase,
What hate of wailing, and what love of laughter,
What hope and fear of worlds to be hereafter,
Would ye cast by that crown of bitter leaves?
And yet, ye say, our very heart it grieves
To see him lying there: how may he save
His life and love if he more pain must have?
And she—how fares it with her? is not earth

From winter's sorrow unto summer's mirth
Grown all too narrow for her yearning heart?
We pray thee, Love, keep these no more apart.
Ye say but sooth: not long may he endure:
And her heart sickeneth past all help or cure
Unless I hasten to the helping—see,
Am I not girt for going speedily?
—The journey lies before me long?—nay, nay,
Upon my feet the dust is lying grey,
The staff is heavy in my hand.—Ye too,
Have ye not slept? or what is this ye do,
Wearying to find the country ye are in?
[The curtain draws up and
shows the same scene
as the last, with the mist clearing, and
PHARAMOND lying there as before.
Look, look! how sun and morn at last do win
Upon the shifting waves of mist! behold
That mountain-wall the earth-fires rent of old,
Grey toward the valley, sun-gilt at the side!
See the black yew-wood that the pass doth hide!
Search through the mist for knoll, and fruited tree,
And winding stream, and highway white—and see,
See, at my feet lies Pharamond the Freed!
A happy journey have we gone indeed!
Hearken, Beloved, over-long, ye deem,
I let these lovers deal with hope and dream
Alone unholpen.—Somewhat sooth ye say:
But now her feet are on this very way
That leadeth from the city: and she saith
One beckoneth her back hitherward—even Death—
And who was that, Beloved, but even I?

278

Yet though her feet and sunlight are drawn nigh
The cold grass where he lieth like the dead,
To ease your hearts a little of their dread
I will abide her coming, and in speech
He knoweth, somewhat of his welfare teach.

LOVE goes on to the Stage and stands at PHARA-
MOND's head.

LOVE
HEARKEN, O Pharamond, why camest thou hither?

KING PHARAMOND
I came seeking Death; I have found him belike.

LOVE
In what land of the world art thou lying, O Pharamond?

KING PHARAMOND
In a land 'twixt two worlds: nor long shall I dwell there.

LOVE
Who am I, Pharamond, that stand here beside thee?

KING PHARAMOND
The Death I have sought—thou art welcome; I greet
thee.

LOVE
Such a name have I had, but another name have I.

KING PHARAMOND

Art thou God then that helps not until the last season?

LOVE
Yea, God am I surely: yet another name have I.

KING PHARAMOND
Methinks as I hearken, thy voice I should wot of.

LOVE
I called thee, and thou cam'st from thy glory and king-
ship.

KING PHARAMOND
I was King Pharamond, and love overcame me.

LOVE
Pharamond, thou say'st it.—I am Love and thy master.

KING PHARAMOND
Sooth didst thou say when thou call'dst thyself Death.

LOVE
Though thou diest, yet thy love and thy deeds shall I
quicken.

KING PHARAMOND
Be thou God, be thou Death, yet I love thee and dread
not.

LOVE
Pharamond, while thou livedst what thing wert thou lov-
ing?

KING PHARAMOND
A dream and a lie—and my death—and I love it.

LOVE
Pharamond, do my bidding, as thy wont was aforetime.

KING PHARAMOND
What wilt thou have of me, for I wend away swiftly?

LOVE
Open thine eyes, and behold where thou liest!

KING PHARAMOND
It is little—the old dream, the old lie is about me.

LOVE
Why faintest thou, Pharamond? is love then unworthy?

KING PHARAMOND
Then hath God made no world now, nor shall make
hereafter.

LOVE
Wouldst thou live if thou mightst in this fair world, O
Pharamond?

KING PHARAMOND
Yea, if she and truth were; nay, if she and truth were not.

LOVE
O long shalt thou live: thou art here in the body,

Where nought but thy spirit I brought in days bygone.
Ah, thou hearkenest!—and where then of old hast thou
heard it?
[Music outside, far off.

KING PHARAMOND
O mock me not, Death; or, Life, hold me no longer!
For that sweet strain I hear that I heard once a-dreaming:
Is it death coming nigher, or life come back that brings
it?
Or rather my dream come again as aforetime?

LOVE
Look up, O Pharamond! canst thou see aught about
thee?

KING PHARAMOND
Yea, surely: all things as aforetime I saw them:
The mist fading out with the first of the sunlight,
And the mountains a-changing as oft in my dreaming,
And the thornbrake anigh blossomed thick with the
May-tide.
[Music again.
O my heart!—I am hearkening thee whereso thou wan-
derest!

LOVE
Put forth thine hand, feel the dew on the daisies!

KING PHARAMOND
So their freshness I felt in the days ere hope perished.
—O me, me, my darling! how fair the world groweth!

Ah, shall I not find thee, if death yet should linger,
Else why grow I so glad now when life seems departing?
What pleasure thus pierceth my heart unto fainting?
—O me, into words now thy melody passeth.

MUSIC with singing (from without)
Dawn talks to-day
Over dew-gleaming flowers,
Night flies away
Till the resting of hours:
Fresh are thy feet
And with dreams thine eyes glistening.
Thy still lips are sweet
Though the world is a-listening.
O Love, set a word in my mouth for our meeting,
Cast thine arms round about me to stay my heart's beat-
ing!
O fresh day, O fair day, O long day made ours!

LOVE
What wilt thou say now of the gifts Love hath given?

KING PHARAMOND
Stay thy whispering, O wind of the morning—she spea-
keth.

THE MUSIC (coming nearer)
Morn shall meet noon
While the flower-stems yet move,
Though the wind dieth soon
And the clouds fade above.

Loved lips are thine
As I tremble and hearken;
Bright thine eyes shine,
Though the leaves thy brow darken.
O Love, kiss me into silence, lest no word avail me,
Stay my head with thy bosom lest breath and life fail me!
O sweet day, O rich day, made long for our love!

LOVE
Was Love then a liar who fashioned thy dreaming?

KING PHARAMOND
O fair-blossomed tree, stay thy rustling—I hearken.

THE MUSIC (coming nearer)
Late day shall greet eve,
And the full blossoms shake,
For the wind will not leave
The tall trees while they wake.
Eyes soft with bliss,
Come nigher and nigher!
Sweet mouth I kiss,
Tell me all thy desire!
Let us speak, love, together some words of our story,
That our lips as they part may remember the glory!
O soft day, O calm day, made clear for our sake!

LOVE
What wouldst thou, Pharamond? why art thou fainting?

KING PHARAMOND
And thou diest, fair daylight, now she draweth near me!

THE MUSIC (close outside)
Eve shall kiss night,
And the leaves stir like rain
As the wind stealeth light
O'er the grass of the plain.
Unseen are thine eyes
Mid the dreamy night's sleeping,
And on my mouth there lies
The dear rain of thy weeping.
Hold, silence, love, speak not of the sweet day departed,
Cling close to me, love, lest I waken sad-hearted!
O kind day, O dear day, short day, come again!

LOVE
Sleep then, O Pharamond, till her kiss shall awake thee,
For, lo, here comes the sun o'er the tops of the mountains,
And she with his light in her hair comes before him,
As solemn and fair as the dawn of the May-tide
On some isle of mid-ocean when all winds are sleeping.
O worthy is she of this hour that awaits her,
And the death of all doubt, and beginning of gladness
Her great heart shall embrace without fear or amaze-
ment.
    —He sleeps, yet his heart's beating measures her foot-
falls;
    And her heart beateth too, as her feet bear her onward:
    Breathe gently between them, O breeze of the morning!
    Wind round them unthought of, sweet scent of the blos-
soms!
    Treasure up every minute of this tide of their meeting,
    O flower-bedecked Earth! with such tales of my triumph

Is your life still renewed, and spring comes back for ever
From that forge of all glory that brought forth my bless-
ing.
  O welcome, Love's darling: Shall this day ever darken,
Whose dawn I have dight for thy longing triumphant?
[Exit LOVE. Enter AZALAIS.

AZALAIS
A song in my mouth, then? my heart full of gladness?
My feet firm on the earth, as when youth was beginning?
And the rest of my early days come back to bless me?—
Who hath brought me these gifts in the midst of the
May-tide?
  What!—three days agone to the city I wandered,
And watched the ships warped to the Quay of the Mer-
chants;
  And wondered why folk should be busy and anxious;
For bitter my heart was, and life seemed a-waning,
With no story told, with sweet longing turned torment,
Love turned to abasement, and rest gone for ever.
And last night I awoke with a pain piercing through me,
And a cry in my ears, and Death passed on before,
As one pointing the way, and I rose up sore trembling,
And by cloud and by night went before the sun's coming,
As one goeth to death,—and lo here the dawning!
And a dawning therewith of a dear joy I know not.
I have given back the day the glad greeting it gave me;
And the gladness it gave me, that too would I give
  Were hands held out to crave it——Fair valley, I greet
thee,
  And the new-wakened voices of all things familiar.
  —Behold, how the mist-bow lies bright on the moun-

286

tain,

Bidding hope as of old since no prison endureth.
Full busy has May been these days I have missed her,
And the milkwort is blooming, and blue falls the speed-
well.

—Lo, here have been footsteps in the first of the morn-
ing,

Since the moon sank all red in the mist now departed.
—Ah! what lieth there by the side of the highway?
Is it death stains the sunlight, or sorrow or sickness?
[Going up to PHARAMOND.

—Not death, for he sleepeth; but beauty sore blemished
By sorrow and sickness, and for all that the sweeter.
I will wait till he wakens and gaze on his beauty,
Lest I never again in the world should behold him.
—Maybe I may help him; he is sick and needs tending,
He is poor, and shall scorn not our simpleness surely.
Whence came he to us-ward—what like has his life
been—

Who spoke to him last—for what is he longing?
—As one hearkening a story I wonder what cometh,
And in what wise my voice to our homestead shall bid
him.

O heart, how thou faintest with hope of the gladness
I may have for a little if there he abide.
Soft there shalt thou sleep, love, and sweet shall thy
dreams be,

And sweet thy awaking amidst of the wonder
Where thou art, who is nigh thee—and then, when thou
seest

How the rose-boughs hang in o'er the little loft window,
And the blue bowl with roses is close to thine hand,

And over thy bed is the quilt sewn with lilies,
And the loft is hung round with the green Southland hangings,
And all smelleth sweet as the low door is opened,
And thou turnest to see me there standing, and holding
Such dainties as may be, thy new hunger to stay—
Then well may I hope that thou wilt not remember
Thine old woes for a moment in the freshness and pleasure,
And that I shall be part of thy rest for a little.
And then—-who shall say—wilt thou tell me thy story,
And what thou hast loved, and for what thou hast striven?
—Thou shalt see me, and my love and my pity, as thou speakest,
And it may be thy pity shall mingle with mine.
—And meanwhile—Ah, love, what hope may my heart hold?
For I see that thou lovest, who ne'er hast beheld me.
And how should thy love change, howe'er the world changeth?
Yet meanwhile, had I dreamed of the bliss of this minute,
How might I have borne to live weary and waiting!
Woe's me! do I fear thee? else should I not wake thee,
For tending thou needest—If my hand touched thy hand
[Touching him.
I should fear thee the less.—O sweet friend, forgive it,
My hand and my tears, for faintly they touched thee!
He trembleth, and waketh not: O me, my darling!
Hope whispers that thou hear'st me through sleep, and wouldst waken,
But for dread that thou dreamest and I should be gone.

Doth it please thee in dreaming that I tremble and dread thee,

That these tears are the tears of one praying vainly,
Who shall pray with no word when thou hast awakened?
—Yet how shall I deal with my life if he love not,
As how should he love me, a stranger, unheard of?
—O bear witness, thou day that hast brought my love hither!

Thou sun that burst out through the mist o'er the mountains,

In that moment mine eyes met the field of his sorrow—
Bear witness, ye fields that have fed me and clothed me,
And air I have breathed, and earth that hast borne me—
Though I find you but shadows, and wrought but for fading,

Though all ye and God fail me,—my love shall not fail!
Yea, even if this love, that seemeth such pleasure
As earth is unworthy of, turneth to pain;
If he wake without memory of me and my weeping,
With a name on his lips not mine—that I know not:
If thus my hand leave his hand for the last time,
And no word from his lips be kind for my comfort—
If all speech fail between us, all sight fail me henceforth,
If all hope and God fail me—my love shall not fail.
—Friend, I may not forbear: we have been here together:
My hand on thy hand has been laid, and thou trembledst.
Think now if this May sky should darken above us,
And the death of the world in this minute should part us—

Think, my love, of the loss if my lips had not kissed thee.
And forgive me my hunger of no hope begotten! [She kisses him.

KING PHARAMOND (awaking)
Who art thou? who art thou, that my dream I might tell thee?
How with words full of love she drew near me, and kissed me.
O thou kissest me yet, and thou clingest about me!
Ah, kiss me and wake me into death and deliverance!

AZALAIS (drawing away from him)
Speak no rough word, I pray thee, for a little, thou love-liest!
But forgive me, for the years of my life have been lonely,
And thou art come hither with the eyes of one seeking.

KING PHARAMOND
Sweet dream of old days, and her very lips speaking
The words of my lips and the night season's longing.
How might I have lived had I known what I longed for!

AZALAIS
I knew thou wouldst love, I knew all thy desire—
Am I she whom thou seekest? may I draw nigh again?

KING PHARAMOND
Ah, lengthen no more the years of my seeking,
For thou knowest my love as thy love lies before me.

AZALAIS (coming near to him again)
O Love, there was fear in thine eyes as thou wakenedst;
Thy first words were of dreaming and death—but we die not.

KING PHARAMOND

In thine eyes was a terror as thy lips' touches faded,
Sore trembled thine arms as they fell away from me;
And thy voice was grown piteous with words of beseech-
ing,
 So that still for a little my search seemed unended.
—Ah, enending, unchanging desire fulfils me!
I cry out for thy comfort as thou clingest about me.
O joy hard to bear, but for memory of sorrow,
But for pity of past days whose bitter is sweet now!
Let us speak, love, together some word of our story,
That our lips as they part may remember the glory.

AZALAIS

O Love, kiss me into silence lest no word avail me;
Stay my head with thy bosom lest breath and life fail me.

THE MUSIC

LOVE IS ENOUGH: while ye deemed him a-sleeping,
There were signs of his coming and sounds of his feet;
His touch it was that would bring you to weeping,
When the summer was deepest and music most sweet:
In his footsteps ye followed the day to its dying,
Ye went forth by his gown-skirts the morning to meet:
In his place on the beaten-down orchard-grass lying,
Of the sweet ways ye pondered yet left for life's trying.

Ah, what was all dreaming of pleasure anear you,
To the time when his eyes on your wistful eyes turned,
And ye saw his lips move, and his head bend to hear you,
As new-born and glad to his kindness ye yearned?

Ah, what was all dreaming of anguish and sorrow,
To the time when the world in his torment was burned,
And no god your heart from its prison might borrow,
And no rest was left, no to-day, no to-morrow?

All wonder of pleasure, all doubt of desire,
All blindness, are ended, and no more ye feel
If your feet tread his flowers or the flames of his fire,
If your breast meet his balms or the edge of his steel.
Change is come, and past over, no more strife, no more
learning:
Now your lips and your forehead are sealed with his seal,
Look backward and smile at the thorns and the burning.
—Sweet rest, O my soul, and no fear of returning!

Enter before the curtain LOVE, clad still as a Pilgrim.

LOVE
How is it with the Fosterer then, when he
Comes back again that rest and peace to see,
And God his latest prayer has granted now?—
Why, as the winds whereso they list shall blow,
So drifts the thought of man, and who shall say
To-morrow shall my thought be as to-day?
—My fosterling is happy, and I too;
Yet did we leave behind things good to do,
Deeds good to tell about when we are dead.
Here is no pain, but rest, and easy bread;
Yet therewith something hard to understand
Dulls the crowned work to which I set my hand.
Ah, patience yet! his longing is well won,
And I shall die at last and all be done.—

Such words unspoken the best man on earth
Still bears about betwixt the lover's mirth;
And now he hath what he went forth to find,
This Pharamond is neither dull nor blind,
And looking upon Oliver, he saith:—
My friend recked nothing of his life or death,
Knew not my anguish then, nor now my pleasure,
And by my crowned joy sets his lessened treasure.
Is risk of twenty days of wind and sea,
Of new-born feeble headless enmity,
I should have scorned once, too great gift to give
To this most faithful man that he may live?
—Yea, was that all? my faithful, you and I,
Still craving, scorn the world too utterly,
The world we want not—yet, our one desire
Fulfilled at last, what next shall feed the fire?
—I say not this to make my altar cold;
Rather that ye, my happy ones, should hold
Enough of memory and enough of fear
Within your hearts to keep its flame full clear;
Rather that ye, still dearer to my heart,
Whom words call hapless, yet should praise your part,
Wherein the morning and the evening sun
Are bright about a story never done;
That those for chastening, these for joy should cling
About the marvels that my minstrels sing.
Well, Pharamond fulfilled of love must turn
Unto the folk that still he deemed would yearn
To see his face, and hear his voice once more;
And he was mindful of the days passed o'er,
And fain had linked them to these days of love;
And he perchance was fain the world to move

While love looked on; and he perchance was fain
Some pleasure of the strife of old to gain.
Easy withal it seemed to him to land,
And by his empty throne awhile to stand
Amid the wonder, and then sit him down
While folk went forth to seek the hidden crown.
Or else his name upon the same wind borne
As smote the world with winding of his horn,
His hood pulled back, his banner flung abroad,
A gleam of sunshine on his half-drawn sword.
—Well, he and you and I have little skill
To know the secret of Fate's worldly will;
Yet can I guess, and you belike may guess,
Yea, and e'en he mid all his lordliness,
That much may be forgot in three years' space
Outside my kingdom.—Gone his godlike face,
His calm voice, and his kindness, half akin
Amid a blind folk to rebuke of sin,
Men 'gin to think that he was great and good,
But hindered them from doing as they would,
And ere they have much time to think on it
Between their teeth another has the bit,
And forth they run with Force and Fate behind.
—Indeed his sword might somewhat heal the blind,
Were I not, and the softness I have given;
With me for him have hope and glory striven
In other days when my tale was beginning;
But sweet life lay beyond then for the winning,
And now what sweetness?—blood of men to spill
Who once believed him God to heal their ill:
To break the gate and storm adown the street
Where once his coming flower-crowned girls did greet:

To deem the cry come from amidst his folk
When his own country tongue should curse his stroke—
Nay, he shall leave to better men or worse
His people's conquered homage and their curse.
So forth they go, his Oliver and he,
One thing at least to learn across the sea,
That whatso needless shadows life may borrow
Love is enough amidst of joy or sorrow.
Love is enough—My Faithful, in your eyes
I see the thought, Our Lord is overwise
Some minutes past in what concerns him not,
And us no more: is all his tale forgot?
—Ah, Well-beloved, I fell asleep e'en now,
And in my sleep some enemy did show
Sad ghosts of bitter things, and names unknown
For things I know—a maze with shame bestrown
And ruin and death; till e'en myself did seem
A wandering curse amidst a hopeless dream.
—Yet see! I live, no older than of old,
What tales soe'er of changing Time has told.
And ye who cling to all my hand shall give,
Sorrow or joy, no less than I shall live.

Scene: Before **KING PHARAMOND'S** Palace.

KING PHARAMOND
A long time it seems since this morn when I met them,
The men of my household and the great man they hon-
our:
Better counsel in king-choosing might I have given
Had ye bided my coming back hither, my people:
And yet who shall say or foretell what Fate meaneth?

For that man there, the stranger, Honorius men called him,
I account him the soul to King Theobald's body,
And the twain are one king; and a goodly king may be
For this people, who grasping at peace and good days,
Careth little who giveth them that which they long for.
Yet what gifts have I given them; I who this even
Turn away with grim face from the fight that should try me?
It is just then, I have lost: lie down, thou supplanter,
In thy tomb in the minster when thy life is well over,
And the well-carven image of latten laid o'er thee
Shall live on as thou livedst, and be worthy the praising
Whereby folk shall remember the days of thy plenty.
Praising Theobald the Good and the peace that he brought them,
But I—I shall live too, though no graven image
On the grass of the hillside shall brave the storms' beating;
Though through days of thy plenty the people remember
As a dim time of war the past days of King Pharamond;
Yet belike as time weareth, and folk turn back a little
To the darkness where dreams lie and live on for ever,
Even there shall be Pharamond who failed not in battle,
But feared to overcome his folk who forgot him,
And turned back and left them a tale for the telling,
A song for the singing, that yet in some battle
May grow to remembrance and rend through the ruin
As my sword rent it through in the days gone for ever.
So, like Enoch of old, I was not, for God took me.
—But lo, here is Oliver, all draws to an ending—
[Enter OLIVER.

Well met, my Oliver! the clocks strike the due minute,
What news hast thou got?—thou art moody of visage.

MASTER OLIVER

In one word, 'tis battle; the days we begun with
Must begin once again with the world waxen baser.

KING PHARAMOND

Ah! battle it may be: but surely no river
Runneth back to its springing: so the world has grown
wiser
And Theobald the Constable is king in our stead,
And contenteth the folk who cried, "Save us, King Pha-
ramond!"

MASTER OLIVER

Hast thou heard of his councillor men call Honorius?
Folk hold him in fear, and in love the tale hath it.

KING PHARAMOND

Much of him have I heard: nay, more, I have seen him
With the men of my household, and the great man they
honour.
They were faring afield to some hunt or disporting,
Few faces were missing, and many I saw there
I was fain of in days past at fray or at feasting;
My heart yearned towards them—but what—days have
changed them,
They must wend as they must down the way they are
driven.

MASTER OLIVER

Yet e'en in these days there remaineth a remnant
That is faithful and fears not the flap of thy banner.

KING PHARAMOND

And a fair crown is faith, as thou knowest, my father;
Fails the world, yet that faileth not; love hath begot it,
Sweet life and contentment at last springeth from it;
No helping these need whose hearts still are with me,
Nay, rather they handle the gold rod of my kingdom.

MASTER OLIVER

Yet if thou leadest forth once more as aforetime
In faith of great deeds will I follow thee, Pharamond,
And thy latter end yet shall be counted more glorious
Than thy glorious beginning; and great shall my gain be
If e'en I must die ere the day of thy triumph.

KING PHARAMOND

Dear is thy heart mid the best and the brightest,
Yet not against these my famed blade will I bare.

MASTER OLIVER

Nay, what hast thou heard of their babble and baseness?

KING PHARAMOND

Full enough, friend—content thee, my lips shall not
speak it,
The same hour wherein they have said that I love thee.
Suffice it, folk need me no more: the deliverance,
Dear bought in the days past, their hearts have forgotten,
But faintly their dim eyes a feared face remember,
Their dull ears remember a stern voice they hated.

What then, shall I waken their fear and their hatred,
And then wait till fresh terror their memory awaketh,
With the semblance of love that they have not to give
me?
Nay, nay, they are safe from my help and my justice,
And I—I am freed, and fresh waxeth my manhood.

MASTER OLIVER
It may not be otherwise since thou wilt have it,
Yet I say it again, if thou shake out thy banner,
Some brave men will be borne unto earth peradventure,
Many dastards go trembling to meet their due doom,
And then shall come fair days and glory upon me
And on all men on earth for thy fame, O King Phara-
mond.

KING PHARAMOND
Yea, I was king once; the songs sung o'er my cradle,
Were ballads of battle and deeds of my fathers:
Yea, I was King Pharamond; in no carpeted court-room
Bore they the corpse of my father before me;
But on grass trodden grey by the hoofs of the war-steeds
Did I kneel to his white lips and sword-cloven bosom,
As from clutch of dead fingers his notched sword I
caught;
For a furlong before us the spear-wood was glistening.
I was king of this city when here where we stand now
Amidst a grim silence I mustered all men folk
Who might yet bear a weapon; and no brawl of kings
was it
That brought war on the city, and silenced the markets
And cumbered the haven with crowd of masts sailless,

But great countries arisen for our ruin and downfall.
I was king of the land, when on all roads were riding
The legates of proud princes to pray help and give ser-
vice—
Yea, I was a great king at last as I sat there,
Peace spread far about me, and the love of all people
To my palace gates wafted by each wind of the heavens.
—And where sought I all this? with what price did I buy
it?
Nay, for thou knowest that this fair fame and fortune
Came stealing soft-footed to give their gifts to me:
And shall I, who was king once, grow griping and weary
In unclosing the clenched fists of niggards who hold
them,
These gifts that I had once, and, having, scarce heeded?
Nay, one thing I have sought, I have sought and have
found it,
And thou, friend, hast helped me and seest me made
happy.

MASTER OLIVER
Farewell then the last time, O land of my fathers!
Farewell, feeble hopes that I once held so mighty.
Yet no more have I need of but this word that thou sayest,
And nought have I to do but to serve thee, my master.
In what land of the world shall we dwell now hencefor-
ward?

KING PHARAMOND
In the land where my love our returning abideth,
The poor land and kingless of the shepherding people,
There is peace there, and all things this land are unlike to.

300

MASTER OLIVER
Before the light waneth will I seek for a passage,
Since for thee and for me the land groweth perilous:
Yea, o'er sweet smell the flowers, too familiar the folk
seem,
Fain I grow of the salt seas, since all things are over here.

KING PHARAMOND
I am fain of one hour's farewell in the twilight,
To the times I lament not: times worser than these times,
To the times that I blame not, that brought on times
better—
Let us meet in our hostel—be brave mid thy kindness,
Let thy heart say, as mine saith, that fair life awaits us.

MASTER OLIVER
Yea, no look in thy face is of ruin, O my master;
Thou art king yet, unchanged yet, nor is my heart chang-
ing;
The world hath no chances to conquer thy glory.
[Exit OLIVER

KING PHARAMOND
Full fair were the world if such faith were remembered.
If such love as thy love had its due, O my fosterer.
Forgive me that giftless from me thou departest,
With thy gifts in my hands left. I might not but take
them;
Thou wilt not begrudge me, I will not forget thee.—
—Long fall the shadows and night draws on apace now,
Day sighs as she sinketh back on to her pillow,

And her last waking breath is full sweet with the rose.
—In such wise depart thou, O daylight of life,
Loved once for the shadows that told of the dreamtide;
Loved still for the longing whereby I remember
That I was lone once in the world of thy making;
Lone wandering about on thy blind way's confusion,
The maze of thy paths that yet led me to love.
All is passed now, and passionless, faint are ye waxen,
Ye hours of blind seeking full of pain clean forgotten.
If it were not that e'en now her eyes I behold not.
That the way lieth long to her feet that would find me,
That the green seas delay yet her fair arms enfolding,
That the long leagues of air will not bear the cry hither
Wherewith she is crying. Come, love, for I love thee.
[A trumpet sounds.
Hark! O days grown a dream of the dream ye have won
me,
    Do ye draw forth the ghosts of old deeds that were noth-
ing,
    That the sound of my trumpet floats down on the even?
    What shows will ye give me to grace my departure?
    Hark!—the beat of the horse-hoofs, the murmur of men
folk!
    Am I riding from battle amidst of my faithful,
    Wild hopes in my heart of the days that are coming;
    Wild longing unsatisfied clinging about me;
    Full of faith that the summer sun elsewhere is ripening
    The fruit grown a pain for my parched lips to think of?
    —Come back, thou poor Pharamond! come back for my
pity!
    Far afield must thou fare before the rest cometh;
    In far lands are they raising the walls of thy prison,

Forging wiles for waylaying, and fair lies for lulling,
The faith and the fire of the heart the world hateth.
In thy way wax streams fordless, and choked passes path-
less,
Fever lurks in the valley, and plague passeth over
The sand of the plain, and with venom and fury
Fulfilled are the woods that thou needs must wend
through:
In the hollow of the mountains the wind is a-storing
Till the keel that shall carry thee hoisteth her sail;
War is crouching unseen round the lands thou shalt
come to,
With thy sword cast away and thy cunning forgotten.
Yea, and e'en the great lord, the great Love of thy fealty,
He who goadeth thee on, weaveth nets to cast o'er thee.
—And thou knowest it all, as thou ridest there lonely,
With the tangles and toils of to-morrow's uprising
Making ready meanwhile for more days of thy kingship.
Faithful heart hadst thou, Pharamond, to hold fast thy
treasure!
I am fain of thee: surely no shame hath destained thee;
Come hither, for thy face all unkissed would I look on!
—Stand we close, for here cometh King Theobald from
the hunting.
Enter KING THEOBALD, HONORIUS, and the
people.

KING THEOBALD
A fair day, my folk, have I had in your fellowship,
And as fair a day cometh to-morrow to greet us,
When the lord of the Golden Land bringeth us tribute:
Grace the gifts of my good-hap with your presence, I

pray you.

THE PEOPLE
God save Theobald the Good, the king of his people!

HONORIUS (aside)
Yea, save him! and send the Gold lords away satisfied,
That the old sword of Pharamond, lying asleep there
In the new golden scabbard, will yet bite as aforetime!
[They pass away into the palace court.

KING PHARAMOND
Troop past in the twilight, O pageant that served me,
Pour through the dark archway to the light that awaits
you
In the chamber of daïs where I once sat among you!
Like the shadows ye are to the shadowless glory
Of the banquet-hall blazing with gold and light go ye:
There blink for a little at your king in his bravery,
Then bear forth your faith to the blackness of night-tide,
And fall asleep fearless of memories of Pharamond,
And in dim dreams dream haply that ye too are kings
—For your dull morrow cometh that is as to-day is.
Pass on in contentment, O king, I discerned not
Through the cloak of your blindness that saw nought be-
side thee,
That feared for no pain and craved for no pleasure!
Pass on, dead-alive, to thy place! thou art worthy:
Nor shalt thou grow wearier than well-worshipped idol
That the incense winds round in the land of the heathen,
While the early and latter rains fall as God listeth,
And on earth that God loveth the sun riseth daily.

—Well art thou: for wert thou the crown of all rulers,
No field shouldst thou ripen, free no frost-bounden river,
Loose no heart from its love, turn no soul to salvation,
Thrust no tempest aside, stay no plague in mid ocean,
Yet grow unto thinking that thou wert God's brother,
Till loveless death gripped thee unloved, unlamented.
—Pass forth, weary King, bear thy crown high to-night!
Then fall asleep, fearing no cry from times bygone,
But in dim dreams dream haply that thou art desired,—
—For thy dull morrow cometh, and is as to-day is.
Ah, hold! now there flashes a link in the archway,
And its light falleth full on thy face, O Honorius,
And I know thee the land's lord, and far away fadeth
My old life of a king at the sight, O thou stranger!
For I know thee full surely the foe the heart hateth
For that barren fulfilment of all that it lacketh.
I may turn away praising that those days long departed
Departed without thee—how long had I piped then
Or e'er thou hadst danced, how long were my weeping
Ere thou hadst lamented!—What dear thing desired
Would thy heart e'er have come to know why I craved
for!
To what crime I could think of couldst thou be consent-
ing?
Yet thou—well I know thee most meet for a ruler—
—Thou lovest not mercy, yet shalt thou be merciful;
Thou joy'st not in justice, yet just shall thy dooms be;
No deep hell thou dreadest, nor dream'st of high heaven;
No gleam of love leads thee: no gift men may give thee;
For no kiss, for no comfort the lone way thou wearest,
A blind will without life, lest thou faint ere the end come.
—Yea, folly it was when I called thee my foeman;

From thee may I turn now with sword in the scabbard
Without shame or misgiving, because God hath made
thee
A ruler for manfolk: pass on then unpitied!
There is darkness between us till the measure's fulfilment.
Amidst singing thou hear'st not, fair sights that thou
seest not,
Think this eve on the deeds thou shalt set in men's hands
To bring fair days about for which thou hast no blessing.
Then fall asleep fearless of dead days that return not;
Yet dream if thou may'st that thou yet hast a hope!
—For thy dull morrow cometh and is as to-day is.
O sweet wind of the night, wherewith now ariseth
The red moon through the garden boughs frail, overlad-
en,
O faint murmuring tongue of the dream-tide trium-
phant,
That wouldst tell me sad tales in the times long passed
over,
If somewhat I sicken and turn to your freshness,
From no shame it is of earth's tangle and trouble,
And deeds done for nought, and change that forgetteth;
But for hope of the lips that I kissed on the sea-strand,
But for hope of the hands that clung trembling about
me,—
And the breast that was heaving with words driven back-
ward,
By longing I longed for, by pain of departing,
By my eyes that knew her pain, my pain that might speak
not—
Yea, for hope of the morn when the sea is passed over,
And for hope of the next moon the elm-boughs shall

306

tangle;

And fresh dawn, and fresh noon, and fresh night of desire
Still following and changing, with nothing forgotten;
For hope of new wonder each morn, when I, waking
Behold her awaking eyes turning to seek me;
For hope of fresh marvels each time the world changing
Shall show her feet moving in noontide to meet me;
For hope of fresh bliss, past all words, half forgotten,

When her voice shall break through the hushed blackness of night.

—O sweet wind of the summer-tide, broad moon a-whitening,

Bear me witness to Love, and the world he has fashioned!

It shall change, we shall change, as through rain and through sunshine

The green rod of the rose-bough to blossoming changeth:

Still lieth in wait with his sweet tale untold of
Each long year of Love, and the first scarce beginneth,
Wherein I have hearkened to the word God hath whispered,
Why the fair world was fashioned mid wonders uncounted.

Breathe soft, O sweet wind, for surely she speaketh:
Weary I wax, and my life is a-waning;
Life lapseth fast, and I faint for thee, Pharamond,
What are thou lacking if Love no more sufficeth?
—Weary not, sweet, as I weary to meet thee;
Look not on the long way but my eyes that were weeping
Faint not in love as thy Pharamond fainteth!—
—Yea, Love were enough if thy lips were not lacking.

THE MUSIC
LOVE IS ENOUGH: ho ye who seek saving,
  Go no further; come hither; there have been who have
found it,
  And these know the House of Fulfilment of Craving;
  These know the Cup with the roses around it;
  These know the World's Wound and the balm that hath
bound it:
  Cry out, the World heedeth not, "Love, lead us home!"

  He leadeth, He hearkeneth, He cometh to you-ward;
  Set your faces as steel to the fears that assemble
  Round his goad for the faint, and his scourge for the fro-
ward:
  Lo his lips, how with tales of last kisses they tremble!
  Lo his eyes of all sorrow that may not dissemble!
  Cry out, for he heedeth, "O Love, lead us home!"

  O hearken the words of his voice of compassion:
  "Come cling round about me, ye faithful who sicken
  Of the weary unrest and the world's passing fashion!
  As the rain in mid-morning your troubles shall thicken,
  But surely within you some Godhead doth quicken,
  As ye cry to me heeding, and leading you home.

  "Come—pain ye shall have, and be blind to the ending!
  Come—fear ye shall have, mid the sky's overcasting!
  Come—change ye shall have, for far are ye wending!
  Come—no crown ye shall have for your thirst and your
fasting,
  But the kissed lips of Love and fair life everlasting!

Cry out, for one heedeth, who leadeth you home!"

Is he gone? was he with us?—ho ye who seek savings
Go no further; come hither; for have we not found it?
Here is the House of Fulfilment of Craving;
Here is the Cup with the roses around it;
The World's Wound well healed, and the balm that hath
bound it:
Cry out! for he heedeth, fair Love that led home.

Enter before the curtain, LOVE, holding a crown and
palm-branch.

LOVE
If love be real, if I whom ye behold
Be aught but glittering wings and gown of gold,
Be aught but singing of an ancient song
Made sweet by record of dead stingless wrong,
How shall we part at that sad garden's end
Through which the ghosts of mighty lovers wend?
How shall ye faint and fade with giftless hands
Who once held fast the life of all the lands?
—Beloved, if so much as this I say,
I know full well ye need it not to-day,
As with full hearts and glorious hope ablaze
Through the thick veil of what shall be ye gaze,
And lacking words to name the things ye see
Turn back with yearning speechless mouths to me.—
—Ah, not to-day—and yet the time has been
When by the bed my wings have waved unseen
Wherein my servant lay who deemed me dead;

My tears have dropped anigh the hapless head
Deep buried in the grass and crying out
For heaven to fall, and end despair or doubt:
Lo, for such days I speak and say, believe
That from these hands reward ye shall receive.
—Reward of what?—Life springing fresh again.—
Life of delight?—I say it not—Of pain?
It may be—Pain eternal?—Who may tell?
Yet pain of Heaven, beloved, and not of Hell.
—What sign, what sign, ye cry, that so it is?
The sign of Earth, its sorrow and its bliss,
Waxing and waning, steadfastness and change;
Too full of life that I should think it strange
Though death hang over it; too sure to die
But I must deem its resurrection nigh.
—In what wise, ah, in what wise shall it be?
How shall the bark that girds the winter tree
Babble about the sap that sleeps beneath,
And tell the fashion of its life and death?
How shall my tongue in speech man's longing wrought
Tell of the things whereof he knoweth nought?
Should I essay it might ye understand
How those I love shall share my promised land!
Then must I speak of little things as great,
Then must I tell of love and call it hate,
Then must I bid you seek what all men shun,
Reward defeat, praise deeds that were not done.
Have faith, and crave and suffer, and all ye
The many mansions of my house shall see
In all content: cast shame and pride away,
Let honour gild the world's eventless day,
Shrink not from change, and shudder not at crime,

Leave lies to rattle in the sieve of Time!
Then, whatsoe'er your workday gear shall stain,
Of me a wedding-garment shall ye gain
No God shall dare cry out at, when at last
Your time of ignorance is overpast;
A wedding garment, and a glorious seat
Within my household, e'en as yet be meet.
Fear not, I say again; believe it true
That not as men mete shall I measure you:
This calm strong soul, whose hidden tale found out
Has grown a spell to conquer fear and doubt,
Is he not mine? yea, surely—mine no less
This well mocked clamourer out of bitterness:
The strong one's strength, from me he had it not;
Let the world keep it that his love forgot;
The weak one's weakness was enough to save,
Let the world hide it in his honour's grave!
For whatso folly is, or wisdom was
Across my threshold naked all must pass.
Fear not; no vessel to dishonour born
Is in my house; there all shall well adorn
The walls whose stones the lapse of Time has laid.
Behold again; this life great stories made;
All cast aside for love, and then and then
Love filched away; the world an adder-den,
And all folk foes: and one, the one desire—
—How shall we name it?—grown a poisoned fire,
God once, God still, but God of wrong and shame
A lying God, a curse without a name.
So turneth love to hate, the wise world saith.
—Folly—I say 'twixt love and hate lies death,
They shall not mingle: neither died this love,

But through a dreadful world all changed must move
With earthly death and wrong, and earthly woe
The only deeds its hand might find to do.
Surely ye deem that this one shall abide
Within the murmuring palace of my pride.
But lo another, how shall he have praise?
Through flame and thorns I led him many days
And nought he shrank, but smiled and followed close,
Till in his path the shade of hate arose
'Twixt him and his desire: with heart that burned
For very love back through the thorns he turned,
His wounds, his tears, his prayers without avail
Forgotten now, nor e'en for him a tale;
Because for love's sake love he cast aside.
—Lo, saith the World, a heart well satisfied
With what I give, a barren love forgot—
—Draw near me, O my child, and heed them not!
The world thou lovest, e'en my world it is,
Thy faithful hands yet reach out for my bliss,
Thou seest me in the night and in the day
Thou canst not deem that I can go astray.
No further, saith the world 'twixt Heaven and Hell
Than 'twixt these twain.—My faithful, heed it well!
For on the great day when the hosts are met
On Armageddon's plain by spears beset,
This is my banner with my sign thereon,
That is my sword wherewith my deeds are done.
But how shall tongue of man tell all the tale
Of faithful hearts who overcome or fail,
But at the last fail nowise to be mine.
In diverse ways they drink the fateful wine
Those twain drank mid the lulling of the storm

Upon the Irish Sea, when love grown warm
Kindled and blazed, and lit the days to come,
The hope and joy and death that led them home.
—In diverse ways; yet having drunk, be sure
The flame thus lighted ever shall endure,
So my feet trod the grapes whereby it glowed.
Lo, Faithful, lo, the door of my abode
Wide open now, and many pressing in
That they the lordship of the World may win!
Hark to the murmuring round my bannered car,
And gird your weapons to you for the war!
For who shall say how soon the day shall be
Of that last fight that swalloweth up the sea?
Fear not, be ready! forth the banners go,
And will not turn again till every foe
Is overcome as though they had not been.
Then, with your memories ever fresh and green,
Come back within the House of Love to dwell;
For ye—the sorrow that no words might tell,
Your tears unheeded, and your prayers made nought
Thus and no otherwise through all have wrought,
That if, the while ye toiled and sorrowed most
The sound of your lamenting seemed all lost,
And from my land no answer came again,
It was because of that your care and pain
A house was building, and your bitter sighs
Came hither as toil-helping melodies,
And in the mortar of our gem-built wall
Your tears were mingled mid the rise and fall
Of golden trowels tinkling in the hands
Of builders gathered wide from all the lands.—
—Is the house finished? Nay, come help to build

Walls that the sun of sorrow once did gild
Through many a bitter morn and hopeless eve,
That so at last in bliss ye may believe;
Then rest with me, and turn no more to tears,
For then no more by days and months and years,
By hours of pain come back, and joy passed o'er
We measure time that was—and is no more.

JOAN
The afternoon is waxen grey
Now these fair shapes have passed away;
And I, who should be merry now
A-thinking of the glorious show,
Feel somewhat sad, and wish it were
To-morrow's mid-morn fresh and fair
About the babble of our stead.

GILES
Content thee, sweet, for nowise dead
Within our hearts the story is;
It shall come back to better bliss
On many an eve of happy spring,
Or midst of summer's flourishing.
Or think—some noon of autumn-tide
Thou wandering on the turf beside
The chestnut-wood may'st find thy song
Fade out, as slow thou goest along,
Until at last thy feet stay there
As though thou bidedst something fair,
And hearkenedst for a coming foot;
While down the hole unto the root
The long leaves flutter loud to thee

The fall of spiky nuts shall be,
And creeping wood-wale's noise above;
For thou wouldst see the wings of Love.

JOAN
Or some November eve belike
Thou wandering back with bow and tyke
From wolf-chase on the wind-swept hill
Shall find that narrow vale and still,
And Pharamond and Azalais
Amidmost of that grassy place
Where we twain met last year, whereby
Red-shafted pine-trunks rise on high,
And changeless now from year to year,
What change soever brought them there,
Great rocks are scattered all around:
—Wouldst thou be frightened at the sound
Of their soft speech? So long ago
It was since first their love did grow.

GILES
Maybe: for e'en now when he turned,
His heart's scorn and his hate outburned,
And love the more for that ablaze,
I shuddered, e'en as in the place
High up the mountains, where men say
Gods dwelt in time long worn away.

JOAN
At Love's voice did I tremble too,
And his bright wings, for all I knew
He was a comely minstrel-lad,

In dainty golden raiment clad.

GILES
Yea, yea; for though to-day he spake
Words measured for our pleasure's sake,
From well-taught mouth not overwise,
Yet did that fount of speech arise
In days that ancient folk called old.
O long ago the tale was told
To mighty men of thought and deed,
Who kindled hearkening their own need,
Set forth by long-forgotten men,
E'en as we kindle: praise we then
Tales of old time, whereby alone
The fairness of the world is shown.

JOAN
A longing yet about me clings,
As I had hearkened half-told things;
And better than the words make plain
I seem to know these lovers twain.
Let us go hence, lest there should fall
Something that yet should mar it all.

GILES
Hist—Master Mayor is drawn anigh;
The Empress speaketh presently.

THE MAYOR
May it please you, your Graces, that I be forgiven,
Over-bold, over-eager to bear forth my speech,
In which yet there speaketh the Good Town, beseeching

That ye tell us of your kindness if ye be contented
With this breath of old tales, and shadowy seemings
Of old times departed.—Overwise for our pleasure
May the rhyme be perchance; but rightly we knew not
How to change it and fashion it fresh into fairness.
And once more, your Graces, we pray your forgiveness
For the boldness Love gave us to set forth this story;
And again, that I say, all that Pharamond sought for,
Through sick dreams and weariness, now have ye found,
Mid health and in wealth, and in might to uphold us;
Midst our love who shall deem you our hope and our
treasure.
Well all is done now; so forget ye King Pharamond,
And Azalais his love, if we set it forth foully,
That fairly set forth were a sweet thing to think of
In the season of summer betwixt labour and sleeping.

THE EMPEROR
Fair Master Mayor, and City well beloved,
Think of us twain as folk no little moved
By this your kindness; and believe it not
That Pharamond the Freed shall be forgot,
By us at least: yea, more than ye may think,
This summer dream into our hearts shall sink.
Lo, Pharamond longed and toiled, nor toiled in vain,
But fame he won: he longed and toiled again,
And Love he won: 'twas a long time ago,
And men did swiftly what we now do slow,
And he, a great man full of gifts and grace,
Wrought out a twofold life in ten years' space.
Ah, fair sir, if for me reward come first,
Yet will I hope that ye have seen the worst

Of that my kingcraft, that I yet shall earn
Some part of that which is so long to learn.
Now of your gentleness I pray you bring
This knife and girdle, deemed a well-wrought thing;
And a king's thanks, whatso they be of worth,
To him who Pharamond this day set forth
In worthiest wise, and made a great man live,
Giving me greater gifts than I may give.

THE EMPRESS
And therewithal I pray you, Master Mayor,
Unto the seeming Azalais to bear
This chain, that she may wear it for my sake,
The memory of my pleasure to awake. [Exit MAYOR.

THE EMPEROR
Gifts such as kings give, sweet! Fain had I been
To see him face to face and his fair Queen,
And thank him friendly; asking him maybe
How the world looks to one with love left free:
It may not be, for as thine eyes say, sweet,
Few folk as friends shall unfreed Pharamond meet.
So is it: we are lonelier than those twain,
Though from their vale they ne'er depart again.

THE EMPRESS
Shall I lament it, love, since thou and I
By all the seeming pride are drawn more nigh?
Lo, love, our toil-girthed garden of desire,
How of its changeless sweetness may we tire,
While round about the storm is in the boughs
And careless change amid the turmoil ploughs

The rugged fields we needs must stumble o'er,
Till the grain ripens that shall change no more.

THE EMPEROR

Yea, and an omen fair we well may deem
This dreamy shadowing of ancient dream,
Of what our own hearts long for on the day
When the first furrow cleaves the fallow grey.

THE EMPRESS

O fair it is! let us go forth, my sweet,
And be alone amid the babbling street;
Yea, so alone that scarce the hush of night
May add one joy unto our proved delight.

GILES

Fair lovers were they: I am fain
To see them both ere long again;
Yea, nigher too, if it might be.

JOAN

Too wide and dim, love, lies the sea,
That we should look on face to face
This Pharamond and Azalais.
Those only from the dead come back
Who left behind them what they lack.

GILES

Nay, I was asking nought so strange,
Since long ago their life did change:
The seeming King and Queen I meant.
And e'en now 'twas my full intent

To bid them home to us straightway,
And crown the joyance of to-day.
He may be glad to see my face,
He first saw mid that waggon race
When the last barley-sheaf came home.

JOAN
A great joy were it, should they come.
They are dear lovers, sure enough.
He deems the summer air too rough
To touch her kissed cheek, howsoe'er
Through winter mountains they must fare,
He would bid spring new flowers to make
Before her feet, that oft must ache
With flinty driftings of the waste.
And sure is she no more abased
Before the face of king and lord,
Than if the very Pharamond's sword
Her love amid the hosts did wield
Above the dinted lilied shield:
O bid them home with us, and we
Their scholars for a while will be
In many a lesson of sweet lore
To learn love's meaning more and more.

GILES
And yet this night of all the year
Happier alone perchance they were,
And better so belike would seem
The glorious lovers of the dream:
So let them dream on lip to lip:
Yet will I gain his fellowship

Ere many days be o'er my head,
And they shall rest them in our stead;
And there we four awhile shall dwell
As though the world were nought but well,
And that old time come back again
When nought in all the earth had pain.
The sun through lime-boughs where we dine
Upon my father's cup shall shine;
The vintage of the river-bank,
That ten years since the sunbeams drank,
Shall fill the mazer bowl carved o'er
With naked shepherd-folk of yore.
Dainty should seem worse fare than ours
As o'er the close-thronged garden flowers
The wind comes to us, and the bees
Complain overhead mid honey-trees.

JOAN
Wherewith shall we be garlanded?

GILES
For thee the buds of roses red.

JOAN
For her white roses widest blown.

GILES
The jasmine boughs for Pharamond's crown.

JOAN
And sops-in-wine for thee, fair love.

GILES
Surely our feast shall deeper move
The kind heart of the summer-tide
Than many a day of pomp and pride;
And as by moon and stars well lit
Our kissing lips shall finish it,
Full satisfied our hearts shall be
With that well-won felicity.

JOAN
Ah, sweetheart, be not all so sure:
Love, who beyond all worlds shall dure,
Mid pleading sweetness still doth keep
A goad to stay his own from sleep;
And I shall long as thou shalt long
For unknown cure of unnamed wrong
As from our happy feast we pass
Along the rose-strewn midnight grass—
—Praise Love who will not be forgot!

GILES
Yea, praise we Love who sleepeth not!
—Come, o'er much gold mine eyes have seen,
And long now for the pathway green,
And rose-hung ancient walls of grey
Yet warm with sunshine gone away.

JOAN
Yea, full fain would I rest thereby,
And watch the flickering martins fly
About the long eave-bottles red
And the clouds lessening overhead:

E'en now meseems the cows are come
Unto the grey gates of our home,
And low to hear the milking-pail:
The peacock spreads abroad his tail
Against the sun, as down the lane
The milkmaids pass the moveless wain,
And stable door, where the roan team
An hour agone began to dream
Over the dusty oats.— Come, love,
Noises of river and of grove
And moving things in field and stall
And night-birds' whistle shall be all
Of the world's speech that we shall hear
By then we come the garth anear:
For then the moon that hangs aloft
These thronged streets, lightless now and soft,
Unnoted, yea, e'en like a shred
Of yon wide white cloud overhead,
Sharp in the dark star-sprinkled sky
Low o'er the willow boughs shall lie;
And when our chamber we shall gain
Eastward our drowsy eyes shall strain
If yet perchance the dawn may show.
—O Love, go with us as we go,
And from the might of thy fair hand
Cast wide about the blooming land
The seed of such-like tales as this!
—O Day, change round about our bliss,
Come, restful night, when day is done!
Come, dawn, and bring a fairer one!

POEMS BY THE WAY

& LOVE IS ENOUGH

BY
WILLIAM MORRIS

NEW IMPRESSION

LONGMANS, GREEN, AND CO.
39 PATERNOSTER ROW, LONDON
NEW YORK, BOMBAY, AND CALCUTTA
1907

BIBLIOGRAPHICAL NOTE

First Edition in this form, June 1896;
Reprinted February 1898, May 1902,
and June 1907

CONTENTS
POEMS BY THE WAY

POEMS BY THE WAY

FROM THE UPLAND TO THE SEA
Shall we wake one morn of spring,
Glad at heart of everything,
Yet pensive with the thought of eve?
Then the white house shall we leave.
Pass the wind-flowers and the bays,
Through the garth, and go our ways,
Wandering down among the meads
Till our very joyance needs
Rest at last; till we shall come
To that Sun-god's lonely home,
Lonely on the hillside grey,
Whence the sheep have gone away;
Lonely till the feast-time is,

When with prayer and praise of bliss,
Thither comes the country side.
There awhile shall we abide,
Sitting low down in the porch
By that image with the torch:
Thy one white hand laid upon
The black pillar that was won
From the far-off Indian mine;
And my hand nigh touching thine,
But not touching; and thy gown
Fair with spring-flowers cast adown
From thy bosom and thy brow.
There the south-west wind shall blow
Through thine hair to reach my cheek,
As thou sittest, nor mayst speak,
Nor mayst move the hand I kiss
For the very depth of bliss;
Nay, nor turn thine eyes to me.
Then desire of the great sea
Nigh enow, but all unheard,
In the hearts of us is stirred,
And we rise, we twain at last,
And the daffodils downcast,
Feel thy feet and we are gone
From the lonely Sun-Crowned one,
Then the meads fade at our back,
And the spring day 'gins to lack
That fresh hope that once it had;
But we twain grow yet more glad,
And apart no more may go
When the grassy slope and low
Dieth in the shingly sand:

Then we wander hand in hand
By the edges of the sea,
And I weary more for thee
Than if far apart we were,
With a space of desert drear
'Twixt thy lips and mine, O love!
Ah, my joy, my joy thereof!

OF THE WOOING OF HALLBIORN THE STRONG
A STORY FROM THE LAND-SETTLING BOOK OF ICELAND, CHAPTER XXX.

At Deildar-Tongue in the autumn-tide,
So many times over comes summer again,
Stood Odd of Tongue his door beside.
What healing in summer if winter be vain?
Dim and dusk the day was grown,
As he heard his folded wethers moan.
Then through the garth a man drew near,
With painted shield and gold-wrought spear.
Good was his horse and grand his gear,
And his girths were wet with Whitewater.
"Hail, Master Odd, live blithe and long!
How fare the folk at Deildar-Tongue?"
"All hail, thou Hallbiorn the Strong!
How fare the folk by the Brothers'-Tongue?"
"Meat have we there, and drink and fire,
Nor lack all things that we desire.
But by the other Whitewater
Of Hallgerd many a tale we hear."
"Tales enow may my daughter make

330

If too many words be said for her sake."
"What saith thine heart to a word of mine,
That I deem thy daughter fair and fine?
Fair and fine for a bride is she,
And I fain would have her home with me."
"Full many a word that at noon goes forth
Comes home at even little worth.
Now winter treadeth on autumn-tide,
So here till the spring shalt thou abide.
Then if thy mind be changed no whit.
And ye still will wed, see ye to it!
And on the first of summer days,
A wedded man, ye may go your ways.
Yet look, howso the thing will fall,
My hand shall meddle nought at all.
Lo, now the night and rain draweth up.
And within doors glimmer stoop and cup.
And hark, a little sound I know,
The laugh of Snæbiorn's fiddle-bow,
My sister's son, and a craftsman good,
When the red rain drives through the iron wood."
Hallbiorn laughed, and followed in,
And a merry feast there did begin.
Hallgerd's hands undid his weed,
Hallgerd's hands poured out the mead.
Her fingers at his breast he felt,
As her hair fell down about his belt.
Her fingers with the cup he took,
And o'er its rim at her did look.
Cold cup, warm hand, and fingers slim.
Before his eyes were waxen dim.
And if the feast were foul or fair,

He knew not, save that she was there.
He knew not if men laughed or wept,
While still 'twixt wall and daïs she stept.
Whether she went or stood that eve,
Not once his eyes her face did leave.
But Snæbiorn laughed and Snæbiorn sang,
And sweet his smitten fiddle rang.
And Hallgerd stood beside him there,
So many times over comes summer again
Nor ever once he turned to her,
What healing in summer if winter be vain?

Master Odd on the morrow spake,
So many times over comes summer again.
"Hearken, O guest, if ye be awake,"
What healing in summer if winter be vain?
"Sure ye champions of the south
Speak many things from a silent mouth.
And thine, meseems, last night did pray
That ye might well be wed to-day.
The year's ingathering feast it is,
A goodly day to give thee bliss.
Come hither, daughter, fine and fair,
Here is a wooer from Whitewater.
Fast away hath he gotten fame,
And his father's name is e'en my name.
Will ye lay hand within his hand,
That blossoming fair our house may stand?"
She laid her hand within his hand;
White she was as the lily wand.
Low sang Snæbiorn's brand in its sheath,
And his lips were waxen grey as death.

"Snæbiorn, sing us a song of worth.
If your song must be silent from now henceforth.
Clear and loud his voice outrang,
And a song of worth at the wedding he sang.
"Sharp sword," he sang, "and death is sure."
So many times over comes summer again,
"But love doth over all endure."
What healing in summer if winter be vain?

Now winter cometh and weareth away,
So many times over comes summer again,
And glad is Hallbiorn many a day.
What healing in summer if winter be vain?
Full soft he lay his love beside;
But dark are the days of winter-tide.
Dark are the days, and the nights are long,
And sweet and fair was Snæbiorn's song.
Many a time he talked with her,
Till they deemed the summer-tide was there.
And they forgat the wind-swept ways
And angry fords of the flitting-days.
While the north wind swept the hillside there
They forgat the other Whitewater.
While nights at Deildar-Tongue were long,
They clean forgat the Brothers'-Tongue.
But whatso falleth 'twixt Hell and Home,
So many times over comes summer again,
Full surely again shall summer come.
What healing in summer if winter be vain?

To Odd spake Hallbiorn on a day
So many times over comes summer again,

"Gone is the snow from everyway."
What healing in summer if winter be vain?
"Now green is grown Whitewater-side,
And I to Whitewater will ride."
Quoth Odd, "Well fare thou winter-guest,
May thine own Whitewater be best
Well is a man's purse better at home
Than open where folk go and come."
"Come ye carles of the south country,
Now shall we go our kin to see!
For the lambs are bleating in the south,
And the salmon swims towards Olfus mouth,
Girth and graithe and gather your gear!
And ho for the other Whitewater!"
Bright was the moon as bright might be,
And Snæbiorn rode to the north country.
And Odd to Reykholt is gone forth,
To see if his mares be ought of worth.
But Hallbiorn into the bower is gone
And there sat Hallgerd all alone.
She was not dight to go nor ride,
She had no joy of the summer-tide.
Silent she sat and combed her hair,
That fell all round about her there.
The slant beam lay upon her head,
And gilt her golden locks to red.
He gazed at her with hungry eyes
And fluttering did his heart arise.
"Full hot," he said, "is the sun to-day,
And the snow is gone from the mountain-way
The king-cup grows above the grass,
And through the wood do the thrushes pass."

Of all his words she hearkened none,
But combed her hair amidst the sun.
"The laden beasts stand in the garth
And their heads are turned to Helliskarth."
The sun was falling on her knee,
And she combed her gold hair silently.
"To-morrow great will be the cheer
At the Brothers'-Tongue by Whitewater."
From her folded lap the sunbeam slid;
She combed her hair, and the word she hid.
"Come, love; is the way so long and drear
From Whitewater to Whitewater?"
The sunbeam lay upon the floor;
She combed her hair and spake no more.
He drew her by the lily hand:
"I love thee better than all the land."
He drew her by the shoulders sweet:
"My threshold is but for thy feet."
He drew her by the yellow hair:
"O why wert thou so deadly fair?
O am I wedded to death?" he cried,
"Is the Dead-strand come to Whitewater side?"
And the sun was fading from the room,
But her eyes were bright in the change and the gloom.
"Sharp sword," she sang, "and death is sure,
But over all doth love endure."
She stood up shining in her place
And laughed beneath his deadly face.
Instead of the sunbeam gleamed a brand,
The hilts were hard in Hallbiorn's hand:
The bitter point was in Hallgerd's breast
That Snæbiorn's lips of love had pressed.

Morn and noon, and nones passed o'er,
And the sun is far from the bower door.
To-morrow morn shall the sun come back,
So many times over comes summer again,
But Hallgerd's feet the floor shall lack.
What healing in summer if winter be vain?

Now Hallbiorn's house-carles ride full fast,
So many times over comes summer again,
Till many a mile of way is past.
What healing in summer if winter be vain?
But when they came over Oxridges,
'Twas, "Where shall we give our horses ease?"
When Shieldbroad-side was well in sight,
'Twas, "Where shall we lay our heads to-night?"
Hallbiorn turned and raised his head;
"Under the stones of the waste," he said.
Quoth one, "The clatter of hoofs anigh."
Quoth the other, "Spears against the sky!"
"Hither ride men from the Wells apace;
Spur we fast to a kindlier place."
Down from his horse leapt Hallbiorn straight:
"Why should the supper of Odin wait?
Weary and chased I will not come
To the table of my fathers' home."
With that came Snæbiorn, who but he,
And twelve in all was his company.
Snæbiorn's folk were on their feet;
He spake no word as they did meet.
They fought upon the northern hill:
Five are the howes men see there still.
Three men of Snæbiorn's fell to earth

And Hallbiorn's twain that were of worth.
And never a word did Snæbiorn say,
Till Hallbiorn's foot he smote away.
Then Hallbiorn cried: "Come, fellow of mine,
To the southern bent where the sun doth shine."
Tottering into the sun he went,
And slew two more upon the bent.
And on the bent where dead he lay
Three howes do men behold to-day.
And never a word spake Snæbiorn yet,
Till in his saddle he was set.
Nor was there any heard his voice,
So many times over comes summer again
Till he came to his ship in Grimsar-oyce.
What healing in summer if winter be vain?

On so fair a day they hoisted sail,
So many times over comes summer again,
And for Norway well did the wind avail.
What healing in summer if winter be vain?
But Snæbiorn looked aloft and said:
"I see in the sail a stripe of red:
Murder, meseems, is the name of it,
And ugly things about it flit.
A stripe of blue in the sail I see:
Cold death of men it seems to me.
And next I see a stripe of black,
For a life fulfilled of bitter lack."
Quoth one, "So fair a wind doth blow
That we shall see Norway soon enow."
"Be blithe, O shipmate," Snæbiorn said,
"Tell Hacon the Earl that I be dead."

337

About the midst of the Iceland main
Round veered the wind to the east again.
And west they drave, and long they ran
Till they saw a land was white and wan.
"Yea," Snæbiorn said, "my home it is,
Ye bear a man shall have no bliss.
Far off beside the Greekish sea
The maidens pluck the grapes in glee.
Green groweth the wheat in the English land,
And the honey-bee flieth on every hand.
In Norway by the cheaping town
The laden beasts go up and down.
In Iceland many a mead they mow
And Hallgerd's grave grows green enow.
But these are Gunnbiorn's skerries wan,
Meet harbour for a hapless man.
In all lands else is love alive,
But here is nought with grief to strive.
Fail not for a while, O eastern wind,
For nought but grief is left behind.
And before me here a rest I know,"
So many times over comes summer again,
"A grave beneath the Greenland snow,"
What healing in summer if winter be vain?

ECHOES OF LOVE'S HOUSE
Love gives every gift whereby we long to live:
"Love takes every gift, and nothing back doth give."

Love unlocks the lips that else were ever dumb:
"Love locks up the lips whence all things good might come."

Love makes clear the eyes that else would never see:
"Love makes blind the eyes to all but me and thee."

Love turns life to joy till nought is left to gain:
"Love turns life to woe till hope is nought and vain."

Love, who changest all, change me nevermore!
"Love, who changest all, change my sorrow sore!"

Love burns up the world to changeless heaven and blest,
"Love burns up the world to a void of all unrest."

And there we twain are left, and no more work we need:
"And I am left alone, and who my work shall heed?"

Ah! I praise thee, Love, for utter joyance won!
"And is my praise nought worth for all my life undone?"

THE BURGHERS' BATTLE

Thick rise the spear-shafts o'er the land
That erst the harvest bore;
The sword is heavy in the hand,
And we return no more.
The light wind waves the Ruddy Fox,
Our banner of the war,
And ripples in the Running Ox,
And we return no more.
Across our stubble acres now
The teams go four and four;
But out-worn elders guide the plough,
And we return no more.

And now the women heavy-eyed
Turn through the open door
From gazing down the highway wide,
Where we return no more.
The shadows of the fruited close
Dapple the feast-hall floor;
There lie our dogs and dream and doze,
And we return no more.
Down from the minster tower to-day
Fall the soft chimes of yore
Amidst the chattering jackdaws' play:
And we return no more.
But underneath the streets are still;
Noon, and the market's o'er!
Back go the goodwives o'er the hill;
For we return no more.
What merchant to our gates shall come?
What wise man bring us lore?
What abbot ride away to Rome,
Now we return no more?
What mayor shall rule the hall we built?
Whose scarlet sweep the floor?
What judge shall doom the robber's guilt,
Now we return no more?
New houses in the street shall rise
Where builded we before,
Of other stone wrought otherwise;
For we return no more.
And crops shall cover field and hill
Unlike what once they bore,
And all be done without our will,
Now we return no more.

Look up! the arrows streak the sky,
The horns of battle roar;
The long spears lower and draw nigh,
And we return no more.
Remember how beside the wain,
We spoke the word of war,
And sowed this harvest of the plain,
And we return no more.
Lay spears about the Ruddy Fox!
The days of old are o'er;
Heave sword about the Running Ox!
For we return no more.

HOPE DIETH: LOVE LIVETH

Strong are thine arms, O love, and strong
Thine heart to live, and love, and long;
But thou art wed to grief and wrong:
Live, then, and long, though hope be dead!
Live on, and labour through the years!
Make pictures through the mist of tears,
Of unforgotten happy fears,
That crossed the time ere hope was dead.
Draw near the place where once we stood
Amid delight's swift-rushing flood,
And we and all the world seemed good
Nor needed hope now cold and dead.
Dream in the dawn I come to thee
Weeping for things that may not be!
Dream that thou layest lips on me!
Wake, wake to clasp hope's body dead!
Count o'er and o'er, and one by one,
The minutes of the happy sun

341

That while agone on kissed lips shone,
Count on, rest not, for hope is dead.
Weep, though no hair's breadth thou shalt move
The living Earth, the heaven above,
By all the bitterness of love!
Weep and cease not, now hope is dead!
Sighs rest thee not, tears bring no ease,
Life hath no joy, and Death no peace:
The years change not, though they decrease,
For hope is dead, for hope is dead.
Speak, love, I listen: far away
I bless the tremulous lips, that say,
"Mock not the afternoon of day,
Mock not the tide when hope is dead!"
I bless thee, O my love, who say'st:
"Mock not the thistle-cumbered waste;
I hold Love's hand, and make no haste
Down the long way, now hope is dead.
With other names do we name pain,
The long years wear our hearts in vain.
Mock not our loss grown into gain,
Mock not our lost hope lying dead.
Our eyes gaze for no morning-star,
No glimmer of the dawn afar;
Full silent wayfarers we are
Since ere the noon-tide hope lay dead.
Behold with lack of happiness
The master, Love, our hearts did bless
Lest we should think of him the less:
Love dieth not, though hope is dead!"

ERROR AND LOSS

Upon an eve I sat me down and wept,
Because the world to me seemed nowise good;
Still autumn was it, and the meadows slept,
The misty hills dreamed, and the silent wood
Seemed listening to the sorrow of my mood:
I knew not if the earth with me did grieve,
Or if it mocked my grief that bitter eve.

Then 'twixt my tears a maiden did I see,
Who drew anigh me on the leaf-strewn grass,
Then stood and gazed upon me pitifully
With grief-worn eyes, until my woe did pass
From me to her, and tearless now I was,
And she mid tears was asking me of one
She long had sought unaided and alone.

I knew not of him, and she turned away
Into the dark wood, and my own great pain
Still held me there, till dark had slain the day,
And perished at the grey dawn's hand again;
Then from the wood a voice cried: "Ah, in vain,
In vain I seek thee, O thou bitter-sweet!
In what lone land are set thy longed-for feet?"

Then I looked up, and lo, a man there came
From midst the trees, and stood regarding me
Until my tears were dried for very shame;
Then he cried out: "O mourner, where is she
Whom I have sought o'er every land and sea?
I love her and she loveth me, and still
We meet no more than green hill meeteth hill."

343

With that he passed on sadly, and I knew
That these had met and missed in the dark night,
Blinded by blindness of the world untrue,
That hideth love and maketh wrong of right.
Then midst my pity for their lost delight,
Yet more with barren longing I grew weak,
Yet more I mourned that I had none to seek.

THE HALL AND THE WOOD
'Twas in the water-dwindling tide
When July days were done,
Sir Rafe of Greenhowes 'gan to ride
In the earliest of the sun.

He left the white-walled burg behind,
He rode amidst the wheat.
The westland-gotten wind blew kind
Across the acres sweet.

Then rose his heart and cleared his brow,
And slow he rode the way:
"As then it was, so is it now,
Not all hath worn away."

So came he to the long green lane
That leadeth to the ford,
And saw the sickle by the wain
Shine bright as any sword.

The brown carles stayed 'twixt draught and draught,
And murmuring, stood aloof,
But one spake out when he had laughed:

"God bless the Green-wood Roof!"

Then o'er the ford and up he fared:
And lo the happy hills!
And the mountain-dale by summer cleared,
That oft the winter fills.

Then forth he rode by Peter's gate,
And smiled and said aloud:
"No more a day doth the Prior wait;
White stands the tower and proud."

There leaned a knight on the gateway side
In armour white and wan,
And after the heels of the horse he cried,
"God keep the hunted man!"

Then quoth Sir Rafe, "Amen, amen!"
For he deemed the word was good;
But never a while he lingered then
Till he reached the Nether Wood.

He rode by ash, he rode by oak,
He rode the thicket round,
And heard no woodman strike a stroke,
No wandering wife he found.

He rode the wet, he rode the dry,
He rode the grassy glade:
At Wood-end yet the sun was high,

345

And his heart was unafraid.

There on the bent his rein he drew,
And looked o'er field and fold,
O'er all the merry meads he knew
Beneath the mountains old.

He gazed across to the good Green Howe
As he smelt the sun-warmed sward;
Then his face grew pale from chin to brow,
And he cried, "God save the sword!"

For there beyond the winding way,
Above the orchards green,
Stood up the ancient gables grey
With ne'er a roof between.

His naked blade in hand he had,
O'er rough and smooth he rode,
Till he stood where once his heart was glad
Amidst his old abode.

Across the hearth a tie-beam lay
Unmoved a weary while.
The flame that clomb the ashlar grey
Had burned it red as tile.

The sparrows bickering on the floor
Fled at his entering in;
The swift flew past the empty door

His winged meat to win.

Red apples from the tall old tree
O'er the wall's rent were shed.
Thence oft, a little lad, would he
Look down upon the lead.

There turned the cheeping chaffinch now
And feared no birding child;
Through the shot-window thrust a bough
Of garden-rose run wild.

He looked to right, he looked to left,
And down to the cold grey hearth,
Where lay an axe with half burned heft
Amidst the ashen dearth.

He caught it up and cast it wide
Against the gable wall;
Then to the daïs did he stride,
O'er beam and bench and all.

Amidst there yet the high-seat stood,
Where erst his sires had sat;
And the mighty board of oaken wood,
The fire had stayed thereat.

Then through the red wrath of his eyne
He saw a sheathed sword,
Laid thwart that wasted field of wine,
Amidmost of the board.

347

And by the hilts a slug-horn lay,
And therebeside a scroll,
He caught it up and turned away
From the lea-land of the bowl.

Then with the sobbing grief he strove,
For he saw his name thereon;
And the heart within his breast uphove
As the pen's tale now he won.

"O Rafe, my love of long ago!
Draw forth thy father's blade,
And blow the horn for friend and foe,
And the good green-wood to aid!"

He turned and took the slug-horn up,
And set it to his mouth,
And o'er that meadow of the cup
Blew east and west and south.

He drew the sword from out the sheath
And shook the fallow brand;
And there a while with bated breath,
And hearkening ear did stand.

Him-seemed the horn's voice he might hear—
Or the wind that blew o'er all.
Him-seemed that footsteps drew anear—
Or the boughs shook round the hall.

Him-seemed he heard a voice he knew—
Or a dream of while agone.

Him-seemed bright raiment towards him drew—
Or bright the sun-set shone.

She stood before him face to face,
With the sun-beam thwart her hand,
As on the gold of the Holy Place
The painted angels stand.

With many a kiss she closed his eyes;
She kissed him cheek and chin:
E'en so in the painted Paradise
Are Earth's folk welcomed in.

There in the door the green-coats stood,
O'er the bows went up the cry,
"O welcome, Rafe, to the free green-wood,
With us to live and die."

It was bill and bow by the high-seat stood,
And they cried above the bows,
"Now welcome, Rafe, to the good green-wood,
And welcome Kate the Rose!"

White, white in the moon is the woodland plash,
White is the woodland glade,
Forth wend those twain, from oak to ash,
With light hearts unafraid.

The summer moon high o'er the hill,
All silver-white is she,
And Sir Rafe's good men with bow and bill,
They go by two and three.

In the fair green-wood where lurks no fear,
Where the King's writ runneth not,
There dwell they, friends and fellows dear,
While summer days are hot.

And when the leaf from the oak-tree falls,
And winds blow rough and strong,
With the carles of the woodland thorps and halls
They dwell, and fear no wrong.

And there the merry yule they make,
And see the winter wane,
And fain are they for true-love's sake,
And the folk thereby are fain.

For the ploughing carle and the straying herd
Flee never for Sir Rafe:
No barefoot maiden wends afeard,
And she deems the thicket safe.

But sore adread do the chapmen ride;
Wide round the wood they go;
And the judge and the sergeants wander wide,
Lest they plead before the bow.

Well learned and wise is Sir Rafe's good sword,
And straight the arrows fly,
And they find the coat of many a lord,
And the crest that rideth high.

THE DAY OF DAYS

Each eve earth falleth down the dark,
As though its hope were o'er;
Yet lurks the sun when day is done
Behind to-morrow's door.

Grey grows the dawn while men-folk sleep,
Unseen spreads on the light,
Till the thrush sings to the coloured things,
And earth forgets the night.

No otherwise wends on our Hope:
E'en as a tale that's told
Are fair lives lost, and all the cost
Of wise and true and bold.

We've toiled and failed; we spake the word;
None hearkened; dumb we lie;
Our Hope is dead, the seed we spread
Fell o'er the earth to die.

What's this? For joy our hearts stand still,
And life is loved and dear,
The lost and found the Cause hath crowned,
The Day of Days is here.

TO THE MUSE OF THE NORTH

O muse that swayest the sad Northern Song,
Thy right hand full of smiting and of wrong,
Thy left hand holding pity; and thy breast
Heaving with hope of that so certain rest:
Thou, with the grey eyes kind and unafraid,
The soft lips trembling not, though they have said

The doom of the World and those that dwell therein.
The lips that smile not though thy children win
The fated Love that draws the fated Death.
O, borne adown the fresh stream of thy breath,
Let some word reach my ears and touch my heart,
That, if it may be, I may have a part
In that great sorrow of thy children dead
That vexed the brow, and bowed adown the head,
Whitened the hair, made life a wondrous dream,
And death the murmur of a restful stream,
But left no stain upon those souls of thine
Whose greatness through the tangled world doth shine.
O Mother, and Love and Sister all in one,
Come thou; for sure I am enough alone
That thou thine arms about my heart shouldst throw,
And wrap me in the grief of long ago.

OF THE THREE SEEKERS
There met three knights on the woodland,
And the first was clad in silk array:
The second was dight in iron and steel,
But the third was rags from head to heel.
"Lo, now is the year and the day come round
When we must tell what we have found."
The first said: "I have found a king
Who grudgeth no gift of anything."
The second said: "I have found a knight
Who hath never turned his back in fight."
But the third said: "I have found a love
That Time and the World shall never move."

Whither away to win good cheer?

"With me," said the first, "for my king is near."
So to the King they went their ways;
But there was a change of times and days.
"What men are ye," the great King said,
"That ye should eat my children's bread?
My waste has fed full many a store,
And mocking and grudge have I gained therefore.
Whatever waneth as days wax old.
Full worthy to win are goods and gold."

Whither away to win good cheer?
"With me," said the second, "my knight is near.
So to the knight they went their ways,
But there was a change of times and days.
He dwelt in castle sure and strong,
For fear lest aught should do him wrong.
Guards by gate and hall there were,
And folk went in and out in fear.
When he heard the mouse run in the wall,
"Hist!" he said, "what next shall befall?
Draw not near, speak under your breath,
For all new-comers tell of death.
Bring me no song nor minstrelsy,
Round death it babbleth still," said he.
"And what is fame and the praise of men,
When lost life cometh not again?"

Whither away to seek good cheer?
"Ah me!" said the third, "that my love were anear!
Were the world as little as it is wide,
In a happy house should ye abide.
Were the world as kind as it is hard,

Ye should behold a fair reward."

So far by high and low have they gone,
They have come to a waste was rock and stone.
But lo, from the waste, a company
Full well bedight came riding by;
And in the midst, a queen, so fair,
That God wrought well in making her.

The first and second knights abode
To gaze upon her as she rode,
Forth passed the third with head down bent,
And stumbling ever as he went.
His shoulder brushed her saddle-bow;
He trembled with his head hung low.
His hand brushed o'er her golden gown,
As on the waste he fell adown.
So swift to earth her feet she set,
It seemed that there her arms he met.
His lips that looked the stone to meet
Were on her trembling lips and sweet.
Softly she kissed him cheek and chin,
His mouth her many tears drank in.
"Where would'st thou wander, love," she said,
"Now I have drawn thee from the dead?"
"I go my ways," he said, "and thine
Have nought to do with grief and pine."
"All ways are one way now," she said,
"Since I have drawn thee from the dead."
Said he, "But I must seek again
Where first I met thee in thy pain:
I am not clad so fair," said he,

"But yet the old hurts thou may'st see.
And thou, but for thy gown of gold,
A piteous tale of thee were told."
"There is no pain on earth," she said,
"Since I have drawn thee from the dead."
"And parting waiteth for us there,"
Said he, "as it was yester-year."
"Yet first a space of love," she said,
"Since I have drawn thee from the dead."
He laughed; said he, "Hast thou a home
Where I and these my friends may come?"
Laughing, "The world's my home," she said,
"Now I have drawn thee from the dead.
Yet somewhere is a space thereof
Where I may dwell beside my love.
There clear the river grows for him
Till o'er its stones his keel shall swim.
There faint the thrushes in their song,
And deem he tarrieth overlong.
There summer-tide is waiting now
Until he bids the roses blow.
Come, tell my flowery fields," she said,
"How I have drawn thee from the dead."

Whither away to win good cheer?
"With me," he said, "for my love is here.
The wealth of my house it waneth not;
No gift it giveth is forgot.
No fear my house may enter in,
For nought is there that death may win.
Now life is little, and death is nought,
Since all is found that erst I sought."

355

LOVE'S GLEANING-TIDE

Draw not away thy hands, my love,
With wind alone the branches move,
And though the leaves be scant above
The Autumn shall not shame us.

Say; Let the world wax cold and drear,
What is the worst of all the year
But life, and what can hurt us, dear,
Or death, and who shall blame us?

Ah, when the summer comes again
How shall we say, we sowed in vain?
The root was joy, the stem was pain,
The ear a nameless blending.

The root is dead and gone, my love,
The stem's a rod our truth to prove;
The ear is stored for nought to move
Till heaven and earth have ending.

THE MESSAGE OF THE MARCH WIND

Fair now is the spring-tide, now earth lies beholding
With the eyes of a lover, the face of the sun;
Long lasteth the daylight, and hope is enfolding
The green-growing acres with increase begun.

Now sweet, sweet it is through the land to be straying
'Mid the birds and the blossoms and the beasts of the
field;
Love mingles with love, and no evil is weighing

On thy heart or mine, where all sorrow is healed.

From township to township, o'er down and by tillage
Fair, far have we wandered and long was the day;
But now cometh eve at the end of the village,
Where over the grey wall the church riseth grey.

There is wind in the twilight; in the white road before us
The straw from the ox-yard is blowing about;
The moon's rim is rising, a star glitters o'er us,
And the vane on the spire-top is swinging in doubt.

Down there dips the highway, toward the bridge crossing
over
    The brook that runs on to the Thames and the sea.
    Draw closer, my sweet, we are lover and lover;
    This eve art thou given to gladness and me.

Shall we be glad always? Come closer and hearken:
    Three fields further on, as they told me down there,
    When the young moon has set, if the March sky should
darken,
    We might see from the hill-top the great city's glare.

Hark, the wind in the elm-boughs! from London it
bloweth,
    And telleth of gold, and of hope and unrest;
    Of power that helps not; of wisdom that knoweth,
    But teacheth not aught of the worst and the best.

Of the rich men it telleth, and strange is the story
    How they have, and they hanker, and grip far and wide;

357

And they live and they die, and the earth and its glory
Has been but a burden they scarce might abide.

Hark! the March wind again of a people is telling;
Of the life that they live there, so haggard and grim,
That if we and our love amidst them had been dwelling
My fondness had faltered, thy beauty grown dim.

This land we have loved in our love and our leisure
For them hangs in heaven, high out of their reach;
The wide hills o'er the sea-plain for them have no plea-
sure,
The grey homes of their fathers no story to teach.

The singers have sung and the builders have builded,
The painters have fashioned their tales of delight;
For what and for whom hath the world's book been gild-
ed,
When all is for these but the blackness of night?

How long, and for what is their patience abiding?
How oft and how oft shall their story be told,
While the hope that none seeketh in darkness is hiding,
And in grief and in sorrow the world groweth old?

Come back to the inn, love, and the lights and the fire,
And the fiddler's old tune and the shuffling of feet;
For there in a while shall be rest and desire,
And there shall the morrow's uprising be sweet.

Yet, love, as we wend, the wind bloweth behind us,
And beareth the last tale it telleth to-night,
How here in the spring-tide the message shall find us;
For the hope that none seeketh is coming to light.

Like the seed of mid-winter, unheeded, unperished,
Like the autumn-sown wheat 'neath the snow lying
green,
Like the love that overtook us, unawares and uncher-
ished,
Like the babe 'neath thy girdle that groweth unseen;

So the hope of the people now buddeth and groweth,
Rest fadeth before it, and blindness and fear;
It biddeth us learn all the wisdom it knoweth;
It hath found us and held us, and biddeth us hear:

For it beareth the message: "Rise up on the morrow
And go on your ways toward the doubt and the strife;
Join hope to our hope and blend sorrow with sorrow.
And seek for men's love in the short days of life."

But lo, the old inn, and the lights, and the fire,
And the fiddler's old tune and the shuffling of feet;
Soon for us shall be quiet and rest and desire,
And to-morrow's uprising to deeds shall be sweet.

A DEATH SONG

What cometh here from west to east awending?
And who are these, the marchers stern and slow?
We bear the message that the rich are sending
Aback to those who bade them wake and know.

Not one, not one, nor thousands must they slay,
But one and all if they would dusk the day.

We asked them for a life of toilsome earning,
They bade us bide their leisure for our bread;
We craved to speak to tell our woeful learning:
We come back speechless, bearing back our dead.
Not one, not one, nor thousands must they slay,
But one and all if they would dusk the day.

They will not learn; they have no ears to hearken.
They turn their faces from the eyes of fate;
Their gay-lit halls shut out the skies that darken.
But, lo! this dead man knocking at the gate.
Not one, not one, nor thousands must they slay,
But one and all if they would dusk the day.

Here lies the sign that we shall break our prison;
Amidst the storm he won a prisoner's rest;
But in the cloudy dawn the sun arisen
Brings us our day of work to win the best.
Not one, not one, nor thousands must they slay,
But one and all if they would dusk the day.

ICELAND FIRST SEEN
Lo from our loitering ship
a new land at last to be seen;
Toothed rocks down the side of the firth
on the east guard a weary wide lea,
And black slope the hillsides above,
striped adown with their desolate green:
And a peak rises up on the west

from the meeting of cloud and of sea,
Foursquare from base unto point
like the building of Gods that have been,
The last of that waste of the mountains
all cloud-wreathed and snow-flecked and grey,
And bright with the dawn that began
just now at the ending of day.

Ah! what came we forth for to see
that our hearts are so hot with desire?
Is it enough for our rest,
the sight of this desolate strand,
And the mountain-waste voiceless as death
but for winds that may sleep not nor tire?
Why do we long to wend forth
through the length and breadth of a land,
Dreadful with grinding of ice,
and record of scarce hidden fire,
But that there 'mid the grey grassy dales
sore scarred by the ruining streams
Lives the tale of the Northland of old
and the undying glory of dreams?

O land, as some cave by the sea
where the treasures of old have been laid,
The sword it may be of a king
whose name was the turning of fight:
Or the staff of some wise of the world
that many things made and unmade.
Or the ring of a woman maybe
whose woe is grown wealth and delight.
No wheat and no wine grows above it,

no orchard for blossom and shade;
The few ships that sail by its blackness
but deem it the mouth of a grave;
Yet sure when the world shall awaken,
this too shall be mighty to save.

Or rather, O land, if a marvel
it seemeth that men ever sought
Thy wastes for a field and a garden
fulfilled of all wonder and doubt,
And feasted amidst of the winter
when the fight of the year had been fought,
Whose plunder all gathered together
was little to babble about;
Cry aloud from thy wastes, O thou land,
"Not for this nor for that was I wrought
Amid waning of realms and of riches
and death of things worshipped and sure,
I abide here the spouse of a God,
and I made and I make and endure."

O Queen of the grief without knowledge,
of the courage that may not avail,
Of the longing that may not attain,
of the love that shall never forget,
More joy than the gladness of laughter
thy voice hath amidst of its wail:
More hope than of pleasure fulfilled
amidst of thy blindness is set;
More glorious than gaining of all
thine unfaltering hand that shall fail:
For what is the mark on thy brow

but the brand that thy Brynhild doth bear?
Lone once, and loved and undone
by a love that no ages outwear.

Ah! when thy Balder comes back,
and bears from the heart of the Sun
Peace and the healing of pain,
and the wisdom that waiteth no more;
And the lilies are laid on thy brow
'mid the crown of the deeds thou hast done;
And the roses spring up by thy feet
that the rocks of the wilderness wore.
Ah! when thy Balder comes back
and we gather the gains he hath won,
Shall we not linger a little
to talk of thy sweetness of old,
Yea, turn back awhile to thy travail
whence the Gods stood aloof to behold?

THE RAVEN AND THE KING'S DAUGHTER

THE RAVEN

King's daughter sitting in tower so high,
Fair summer is on many a shield.
Why weepest thou as the clouds go by?
Fair sing the swans 'twixt firth and field.
Why weepest thou in the window-seat
Till the tears run through thy fingers sweet?

THE KING'S DAUGHTER

I weep because I sit alone
Betwixt these walls of lime and stone.
Fair folk are in my father's hall,
But for me he built this guarded wall.
And here the gold on the green I sew
Nor tidings of my true-love know.

THE RAVEN

King's daughter, sitting above the sea,
I shall tell thee a tale shall gladden thee.
Yestreen I saw a ship go forth
When the wind blew merry from the north.
And by the tiller Steingrim sat,
And O, but my heart was glad thereat!
For 'twixt ashen plank and dark blue sea
His sword sang sweet of deeds to be.

THE KING'S DAUGHTER

O barren sea, thou bitter bird,
And a barren tale my ears have heard.

THE RAVEN

Thy father's men were hard thereby
In byrny bright and helmet high.

THE KING'S DAUGHTER

O worser waxeth thy story far,
For these drew upon me bolt and bar.

Fly south, O fowl, to the field of death
For nothing sweet thy grey neb saith.

THE RAVEN

O, there was Olaf the lily-rose,
As fair as any oak that grows.

THE KING'S DAUGHTER

O sweet bird, what did he then
Among the spears of my father's men?

THE RAVEN

'Twixt ashen plank and dark blue sea,
He sang: My true love waiteth me.

THE KING'S DAUGHTER

As well as this dull floor knows my feet,
I am not weary yet, my sweet.

THE RAVEN

He sang: As once her hand I had,
Her lips at last shall make me glad.

THE KING'S DAUGHTER

As once our fingers met, O love,

365

So shall our lips be fain thereof.

THE RAVEN

He sang: Come wrack and iron and flame,
For what shall breach the wall but fame?

THE KING'S DAUGHTER

Be swift to rise and set, O Sun,
Lest life 'twixt hope and death be done.

THE RAVEN

King's daughter sitting in tower so high,
A gift for my tale ere forth I fly,
The gold from thy finger fair and fine,
Thou hadst it from no love of thine.

THE KING'S DAUGHTER

By my father's ring another there is,
I had it with my mother's kiss.
Fly forth, O fowl, across the sea
To win another gift of me.
Fly south to bring me tidings true,
Fair summer is on many a shield.
Of the eve grown red with the battle-dew,
Fair sing the swans 'twixt firth and field.

THE RAVEN

King's daughter sitting in tower so high,
Fair summer is on many a shield.
Tidings to hearken ere thou die,
Fair sing the swans 'twixt firth and field.
In the Frankish land the spear points met,
And wide about the field was wet.
And high ere the cold moon quenched the sun,
Blew Steingrim's horn for battle won.

THE KING'S DAUGHTER

Fair fall thee, fowl! Tell tidings true
Of deeds that men that day did do.

THE RAVEN

Steingrim before his banner went,
And helms were broke and byrnies rent.

THE KING'S DAUGHTER

A doughty man and good at need;
Tell men of any other's deed?

THE RAVEN

Where Steingrim through the battle bore
Still Olaf went a foot before.

THE KING'S DAUGHTER

O fair with deeds the world doth grow!
Where is my true-love gotten now?

THE RAVEN

Upon the deck beside the mast
He lieth now, and sleepeth fast.

THE KING'S DAUGHTER

Heard'st thou before his sleep began
That he spake word of any man?

THE RAVEN

Methought of thee he sang a song,
But nothing now he saith for long.

THE KING'S DAUGHTER

And wottest thou where he will wend
With the world before him from end to end?

THE RAVEN

Before the battle joined that day
Steingrim a word to him did say:
"If we bring the banner back in peace,
In the King's house much shall my fame increase;
Till there no guarded door shall be
But it shall open straight to me.

Then to the bower we twain shall go
Where thy love the golden seam doth sew.
I shall bring thee in and lay thine hand
About the neck of that lily-wand.
And let the King be lief or loth
One bed that night shall hold you both."
Now north belike runs Steingrim's prow,
And the rain and the wind from the south do blow.

THE KING'S DAUGHTER

Lo, fowl of death, my mother's ring,
But the bridal song I must learn to sing.
And fain were I for a space alone,
For O the wind, and the wind doth moan.
And I must array the bridal bed,
Fair summer is on many a shield.
For O the rain, and the rain drifts red!
Fair sing the swans 'twixt firth and field.

Before the day from the night was born,
Fair summer is on many a shield.
She heard the blast of Steingrim's horn,
Fair sing the swans 'twixt firth and field.
Before the day was waxen fair
Were Steingrim's feet upon the stair.
"O bolt and bar they fall away,
But heavy are Steingrim's feet to-day."
"O heavy the feet of one who bears

The longing of days and the grief of years!
Lie down, lie down, thou lily-wand
That on thy neck I may lay his hand.
Whether the King be lief or loth
To-day one bed shall hold you both.
O thou art still as he is still,
So sore as ye longed to talk your fill
And good it were that I depart,
Now heart is laid so close to heart.
For sure ye shall talk so left alone
Fair summer is on many a shield.
Of days to be below the stone."
Fair sing the swans 'twixt firth and field.

SPRING'S BEDFELLOW

Spring went about the woods to-day,
The soft-foot winter-thief,
And found where idle sorrow lay
'Twixt flower and faded leaf.

She looked on him, and found him fair
For all she had been told;
She knelt adown beside him there,
And sang of days of old.

His open eyes beheld her nought,
Yet 'gan his lips to move;
But life and deeds were in her thought,
And he would sing of love.

So sang they till their eyes did meet,
And faded fear and shame;

More bold he grew, and she more sweet,
Until they sang the same.

Until, say they who know the thing,
Their very lips did kiss,
And Sorrow laid abed with Spring
Begat an earthly bliss.

MEETING IN WINTER
Winter in the world it is,
Round about the unhoped kiss
Whose dream I long have sorrowed o'er;
Round about the longing sore,
That the touch of thee shall turn
Into joy too deep to burn.

Round thine eyes and round thy mouth
Passeth no murmur of the south,
When my lips a little while
Leave thy quivering tender smile,
As we twain, hand holding hand,
Once again together stand.

Sweet is that, as all is sweet;
For the white drift shalt thou meet,
Kind and cold-cheeked and mine own,
Wrapped about with deep-furred gown
In the broad-wheeled chariot:
Then the north shall spare us not;
The wide-reaching waste of snow
Wilder, lonelier yet shall grow
As the reddened sun falls down.

But the warders of the town,
When they flash the torches out
O'er the snow amid their doubt,
And their eyes at last behold
Thy red-litten hair of gold;
Shall they open, or in fear
Cry, "Alas! what cometh here?
Whence hath come this Heavenly One
To tell of all the world undone?"

They shall open, and we shall see
The long street litten scantily
By the long stream of light before
The guest-hall's half-open door;
And our horses' bells shall cease
As we reach the place of peace;
Thou shalt tremble, as at last
The worn threshold is o'er-past,
And the fire-light blindeth thee:
Trembling shalt thou cling to me
As the sleepy merchants stare
At thy cold hands slim and fair
Thy soft eyes and happy lips
Worth all lading of their ships.

O my love, how sweet and sweet
That first kissing of thy feet,
When the fire is sunk alow,
And the hall made empty now
Groweth solemn, dim and vast!
O my love, the night shall last
Longer than men tell thereof

Laden with our lonely love!

THE TWO SIDES OF THE RIVER

THE YOUTHS

O winter, O white winter, wert thou gone,
No more within the wilds were I alone,
Leaping with bent bow over stock and stone!

No more alone my love the lamp should burn,
Watching the weary spindle twist and turn,
Or o'er the web hold back her tears and yearn:
O winter, O white winter, wert thou gone!

THE MAIDENS

Sweet thoughts fly swiftlier than the drifting snow,
And with the twisting threads sweet longings grow,
And o'er the web sweet pictures come and go,
For no white winter are we long alone.

THE YOUTHS

O stream so changed, what hast thou done to me,
That I thy glittering ford no more can see
Wreathing with white her fair feet lovingly?

See, in the rain she stands, and, looking down
With frightened eyes upon thy whirlpools brown,
Drops to her feet again her girded gown.
O hurrying turbid stream, what hast thou done?

THE MAIDENS

The clouds lift, telling of a happier day
When through the thin stream I shall take my way,
Girt round with gold, and garlanded with may,
What rushing stream can keep us long alone?

THE YOUTHS

O burning Sun, O master of unrest,
Why must we, toiling, cast away the best,
Now, when the bird sleeps by her empty nest?

See, with my garland lying at her feet,
In lonely labour stands mine own, my sweet,
Above the quern half-filled with half-ground wheat.
O red taskmaster, that thy flames were done!

THE MAIDENS

O love, to-night across the half-shorn plain
Shall I not go to meet the yellow wain,
A look of love at end of toil to gain?
What flaming sun can keep us long alone?

THE YOUTHS

To-morrow, said I, is grape gathering o'er;
To-morrow, and our loves are twinned no more.
To-morrow came, to bring us woe and war.

What have I done, that I should stand with these
Hearkening the dread shouts borne upon the breeze,
While she, far off, sits weeping 'neath her trees?
Alas, O kings, what is it ye have done?

THE MAIDENS

Come, love, delay not; come, and slay my dread!
Already is the banquet table spread;
In the cool chamber flower-strewn is my bed:
Come, love, what king shall keep us long alone?

THE YOUTHS

O city, city, open thou thy gate!
See, with life snatched from out the hand of fate!
How on thy glittering triumph I must wait!

Are not her hands stretched out to me? Her eyes,
Grow they not weary as each new hope dies,
And lone before her still the long road lies?
O golden city, fain would I be gone!

THE MAIDENS

And thou art happy, amid shouts and songs,
And all that unto conquering men belongs.
Night hath no fear for me, and day no wrongs.
What brazen city gates can keep us, lone?

THE YOUTHS

O long, long road, how bare thou art, and grey!
Hill after hill thou climbest, and the day
Is ended now, O moonlit endless way!

And she is standing where the rushes grow,
And still with white hand shades her anxious brow,
Though 'neath the world the sun is fallen now,
O dreary road, when will thy leagues be done?

THE MAIDENS

O tremblest thou, grey road, or do my feet
Tremble with joy, thy flinty face to meet?
Because my love's eyes soon mine eyes shall greet?
No heart thou hast to keep us long alone.

THE YOUTHS

O wilt thou ne'er depart, thou heavy night?
When will thy slaying bring on the morning bright,
That leads my weary feet to my delight?

Why lingerest thou, filling with wandering fears
My lone love's tired heart; her eyes with tears
For thoughts like sorrow for the vanished years?
Weaver of ill thoughts, when wilt thou be gone?

THE MAIDENS

Love, to the east are thine eyes turned as mine,
In patient watching for the night's decline?
And hast thou noted this grey widening line?

Can any darkness keep us long alone?

THE YOUTHS

O day, O day, is it a little thing
That thou so long unto thy life must cling,
Because I gave thee such a welcoming?

I called thee king of all felicity,
I praised thee that thou broughtest joy so nigh;
Thine hours are turned to years, thou wilt not die;
O day so longed for, would that thou wert gone!

THE MAIDENS

The light fails, love; the long day soon shall be
Nought but a pensive happy memory
Blessed for the tales it told to thee and me.
How hard it was, O love, to be alone.

LOVE FULFILLED

Hast thou longed through weary days
For the sight of one loved face?
Hast thou cried aloud for rest,
Mid the pain of sundering hours;
Cried aloud for sleep and death,
Since the sweet unhoped for best
Was a shadow and a breath?
O, long now, for no fear lowers
O'er these faint feet-kissing flowers.
O, rest now; and yet in sleep
All thy longing shalt thou keep.

377

Thou shalt rest and have no fear
Of a dull awaking near,
Of a life for ever blind,
Uncontent and waste and wide.
Thou shalt wake and think it sweet
That thy love is near and kind.
Sweeter still for lips to meet;
Sweetest that thine heart doth hide
Longing all unsatisfied
With all longing's answering
Howsoever close ye cling.

Thou rememberest how of old
E'en thy very pain grew cold,
How thou might'st not measure bliss
E'en when eyes and hands drew nigh.
Thou rememberest all regret
For the scarce remembered kiss.
The lost dream of how they met,
Mouths once parched with misery.
Then seemed Love born but to die,
Now unrest, pain, bliss are one,
Love, unhidden and alone.

THE KING OF DENMARK'S SONS

In Denmark gone is many a year,
So fair upriseth the rim of the sun,
Two sons of Gorm the King there were,
So grey is the sea when day is done.

Both these were gotten in lawful bed

Of Thyrre Denmark's Surety-head.

Fair was Knut of face and limb
As the breast of the Queen that suckled him.

But Harald was hot of hand and heart
As lips of lovers ere they part.

Knut sat at home in all men's love,
But over the seas must Harald rove.

And for every deed by Harald won,
Gorm laid more love on Knut alone.

On a high-tide spake the King in hall,
"Old I grow as the leaves that fall.

"Knut shall reign when I am dead,
So shall the land have peace and aid.

"But many a ship shall Harald have,
For I deem the sea well wrought for his grave."

Then none spake save the King again,
"If Knut die all my days be vain.

"And whoso the tale of his death shall tell,
Hath spoken a word to gain him hell.

"Lo here a doom I will not break,"
So fair upriseth the rim of the sun.
"For life or death or any man's sake,"

So grey is the sea when day is done.

O merry days in the summer-tide!
So fair upriseth the rim of the sun.
When the ships sail fair and the young men ride,
So grey is the sea when day is done.

Now Harald has got him east away,
And each morrow of fight was a gainful day.

But Knut is to his fosterer gone
To deal in deeds of peace alone.

So wear the days, and well it is
Such lovely lords should dwell in bliss.

O merry in the winter-tide
When men to Yule-feast wend them wide.

And here lieth Knut in the Lima-firth
When the lift is low o'er the Danish earth.

"Tell me now, Shipmaster mine,
What are yon torches there that shine?"

"Lord, no torches may these be
But golden prows across the sea.

"For over there the sun shines now
And the gold worms gape from every prow."

The sun and the wind came down o'er the sea,
"Tell them over how many they be!"

"Ten I tell with shield-hung sides.
Nought but a fool his death abides."

"Ten thou tellest, and we be three,
Good need that we do manfully.

"Good fellows, grip the shield and spear
For Harald my brother draweth near.

"Well breakfast we when night is done,
And Valhall's cock crows up the sun."

Up spoke Harald in wrathful case:
"I would have word with this waxen face!

"What wilt thou pay, thou huckstered
That I let thee live another year?

"For oath that thou wilt never reign
Will I let thee live a year or twain."

"Kisses and love shalt thou have of me
If yet my liegeman thou wilt be.

"But stroke of sword, and dint of axe,
Or ere thou makest my face as wax."

As thick the arrows fell around

As fall sere leaves on autumn ground.

In many a cheek the red did wane
No maid might ever kiss again.

"Lay me aboard," Lord Harald said,
"The winter day will soon be dead!

"Lay me aboard the bastard's ship,
And see to it lest your grapnels slip!"

Then some they knelt and some they drowned,
And some lay dead Lord Knut around.

"Look here at the wax-white corpse of him,
As fair as the Queen in face and limb!

"Make now for the shore, for the moon is bright,
And I would be home ere the end of night.

"Two sons last night had Thyrre the Queen,
So fair upriseth the rim of the sun.
And both she may lack ere the woods wax green,"
So grey is the sea when day is done.

A little before the morning tide,
So fair upriseth the rim of the sun,
Queen Thyrre looked out of her window-side,
So grey is the sea when day is done.

"O men-at-arms, what men be ye?"
"Harald thy son come over the sea."

"Why is thy face so pale, my son?"
"It may be red or day is done."

"O evil words of an evil hour!
Come, sweet son, to thy mother's bower!"

None from the Queen's bower went that day
Till dark night over the meadows lay.

None thenceforth heard wail or cry
Till the King's feast was waxen high.

Then into the hall Lord Harald came
When the great wax lights were all aflame.

"What tidings, son, dost thou bear to me?
Speak out before I drink with thee."

"Tidings small for a seafarer.
Two falcons in the sea-cliffs were;

"And one was white and one was grey,
And they fell to battle on a day;

"They fought in the sun, they fought in the wind,
No boot the white fowl's wounds to bind.

"They fought in the wind, they fought in the sun,
And the white fowl died when the play was done."

"Small tidings these to bear o'er the sea!
Good hap that nothing worser they be!

"Small tidings for a travelled man!
Drink with me, son, whiles yet ye can!

"Drink with me ere thy day and mine,
So fair upriseth the rim of the sun,
Be nought but a tale told over the wine."
So grey is the sea when day is done.

Now fareth the King with his men to sleep,
So fair upriseth the rim of the sun,
And dim the maids from the Queen's bower creep,
So grey is the sea when day is done.

And in the hall is little light,
And there standeth the Queen with cheeks full white.

And soft the feet of women fall
From end to end of the King's great hall.

These bear the gold-wrought cloths away,
And in other wise the hall array;

Till all is black that hath been gold
So heavy a tale there must be told.

The morrow men looked on King Gorm and said,

"Hath he dreamed a dream or beheld the dead?

"Why is he sad who should be gay?
Why are the old man's lips so grey?"

Slow paced the King adown the hall,
Nor looked aside to either wall,

Till in high-seat there he sat him down,
And deadly old men deemed him grown.

"O Queen, what thrall's hands durst do this,
To strip my hall of mirth and bliss?"

"No thrall's hands in the hangings were,
No thrall's hands made the tenters bare.

"King's daughters' hands have done the deed,
The hands of Denmark's Surety-head."

"Nought betters the deed thy word unsaid.
Tell me that Knut my son is dead!"

She said: "The doom on thee, O King!
For thine own lips have said the thing."

Men looked to see the King arise,
The death of men within his eyes.

Men looked to see his bitter sword
That once cleared ships from board to board.

But in the hall no sword gleamed wide,
His hand fell down along his side.

No red there came into his cheek,
He fell aback as one made weak.

His wan cheek brushed the high-seat's side,
And in the noon of day he died.

So lieth King Gorm beneath the grass,
But from mouth to mouth this tale did pass.

And Harald reigned and went his way,
So fair upriseth the rim of the sun.
And still is the story told to-day,
So grey is the sea when day is done.

ON THE EDGE OF THE WILDERNESS
PUELLÆ

Whence comest thou, and whither goest thou?
Abide! abide! longer the shadows grow;
What hopest thou the dark to thee will show?

Abide! abide! for we are happy here.

AMANS

Why should I name the land across the sea
Wherein I first took hold on misery?
Why should I name the land that flees from me?

Let me depart, since ye are happy here.

PUELLÆ

What wilt thou do within the desert place
Whereto thou turnest now thy careful face?
Stay but a while to tell us of thy case.

Abide! abide! for we are happy here.

AMANS

What, nigh the journey's end shall I abide,
When in the waste mine own love wanders wide,
When from all men for me she still doth hide?

Let me depart, since ye are happy here.

PUELLÆ

Nay, nay; but rather she forgetteth thee,
To sit upon the shore of some warm sea,
Or in green gardens where sweet fountains be.

Abide! abide! for we are happy here.

AMANS

Will ye then keep me from the wilderness,
Where I at least, alone with my distress,
The quiet land of changing dreams may bless?

Let me depart, since ye are happy here.

PUELLÆ

Forget the false forgetter and be wise,
And 'mid these clinging hands and loving eyes,
Dream, not in vain, thou knowest paradise.

Abide! abide! for we are happy here.

AMANS

Ah! with your sweet eyes shorten not the day,
Nor let your gentle hands my journey stay!
Perchance love is not wholly cast away.

Let me depart, since ye are happy here.

PUELLÆ

Pluck love away as thou wouldst pluck a thorn
From out thy flesh; for why shouldst thou be born
To bear a life so wasted and forlorn?

Abide! abide! for we are happy here.

AMANS

Yea, why then was I born, since hope is pain,
And life a lingering death, and faith but vain,
And love the loss of all I seemed to gain?

Let me depart, since ye are happy here.

PUELLÆ

Dost thou believe that this shall ever be,
That in our land no face thou e'er shalt see,
No voice thou e'er shalt hear to gladden thee?

Abide! abide! for we are happy here.

AMANS

No longer do I know of good or bad,
I have forgotten that I once was glad;
I do but chase a dream that I have had.

Let me depart, since ye are happy here.

PUELLÆ

Stay! take one image for thy dreamful night;
Come, look at her, who in the world's despite
Weeps for delaying love and lost delight.

Abide! abide! for we are happy here.

AMANS

Mock me not till to-morrow. Mock the dead,
They will not heed it, or turn round the head,
To note who faithless are, and who are wed.

Let me depart, since ye are happy here.

PUELLÆ

We mock thee not. Hast thou not heard of those
Whose faithful love the loved heart holds so close,
That death must wait till one word lets it loose?

Abide! abide! for we are happy here.

AMANS

I hear you not: the wind from off the waste
Sighs like a song that bids me make good haste
The wave of sweet forgetfulness to taste.

Let me depart, since ye are happy here.

PUELLÆ

Come back! like such a singer is the wind,
As to a sad tune sings fair words and kind,
That he with happy tears all eyes may blind!

Abide! abide! for we are happy here.

AMANS

Did I not hear her sweet voice cry from far,
That o'er the lonely waste fair fields there are,
Fair days that know not any change or care?

Let me depart, since ye are happy here.

PUELLÆ

Oh, no! not far thou heardest her, but nigh;
Nigh, 'twixt the waste's edge and the darkling sky.
Turn back again, too soon it is to die.

Abide! a little while be happy here.

AMANS

How with the lapse of lone years could I strive,
And can I die now that thou biddest live?
What joy this space 'twixt birth and death can give.

Can we depart, who are so happy here?

A GARDEN BY THE SEA
I know a little garden-close,
Set thick with lily and red rose,
Where I would wander if I might
From dewy morn to dewy night,
And have one with me wandering.

And though within it no birds sing,
And though no pillared house is there,
And though the apple-boughs are bare
Of fruit and blossom, would to God
Her feet upon the green grass trod,
And I beheld them as before.

There comes a murmur from the shore,
And in the close two fair streams are,
Drawn from the purple hills afar,
Drawn down unto the restless sea:
Dark hills whose heath-bloom feeds no bee,
Dark shore no ship has ever seen,
Tormented by the billows green
Whose murmur comes unceasingly
Unto the place for which I cry.

For which I cry both day and night,
For which I let slip all delight,
Whereby I grow both deaf and blind,
Careless to win, unskilled to find,
And quick to lose what all men seek.

Yet tottering as I am and weak,
Still have I left a little breath
To seek within the jaws of death
An entrance to that happy place,
To seek the unforgotten face,
Once seen, once kissed, once reft from me
Anigh the murmuring of the sea.

MOTHER AND SON
Now sleeps the land of houses,
and dead night holds the street,
And there thou liest, my baby,
and sleepest soft and sweet;
My man is away for awhile,
but safe and alone we lie,
And none heareth thy breath but thy mother,

and the moon looking down from the sky
On the weary waste of the town,
as it looked on the grass-edged road
Still warm with yesterday's sun,
when I left my old abode;
Hand in hand with my love,
that night of all nights in the year;
When the river of love o'erflowed
and drowned all doubt and fear,
And we two were alone in the world,
and once if never again,
We knew of the secret of earth
and the tale of its labour and pain.

Lo amidst London I lift thee,
and how little and light thou art,
And thou without hope or fear
thou fear and hope of my heart!
Lo here thy body beginning,
O son, and thy soul and thy life;
But how will it be if thou livest,
and enterest into the strife,
And in love we dwell together
when the man is grown in thee,
When thy sweet speech I shall hearken,
and yet 'twixt thee and me
Shall rise that wall of distance,
that round each one doth grow,
And maketh it hard and bitter
each other's thought to know.

Now, therefore, while yet thou art little

and hast no thought of thine own,
I will tell thee a word of the world;
of the hope whence thou hast grown;
Of the love that once begat thee,
of the sorrow that hath made
Thy little heart of hunger,
and thy hands on my bosom laid.
Then mayst thou remember hereafter,
as whiles when people say
All this hath happened before
in the life of another day;
So mayst thou dimly remember
this tale of thy mother's voice,
As oft in the calm of dawning
I have heard the birds rejoice,
As oft I have heard the storm-wind
go moaning through the wood;
And I knew that earth was speaking,
and the mother's voice was good.

Now, to thee alone will I tell it
that thy mother's body is fair,
In the guise of the country maidens
Who play with the sun and the air;
Who have stood in the row of the reapers
in the August afternoon,
Who have sat by the frozen water
in the high day of the moon,
When the lights of the Christmas feasting
were dead in the house on the hill,
And the wild geese gone to the salt-marsh
had left the winter still.

Yea, I am fair, my firstling;
if thou couldst but remember me!
The hair that thy small hand clutcheth
is a goodly sight to see;
I am true, but my face is a snare;
soft and deep are my eyes,
And they seem for men's beguiling
fulfilled with the dreams of the wise.
Kind are my lips, and they look
as though my soul had learned
Deep things I have never heard of.
My face and my hands are burned
By the lovely sun of the acres;
three months of London town
And thy birth-bed have bleached them indeed,
"But lo, where the edge of the gown"
(So said thy father) "is parting
the wrist that is white as the curd
From the brown of the hand that I love,
bright as the wing of a bird."

Such is thy mother, O firstling,
yet strong as the maidens of old,
Whose spears and whose swords were the warders
of homestead, of field, and of fold.
Oft were my feet on the highway,
often they wearied the grass;
From dusk unto dusk of the summer
three times in a week would I pass
To the downs from the house on the river
through the waves of the blossoming corn.
Fair then I lay down in the even,

and fresh I arose on the morn,
And scarce in the noon was I weary.
Ah, son, in the days of thy strife,
If thy soul could but harbour a dream
of the blossom of my life!
It would be as the sunlit meadows
beheld from a tossing sea,
And thy soul should look on a vision
of the peace that is to be.

Yet, yet the tears on my cheek!
and what is this doth move
My heart to thy heart, beloved,
save the flood of yearning love?
For fair and fierce is thy father,
and soft and strange are his eyes
That look on the days that shall be
with the hope of the brave and the wise.
It was many a day that we laughed,
as over the meadows we walked,
And many a day I hearkened
and the pictures came as he talked;
It was many a day that we longed,
and we lingered late at eve
Ere speech from speech was sundered,
and my hand his hand could leave.
Then I wept when I was alone,
and I longed till the daylight came;
And down the stairs I stole,
and there was our housekeeping dame
(No mother of me, the foundling)
kindling the fire betimes

Ere the haymaking folk went forth
to the meadows down by the limes;
All things I saw at a glance;
the quickening fire-tongues leapt
Through the crackling heap of sticks,
and the sweet smoke up from it crept,
And close to the very hearth
the low sun flooded the floor,
And the cat and her kittens played
in the sun by the open door.
The garden was fair in the morning,
and there in the road he stood
Beyond the crimson daisies
and the bush of southernwood.
Then side by side together
through the grey-walled place we went,
And O the fear departed,
and the rest and sweet content!

Son, sorrow and wisdom he taught me,
and sore I grieved and learned
As we twain grew into one;
and the heart within me burned
With the very hopes of his heart.
Ah, son, it is piteous,
But never again in my life
shall I dare to speak to thee thus;
So may these lonely words
about thee creep and cling,
These words of the lonely night
in the days of our wayfaring.
Many a child of woman

to-night is born in the town,
The desert of folly and wrong;
and of what and whence are they grown?
Many and many an one
of wont and use is born;
For a husband is taken to bed
as a hat or a ribbon is worn.
Prudence begets her thousands;
"good is a housekeeper's life,
So shall I sell my body
that I may be matron and wife."
"And I shall endure foul wedlock
and bear the children of need."
Some are there born of hate,
many the children of greed.
"I, I too can be wedded,
though thou my love hast got."
"I am fair and hard of heart,
and riches shall be my lot."
And all these are the good and the happy,
on whom the world dawns fair.
O son, when wilt thou learn
of those that are born of despair,
As the fabled mud of the Nile
that quickens under the sun
With a growth of creeping things,
half dead when just begun?
E'en such is the care of Nature
that man should never die,
Though she breed of the fools of the earth,
and the dregs of the city sty.

But thou, O son, O son,
of very love wert born,
When our hope fulfilled bred hope,
and fear was a folly outworn.
On the eve of the toil and the battle
all sorrow and grief we weighed,
We hoped and we were not ashamed,
we knew and we were not afraid.

Now waneth the night and the moon;
ah, son, it is piteous
That never again in my life
shall I dare to speak to thee thus.
But sure from the wise and the simple
shall the mighty come to birth;
And fair were my fate, beloved,
if I be yet on the earth
When the world is awaken at last,
and from mouth to mouth they tell
Of thy love and thy deeds and thy valour,
and thy hope that nought can quell.

THUNDER IN THE GARDEN

When the boughs of the garden hang heavy with rain
And the blackbird reneweth his song,
And the thunder departing yet rolleth again,
I remember the ending of wrong.

When the day that was dusk while his death was aloof
Is ending wide-gleaming and strange
For the clearness of all things beneath the world's roof,
I call back the wild chance and the change.

For once we twain sat through the hot afternoon
While the rain held aloof for a while,
Till she, the soft-clad, for the glory of June
Changed all with the change of her smile.

For her smile was of longing, no longer of glee,
And her fingers, entwined with mine own,
With caresses unquiet sought kindness of me
For the gift that I never had known.

Then down rushed the rain, and the voice of the thunder
Smote dumb all the sound of the street,
And I to myself was grown nought but a wonder,
As she leaned down my kisses to meet.

That she craved for my lips that had craved her so often,
And the hand that had trembled to touch,
That the tears filled her eyes I had hoped not to soften
In this world was a marvel too much.

It was dusk 'mid the thunder, dusk e'en as the night,
When first brake out our love like the storm,
But no night-hour was it, and back came the light
While our hands with each other were warm.

And her smile killed with kisses, came back as at first
As she rose up and led me along,
And out to the garden, where nought was athirst,
And the blackbird renewing his song.

Earth's fragrance went with her, as in the wet grass,

Her feet little hidden were set;
She bent down her head, 'neath the roses to pass,
And her arm with the lily was wet.

In the garden we wandered while day waned apace
And the thunder was dying aloof;
Till the moon o'er the minster-wall lifted his face,
And grey gleamed out the lead of the roof.

Then we turned from the blossoms, and cold were they
grown:
In the trees the wind westering moved;
Till over the threshold back fluttered her gown,
And in the dark house was I loved.

THE GOD OF THE POOR
There was a lord that hight Maltete,
Among great lords he was right great,
On poor folk trod he like the dirt,
None but God might do him hurt.
Deus est Deus pauperum.

With a grace of prayers sung loud and late
Many a widow's house he ate;
Many a poor knight at his hands
Lost his house and narrow lands.
Deus est Deus pauperum.

He burnt the harvests many a time,
He made fair houses heaps of lime;
Whatso man loved wife or maid
Of Evil-head was sore afraid.

Deus est Deus pauperum.

He slew good men and spared the bad;
Too long a day the foul dog had,
E'en as all dogs will have their day;
But God is as strong as man, I say.
Deus est Deus pauperum.

For a valiant knight, men called Boncoeur,
Had hope he should not long endure,
And gathered to him much good folk,
Hardy hearts to break the yoke.
Deus est Deus pauperum.

But Boncoeur deemed it would be vain
To strive his guarded house to gain;
Therefore, within a little while,
He set himself to work by guile.
Deus est Deus pauperum.

He knew that Maltete loved right well
Red gold and heavy. If from hell
The Devil had cried, "Take this gold cup,"
Down had he gone to fetch it up.
Deus est Deus pauperum.

Twenty poor men's lives were nought
To him, beside a ring well wrought.
The pommel of his hunting-knife
Was worth ten times a poor man's life.
Deus est Deus pauperum.

A squire new-come from over-sea
Boncoeur called to him privily,
And when he knew his lord's intent,
Clad like a churl therefrom he went
Deus est Deus pauperum.

But when he came where dwelt Maltete,
With few words did he pass the gate,
For Maltete built him walls anew,
And, wageless, folk from field he drew.
Deus est Deus pauperum.

Now passed the squire through this and that,
Till he came to where Sir Maltete sat,
And over red wine wagged his beard:
Then spoke the squire as one afeard.
Deus est Deus pauperum.

"Lord, give me grace, for privily
I have a little word for thee."
"Speak out," said Maltete, "have no fear,
For how can thy life to thee be dear?"
Deus est Deus pauperum.

"Such an one I know," he said,
"Who hideth store of money red."
Maltete grinned at him cruelly:
"Thou florin-maker, come anigh."
Deus est Deus pauperum.

"E'en such as thou once preached of gold,
And showed me lies in books full old,

Nought gat I but evil brass,
Therefore came he to the worser pass."
Deus est Deus pauperum.

"Hast thou will to see his skin?
I keep my heaviest marks therein,
For since nought else of wealth had he,
I deemed full well he owed it me."
Deus est Deus pauperum.

"Nought know I of philosophy,"
The other said, "nor do I lie.
Before the moon begins to shine,
May all this heap of gold be thine."
Deus est Deus pauperum.

"Ten leagues from this a man there is,
Who seemeth to know but little bliss,
And yet full many a pound of gold
A dry well nigh his house doth hold."
Deus est Deus pauperum.

"John-a-Wood is he called, fair lord,
Nor know I whence he hath this hoard."
Then Maltete said, "As God made me,
A wizard over-bold is he!"
Deus est Deus pauperum.

"It were a good deed, as I am a knight,
To burn him in a fire bright;
This John-a-Wood shall surely die,
And his gold in my strong chest shall lie."

Deus est Deus pauperum.

"This very night, I make mine avow.
The truth of this mine eyes shall know."
Then spoke an old knight in the hall,
"Who knoweth what things may befall?"
Deus est Deus pauperum.

"I rede thee go with a great rout,
For thy foes they ride thick about."
"Thou and the devil may keep my foes,
Thou redest me this gold to lose."
Deus est Deus pauperum.

"I shall go with but some four or five,
So shall I take my thief alive.
For if a great rout he shall see,
Will he not hide his wealth from me?"
Deus est Deus pauperum.

The old knight muttered under his breath,
"Then mayhap ye shall but ride to death."
But Maltete turned him quickly round,
"Bind me this grey-beard under ground!"
Deus est Deus pauperum.

"Because ye are old, ye think to jape.
Take heed, ye shall not long escape.
When I come back safe, old carle, perdie,
Thine head shall brush the linden-tree."
Deus est Deus pauperum.

Therewith he rode with his five men,
And Boncoeur's spy, for good leagues ten,
Until they left the beaten way,
And dusk it grew at end of day.
Deus est Deus pauperum.

There, in a clearing of the wood,
Was John's house, neither fair nor good.
In a ragged plot his house anigh,
Thin coleworts grew but wretchedly.
Deus est Deus pauperum.

John-a-Wood in his doorway sat,
Turning over this and that,
And chiefly how he best might thrive,
For he had will enough to live.
Deus est Deus pauperum.

Green coleworts from a wooden bowl
He ate; but careful was his soul,
For if he saw another day,
Thenceforth was he in Boncoeur's pay.
Deus est Deus pauperum.

So when he saw how Maltete came,
He said, "Beginneth now the game!"
And in the doorway did he stand
Trembling, with hand joined fast to hand.
Deus est Deus pauperum.

When Maltete did this carle behold
Somewhat he doubted of his gold,

But cried out, "Where is now thy store
Thou hast through books of wicked lore?"
Deus est Deus pauperum.

Then said the poor man, right humbly,
"Fair lord, this was not made by me,
I found it in mine own dry well,
And had a mind thy grace to tell.
Deus est Deus pauperum.

"Therefrom, my lord, a cup I took
This day, that thou thereon mightst look,
And know me to be leal and true,"
And from his coat the cup he drew.
Deus est Deus pauperum.

Then Maltete took it in his hand,
Nor knew he aught that it used to stand
On Boncoeur's cupboard many a day.
"Go on," he said, "and show the way.
Deus est Deus pauperum.

"Give me thy gold, and thou shalt live,
Yea, in my house thou well mayst thrive."
John turned about and 'gan to go
Unto the wood with footsteps slow.
Deus est Deus pauperum.

But as they passed by John's woodstack,
Growled Maltete, "Nothing now doth lack
Wherewith to light a merry fire,
And give my wizard all his hire."

Deus est Deus pauperum.

The western sky was red as blood,
Darker grew the oaken-wood;
"Thief and carle, where are ye gone?
Why are we in the wood alone?
Deus est Deus pauperum.

"What is the sound of this mighty horn?
Ah, God! that ever I was born!
The basnets flash from tree to tree;
Show me, thou Christ, the way to flee!"
Deus est Deus pauperum.

Boncoeur it was with fifty men;
Maltete was but one to ten,
And his own folk prayed for grace,
With empty hands in that lone place.
Deus est Deus pauperum.

"Grace shall ye have," Boncoeur said,
"All of you but Evil-head."
Lowly could that great lord be,
Who could pray so well as he?
Deus est Deus pauperum.

Then could Maltete howl and cry,
Little will he had to die.
Soft was his speech, now it was late,
But who had will to save Maltete?

Deus est Deus pauperum.

They brought him to the house again,
And toward the road he looked in vain.
Lonely and bare was the great highway,
Under the gathering moonlight grey.
Deus est Deus pauperum.

They took off his gilt basnet,
That he should die there was no let;
They took off his coat of steel,
A damned man he well might feel.
Deus est Deus pauperum.

"Will ye all be rich as kings,
Lacking naught of all good things?"
"Nothing do we lack this eve;
When thou art dead, how can we grieve?"
Deus est Deus pauperum.

"Let me drink water ere I die,
None henceforth comes my lips anigh."
They brought it him in that bowl of wood.
He said, "This is but poor men's blood!"
Deus est Deus pauperum.

They brought it him in the cup of gold.
He said, "The women I have sold
Have wept it full of salt for me;
I shall die gaping thirstily."
Deus est Deus pauperum.

On the threshold of that poor homestead
They smote off his evil head;
They set it high on a great spear,
And rode away with merry cheer.
Deus est Deus pauperum.

At the dawn, in lordly state,
They rode to Maltete's castle-gate.
"Whoso willeth laud to win,
Make haste to let your masters in!"
Deus est Deus pauperum.

Forthwith opened they the gate,
No man was sorry for Maltete.
Boncoeur conquered all his lands,
A good knight was he of his hands.
Deus est Deus pauperum.

Good men he loved, and hated bad;
Joyful days and sweet he had;
Good deeds did he plenteously;
Beneath him folk lived frank and free.
Deus est Deus pauperum.

He lived long, with merry days;
None said aught of him but praise.
God on him have full mercy;
A good knight merciful was he.
Deus est Deus pauperum.

The great lord, called Maltete, is dead;
Grass grows above his feet and head,
And a holly-bush grows up between
His rib-bones gotten white and clean.
Deus est Deus pauperum.

A carle's sheep-dog certainly
Is a mightier thing than he.
Till London-bridge shall cross the Nen,
Take we heed of such-like men.
Deus est Deus pauperum.

LOVE'S REWARD

It was a knight of the southern land
Rode forth upon the way
When the birds sang sweet on either hand
About the middle of the May.

But when he came to the lily-close,
Thereby so fair a maiden stood,
That neither the lily nor the rose
Seemed any longer fair nor good.

"All hail, thou rose and lily-bough!
What dost thou weeping here,
For the days of May are sweet enow,
And the nights of May are dear?"

"Well may I weep and make my moan.
Who am bond and captive here;
Well may I weep who lie alone,
Though May be waxen dear."

411

"And is there none shall ransom thee?
Mayst thou no borrow find?"
"Nay, what man may my borrow be,
When all my wealth is left behind?"

"Perchance some ring is left with thee,
Some belt that did thy body bind?"
"Nay, no man may my borrow be,
My rings and belt are left behind."

"The shoes that the May-blooms kissed on thee
Might yet be things to some men's mind."
"Nay, no man may my borrow be,
My golden shoes are left behind."

"The milk-white sark that covered thee
A dear-bought token some should find."
"Nay, no man may my borrow be,
My silken sark is left behind."

"The kiss of thy mouth and the love of thee
Better than world's wealth should I find."
"Nay, thou mayst not my borrow be,
For all my love is left behind.

"A year agone come Midsummer-night
I woke by the Northern sea;
I lay and dreamed of my delight
Till love no more would let me be.

"Seaward I went by night and cloud

To hear the white swans sing;
But though they sang both clear and loud,
I hearkened a sweeter thing.

"O sweet and sweet as none may tell
Was the speech so close 'twixt lip and lip:
But fast, unseen, the black oars fell
That drave to shore the rover's ship.

"My love lay bloody on the strand
Ere stars were waxen wan:
Naught lacketh graves the Northern land
If to-day it lack a lovelier man.

"I sat and wept beside the mast
When the stars were gone away.
Naught lacketh the Northland joy gone past
If it lack the night and day."

"Is there no place in any land
Where thou wouldst rather be than here?"
"Yea, a lone grave on a cold sea-strand
My heart for a little holdeth dear."

"Of all the deeds that women do
Is there none shall bring thee some delight?"
"To lie down and die where lay we two
Upon Midsummer night."

"I will bring thee there where thou wouldst be,

A borrow shalt thou find."
"Wherewith shall I reward it thee
For wealth and good-hap left behind?"

"A kiss from lips that love not me,
A good-night somewhat kind;
A narrow house to share with thee
When we leave the world behind."

They have taken ship and sailed away
Across the Southland main;
They have sailed by hills were green and gay,
A land of goods and gain.

They have sailed by sea-cliffs stark and white
And hillsides fair enow;
They have sailed by lands of little night
Where great the groves did grow.

They have sailed by islands in the sea
That the clouds lay thick about;
And into a main where few ships be
Amidst of dread and doubt.

With broken mast and battered side
They drave amidst the tempest's heart;
But why should death to these betide
Whom love did hold so well apart?

The flood it drave them toward the strand,

The ebb it drew them fro;
The swallowing seas that tore the land
Cast them ashore and let them go.

"Is this the land? is this the land,
Where life and I must part a-twain?"
"Yea, this is e'en the sea-washed strand
That made me yoke-fellow of pain.

"The strand is this, the sea is this,
The grey bent and the mountains grey;
But no mound here his grave-mound is;
Where have they borne my love away?"

"What man is this with shield and spear
Comes riding down the bent to us?
A goodly man forsooth he were
But for his visage piteous."

"Ghost of my love, so kind of yore,
Art thou not somewhat gladder grown
To feel my feet upon this shore?
O love, thou shalt not long be lone."

"Ghost of my love, each day I come
To see where God first wrought us wrong:
Now kind thou com'st to call me home.
Be sure I shall not tarry long."

"Come here, my love; come here for rest,

So sore as my body longs for thee!
My heart shall beat against thy breast,
As arms of thine shall comfort me."

"Love, let thy lips depart no more
From those same eyes they once did kiss,
The very bosom wounded sore
When sorrow clave the heart of bliss!"

O was it day, or was it night,
As there they told their love again?
The high-tide of the sun's delight,
Or whirl of wind and drift of rain?

"Speak sweet, my love, of how it fell,
And how thou cam'st across the sea,
And what kind heart hath served thee well,
And who thy borrow there might be?"

Naught but the wind and sea made moan
As hastily she turned her round;
From light clouds wept the morn alone,
Not the dead corpse upon the ground.

"O look, my love, for here is he
Who once of all the world was kind,
And led my sad heart o'er the sea!
And now must he be left behind."

She kissed his lips that yet did smile,
She kissed his eyes that were not sad:
"O thou who sorrow didst beguile,

And now wouldst have me wholly glad!

"A little gift is this," she said,
"Thou once hadst deemed great gift enow;
Yet surely shalt thou rest thine head
Where I one day shall lie alow.

"There shalt thou wake to think of me,
And by thy face my face shall find;
And I shall then thy borrow be
When all the world is left behind."

THE FOLK-MOTE BY THE RIVER

It was up in the morn we rose betimes
From the hall-floor hard by the row of limes.

It was but John the Red and I,
And we were the brethren of Gregory;

And Gregory the Wright was one
Of the valiant men beneath the sun,

And what he bade us that we did
For ne'er he kept his counsel hid.

So out we went, and the clattering latch
Woke up the swallows under the thatch.

It was dark in the porch, but our scythes we felt,
And thrust the whetstone under the belt.

Through the cold garden boughs we went

Where the tumbling roses shed their scent.

Then out a-gates and away we strode
O'er the dewy straws on the dusty road,

And there was the mead by the town-reeve's close
Where the hedge was sweet with the wilding rose.

Then into the mowing grass we went
Ere the very last of the night was spent.

Young was the moon, and he was gone,
So we whet our scythes by the stars alone:

But or ever the long blades felt the hay
Afar in the East the dawn was grey.

Or ever we struck our earliest stroke
The thrush in the hawthorn-bush awoke.

While yet the bloom of the swathe was dim
The blackbird's bill had answered him.

Ere half of the road to the river was shorn
The sunbeam smote the twisted thorn.

Now wide was the way 'twixt the standing grass
For the townsfolk unto the mote to pass,

And so when all our work was done

We sat to breakfast in the sun,

While down in the stream the dragon-fly
'Twixt the quivering rushes flickered by;

And though our knives shone sharp and white
The swift bleak heeded not the sight.

So when the bread was done away
We looked along the new-shorn hay,

And heard the voice of the gathering-horn
Come over the garden and the corn;

For the wind was in the blossoming wheat
And drave the bees in the lime-boughs sweet.

Then loud was the horn's voice drawing near,
And it hid the talk of the prattling weir.

And now was the horn on the pathway wide
That we had shorn to the river-side.

So up we stood, and wide around
We sheared a space by the Elders' Mound;

And at the feet thereof it was
That highest grew the June-tide grass;

And over all the mound it grew
With clover blent, and dark of hue.

But never aught of the Elders' Hay
To rick or barn was borne away.

But it was bound and burned to ash
In the barren close by the reedy plash.

For 'neath that mound the valiant dead
Lay hearkening words of valiance said

When wise men stood on the Elders' Mound,
And the swords were shining bright around.

And now we saw the banners borne
On the first of the way that we had shorn;
So we laid the scythe upon the sward
And girt us to the battle-sword.

For after the banners well we knew
Were the Freemen wending two and two.

There then that highway of the scythe
With many a hue was brave and blythe.

And first below the Silver Chief
Upon the green was the golden sheaf.

And on the next that went by it
The White Hart in the Park did sit.

Then on the red the White Wings flew,

And on the White was the Cloud-fleck blue.

Last went the Anchor of the Wrights
Beside the Ship of the Faring-Knights.

Then thronged the folk the June-tide field
With naked sword and painted shield,

Till they came adown to the river-side,
And there by the mound did they abide.

Now when the swords stood thick and white
As the mace reeds stand in the streamless bight,

There rose a man on the mound alone
And over his head was the grey mail done.

When over the new-shorn place of the field
Was nought but the steel hood and the shield.

The face on the mound shone ruddy and hale,
But the hoar hair showed from the hoary mail.

And there rose a hand by the ruddy face
And shook a sword o'er the peopled place.

And there came a voice from the mound and said:
"O sons, the days of my youth are dead,

And gone are the faces I have known
In the street and the booths of the goodly town.

O sons, full many a flock have I seen
Feed down this water-girdled green.

Full many a herd of long-horned neat
Have I seen 'twixt water-side and wheat.

Here by this water-side full oft
Have I heaved the flowery hay aloft.

And oft this water-side anigh
Have I bowed adown the wheat-stalks high.

And yet meseems I live and learn
And lore of younglings yet must earn.

For tell me, children, whose are these
Fair meadows of the June's increase?

Whose are these flocks and whose the neat,
And whose the acres of the wheat?"

Scarce did we hear his latest word,
On the wide shield so rang the sword.

So rang the sword upon the shield
That the lark was hushed above the field.

Then sank the shouts and again we heard
The old voice come from the hoary beard:

"Yea, whose are yonder gables then,
And whose the holy hearths of men?
Whose are the prattling children there,
And whose the sunburnt maids and fair?

Whose thralls are ye, hereby that stand,
Bearing the freeman's sword in hand?"

As glitters the sun in the rain-washed grass,
So in the tossing swords it was;

As the thunder rattles along and adown
E'en so was the voice of the weaponed town.

And there was the steel of the old man's sword.
And there was his hollow voice, and his word:

"Many men, many minds, the old saw saith,
Though hereof ye be sure as death.

For what spake the herald yestermorn
But this, that ye were thrall-folk born;

That the lord that owneth all and some
Would send his men to fetch us home

Betwixt the haysel, and the tide
When they shear the corn in the country-side?

423

O children, Who was the lord? ye say,
What prayer to him did our fathers pray?

Did they hold out hands his gyves to bear?
Did their knees his high hall's pavement wear?

Is his house built up in heaven aloft?
Doth he make the sun rise oft and oft?

Doth he hold the rain in his hollow hand?
Hath he cleft this water through the land?

Or doth he stay the summer-tide,
And make the winter days abide?

O children, Who is the lord? ye say,
Have we heard his name before to-day?

O children, if his name I know,
He hight Earl Hugh of the Shivering Low:

For that herald bore on back and breast
The Black Burg under the Eagle's Nest."

As the voice of the winter wind that tears
At the eaves of the thatch and its emptied ears,

E'en so was the voice of laughter and scorn
By the water-side in the mead new-shorn;

And over the garden and the wheat
Went the voice of women shrilly-sweet.

But now by the hoary elder stood
A carle in raiment red as blood.

Red was his weed and his glaive was white,
And there stood Gregory the Wright.

So he spake in a voice was loud and strong:
"Young is the day though the road is long;

There is time if we tarry nought at all
For the kiss in the porch and the meat in the hall.

And safe shall our maidens sit at home
For the foe by the way we wend must come.

Through the three Lavers shall we go
And raise them all against the foe.

Then shall we wend the Downland ways,
And all the shepherd spearmen raise.

To Cheaping Raynes shall we come adown
And gather the bowmen of the town;

And Greenstead next we come unto
Wherein are all folk good and true.

When we come our ways to the Outer Wood
We shall be an host both great and good;

Yea when we come to the open field
There shall be a many under shield.

And maybe Earl Hugh shall lie alow
And yet to the house of Heaven shall go.

But we shall dwell in the land we love
And grudge no hallow Heaven above.

Come ye, who think the time o'er long
Till we have slain the word of wrong!

Come ye who deem the life of fear
On this last day hath drawn o'er near!

Come after me upon the road
That leadeth to the Erne's abode."

Down then he leapt from off the mound
And back drew they that were around

Till he was foremost of all those
Betwixt the river and the close.

And uprose shouts both glad and strong
As followed after all the throng;

And overhead the banners flapped,
As we went on our ways to all that happed.

The fields before the Shivering Low
Of many a grief of manfolk know;

There may the autumn acres tell
Of how men met, and what befell.

The Black Burg under the Eagle's nest
Shall tell the tale as it liketh best.

And sooth it is that the River-land
Lacks many an autumn-gathering hand.

And there are troth-plight maids unwed
Shall deem awhile that love is dead;

And babes there are to men shall grow
Nor ever the face of their fathers know.

And yet in the Land by the River-side
Doth never a thrall or an earl's man bide;

For Hugh the Earl of might and mirth
Hath left the merry days of Earth;

And we live on in the land we love,
And grudge no hallow Heaven above.

427

THE VOICE OF TOIL
I heard men saying, Leave hope and praying,
All days shall be as all have been;
To-day and to-morrow bring fear and sorrow,
The never-ending toil between.

When Earth was younger mid toil and hunger,
In hope we strove, and our hands were strong;
Then great men led us, with words they fed us,
And bade us right the earthly wrong.

Go read in story their deeds and glory,
Their names amidst the nameless dead;
Turn then from lying to us slow-dying
In that good world to which they led;

Where fast and faster our iron master,
The thing we made, for ever drives,
Bids us grind treasure and fashion pleasure
For other hopes and other lives.

Where home is a hovel and dull we grovel,
Forgetting that the world is fair;
Where no babe we cherish, lest its very soul perish;
Where mirth is crime, and love a snare.

Who now shall lead us, what god shall heed us
As we lie in the hell our hands have won?
For us are no rulers but fools and befoolers,
The great are fallen, the wise men gone.

I heard men saying, Leave tears and praying,
The sharp knife heedeth not the sheep;
Are we not stronger than the rich and the wronger,
When day breaks over dreams and sleep?

Come, shoulder to shoulder ere the world grows older!
Help lies in nought but thee and me;
Hope is before us, the long years that bore us
Bore leaders more than men may be.

Let dead hearts tarry and trade and marry,
And trembling nurse their dreams of mirth,
While we the living our lives are giving
To bring the bright new world to birth.

Come, shoulder to shoulder ere earth grows older!
The Cause spreads over land and sea;
Now the world shaketh, and fear awaketh,
And joy at last for thee and me.

GUNNAR'S HOWE ABOVE THE HOUSE AT LI-THEND

Ye who have come o'er the sea
to behold this grey minster of lands,
Whose floor is the tomb of time past,
and whose walls by the toil of dead hands
Show pictures amidst of the ruin
of deeds that have overpast death,
Stay by this tomb in a tomb
to ask of who lieth beneath.

Ah! the world changeth too soon,
that ye stand there with unbated breath,
As I name him that Gunnar of old,
who erst in the haymaking tide
Felt all the land fragrant and fresh,
as amidst of the edges he died.
Too swiftly fame fadeth away,
if ye tremble not lest once again
The grey mound should open and show him
glad-eyed without grudging or pain.
Little labour methinks to behold him
but the tale-teller laboured in vain.
Little labour for ears that may hearken
to hear his death-conquering song,
Till the heart swells to think of the gladness
undying that overcame wrong.
O young is the world yet meseemeth
and the hope of it flourishing green,
When the words of a man unremembered
so bridge all the days that have been,
As we look round about on the land
that these nine hundred years he hath seen.

Dusk is abroad on the grass
of this valley amidst of the hill:
Dusk that shall never be dark
till the dawn hard on midnight shall fill
The trench under Eyiafell's snow,
and the grey plain the sea meeteth grey.
White, high aloft hangs the moon
that no dark night shall brighten ere day,
For here day and night toileth the summer

lest deedless his time pass away.

THE DAY IS COMING

Come hither, lads, and hearken,
for a tale there is to tell,
Of the wonderful days a-coming, when all
shall be better than well.

And the tale shall be told of a country,
a land in the midst of the sea,
And folk shall call it England
in the days that are going to be.

There more than one in a thousand
in the days that are yet to come,
Shall have some hope of the morrow,
some joy of the ancient home.

For then, laugh not, but listen
to this strange tale of mine,
All folk that are in England
shall be better lodged than swine.

Then a man shall work and bethink him,
and rejoice in the deeds of his hand,
Nor yet come home in the even
too faint and weary to stand.

Men in that time a-coming
shall work and have no fear

For to-morrow's lack of earning
and the hunger-wolf anear.

I tell you this for a wonder,
that no man then shall be glad
Of his fellow's fall and mishap
to snatch at the work he had.

For that which the worker winneth
shall then be his indeed,
Nor shall half be reaped for nothing
by him that sowed no seed.

O strange new wonderful justice!
But for whom shall we gather the gain?
For ourselves and for each of our fellows,
and no hand shall labour in vain.

Then all Mine and all Thine shall be Ours,
and no more shall any man crave
For riches that serve for nothing
but to fetter a friend for a slave.

And what wealth then shall be left us
when none shall gather gold
To buy his friend in the market,
and pinch and pine the sold?

Nay, what save the lovely city,
and the little house on the hill,
And the wastes and the woodland beauty,
and the happy fields we till;

And the homes of ancient stories,
the tombs of the mighty dead;
And the wise men seeking out marvels,
and the poet's teeming head;

And the painter's hand of wonder;
and the marvellous fiddle-bow,
And the banded choirs of music:
all those that do and know.

For all these shall be ours and all men's,
nor shall any lack a share
Of the toil and the gain of living
in the days when the world grows fair.

Ah! such are the days that shall be!
But what are the deeds of to-day
In the days of the years we dwell in,
that wear our lives away?

Why, then, and for what are we waiting?
There are three words to speak;
WE WILL IT, and what is the foeman
but the dream-strong wakened and weak?

O why and for what are we waiting?
while our brothers droop and die,
And on every wind of the heavens
a wasted life goes by.

How long shall they reproach us
where crowd on crowd they dwell,
Poor ghosts of the wicked city,
the gold-crushed hungry hell?

Through squalid life they laboured,
in sordid grief they died,
Those sons of a mighty mother,
those props of England's pride.

They are gone; there is none can undo it,
nor save our souls from the curse;
But many a million cometh,
and shall they be better or worse?

It is we must answer and hasten,
and open wide the door
For the rich man's hurrying terror,
and the slow-foot hope of the poor.

Yea, the voiceless wrath of the wretched,
and their unlearned discontent,
We must give it voice and wisdom
till the waiting-tide be spent.

Come, then, since all things call us,
the living and the dead,
And o'er the weltering tangle
a glimmering light is shed.

Come, then, let us cast off fooling,
and put by ease and rest,
For the Cause alone is worthy
till the good days bring the best.

Come, join in the only battle
wherein no man can fail,
Where whoso fadeth and dieth,
yet his deed shall still prevail.

Ah! come, cast off all fooling,
for this, at least, we know:
That the Dawn and the Day is coming,
and forth the Banners go.

EARTH THE HEALER, EARTH THE KEEPER

So swift the hours are moving
Unto the time un-proved:
Farewell my love unloving,
Farewell my love beloved!

What! are we not glad-hearted?
Is there no deed to do?
Is not all fear departed
And Spring-tide blossomed new?

The sails swell out above us,
The sea-ridge lifts the keel;
For They have called who love us,
Who bear the gifts that heal:

A crown for him that winneth,
A bed for him that fails,
A glory that beginneth
In never-dying tales.

Yet now the pain is ended
And the glad hand grips the sword,
Look on thy life amended
And deal out due award.

Think of the thankless morning,
The gifts of noon unused;
Think of the eve of scorning,
The night of prayer refused.

And yet. The life before it,
Dost thou remember aught,
What terrors shivered o'er it
Born from the hell of thought?

And this that cometh after:
How dost thou live, and dare
To meet its empty laughter,
To face its friendless care?

In fear didst thou desire,
At peace dost thou regret,
The wasting of the fire,
The tangling of the net.

Love came and gat fair greeting;
Love went; and left no shame.

Shall both the twilights meeting
The summer sunlight blame?

What! cometh love and goeth
Like the dark night's empty wind,
Because thy folly soweth
The harvest of the blind?

Hast thou slain love with sorrow?
Have thy tears quenched the sun?
Nay even yet to-morrow
Shall many a deed be done.

This twilight sea thou sailest,
Has it grown dim and black
For that wherein thou failest,
And the story of thy lack?

Peace then! for thine old grieving
Was born of Earth the kind,
And the sad tale thou art leaving
Earth shall not leave behind.

Peace! for that joy abiding
Whereon thou layest hold
Earth keepeth for a tiding
For the day when this is old.

Thy soul and life shall perish,
And thy name as last night's wind;
But Earth the deed shall cherish
That thou to-day shalt find.

And all thy joy and sorrow
So great but yesterday,
So light a thing to-morrow,
Shall never pass away.

Lo! lo! the dawn-blink yonder,
The sunrise draweth nigh,
And men forget to wonder
That they were born to die.

Then praise the deed that wendeth
Through the daylight and the mirth!
The tale that never endeth
Whoso may dwell on earth.

ALL FOR THE CAUSE
Hear a word, a word in season,
for the day is drawing nigh,
When the Cause shall call upon us,
some to live, and some to die!

He that dies shall not die lonely,
many an one hath gone before;
He that lives shall bear no burden
heavier than the life they bore.

Nothing ancient is their story,
e'en but yesterday they bled,
Youngest they of earth's beloved,
last of all the valiant dead.

E'en the tidings we are telling
was the tale they had to tell,
E'en the hope that our hearts cherish,
was the hope for which they fell.

In the grave where tyrants thrust them,
lies their labour and their pain,
But undying from their sorrow
springeth up the hope again.

Mourn not therefore, nor lament it,
that the world outlives their life;
Voice and vision yet they give us,
making strong our hands for strife.

Some had name, and fame, and honour,
learn'd they were, and wise and strong;
Some were nameless, poor, unlettered,
weak in all but grief and wrong.

Named and nameless all live in us;
one and all they lead us yet
Every pain to count for nothing,
every sorrow to forget.

Hearken how they cry, "O happy,
happy ye that ye were born
In the sad slow night's departing,
in the rising of the morn.

"Fair the crown the Cause hath for you,
well to die or well to live

Through the battle, through the tangle,
peace to gain or peace to give."

Ah, it may be! Oft meseemeth,
in the days that yet shall be,
When no slave of gold abideth
'twixt the breadth of sea to sea,

Oft, when men and maids are merry,
ere the sunlight leaves the earth,
And they bless the day beloved,
all too short for all their mirth,

Some shall pause awhile and ponder
on the bitter days of old,
Ere the toil of strife and battle
overthrew the curse of gold;

Then 'twixt lips of loved and lover
solemn thoughts of us shall rise;
We who once were fools defeated,
then shall be the brave and wise.

There amidst the world new-builded
shall our earthly deeds abide,
Though our names be all forgotten,
and the tale of how we died.

Life or death then, who shall heed it,
what we gain or what we lose?
Fair flies life amid the struggle,
and the Cause for each shall choose.

Hear a word, a word in season,
for the day is drawing nigh,
When the Cause shall call upon us,
some to live, and some to die!

PAIN AND TIME STRIVE NOT

What part of the dread eternity
Are those strange minutes that I gain,
Mazed with the doubt of love and pain,
When I thy delicate face may see,
A little while before farewell?

What share of the world's yearning-tide
That flash, when new day bare and white
Blots out my half-dream's faint delight,
And there is nothing by my side,
And well remembered is farewell?

What drop in the grey flood of tears
That time, when the long day toiled through,
Worn out, shows nought for me to do,
And nothing worth my labour bears
The longing of that last farewell?

What pity from the heavens above,
What heed from out eternity,
What word from the swift world for me?
Speak, heed, and pity, O tender love,
Who knew'st the days before farewell!

DRAWING NEAR THE LIGHT

Lo, when we wade the tangled wood,
In haste and hurry to be there,
Nought seem its leaves and blossoms good,
For all that they be fashioned fair.

But looking up, at last we see
The glimmer of the open light,
From o'er the place where we would be:
Then grow the very brambles bright.

So now, amidst our day of strife,
With many a matter glad we play,
When once we see the light of life
Gleam through the tangle of to-day.

VERSES FOR PICTURES
DAY

I am Day; I bring again
Life and glory, Love and pain:
Awake, arise! from death to death
Through me the World's tale quickeneth.

SPRING

Spring am I, too soft of heart
Much to speak ere I depart:
Ask the Summer-tide to prove
The abundance of my love.

SUMMER

Summer looked for long am I;
Much shall change or e'er I die.
Prithee take it not amiss
Though I weary thee with bliss.

AUTUMN

Laden Autumn here I stand
Worn of heart, and weak of hand:
Nought but rest seems good to me,
Speak the word that sets me free.

WINTER

I am Winter, that do keep
Longing safe amidst of sleep:
Who shall say if I were dead
What should be remembered?

NIGHT

I am Night: I bring again
Hope of pleasure, rest from pain:
Thoughts unsaid 'twixt Life and Death
My fruitful silence quickeneth.

FOR THE BRIAR ROSE
THE BRIARWOOD

The fateful slumber floats and flows
About the tangle of the rose;
But lo! the fated hand and heart

To rend the slumberous curse apart!

THE COUNCIL ROOM

The threat of war, the hope of peace,
The Kingdom's peril and increase
Sleep on, and bide the latter day,
When Fate shall take her chain away.

THE GARDEN COURT

The maiden pleasance of the land
Knoweth no stir of voice or hand,
No cup the sleeping waters fill,
The restless shuttle lieth still.

THE ROSEBOWER

Here lies the hoarded love, the key
To all the treasure that shall be;
Come fated hand the gift to take,
And smite this sleeping world awake.

ANOTHER FOR THE BRIAR ROSE

O treacherous scent, O thorny sight,
O tangle of world's wrong and right,
What art thou 'gainst my armour's gleam
But dusky cobwebs of a dream?

Beat down, deep sunk from every gleam
Of hope, they lie and dully dream;

Men once, but men no more, that Love
Their waste defeated hearts should move.

Here sleeps the world that would not love!
Let it sleep on, but if He move
Their hearts in humble wise to wait
On his new-wakened fair estate.

O won at last is never late!
Thy silence was the voice of fate;
Thy still hands conquered in the strife;
Thine eyes were light; thy lips were life.

THE WOODPECKER
I once a King and chief
Now am the tree-bark's thief,
Ever 'twixt trunk and leaf
Chasing the prey.

THE LION
The Beasts that be
In wood and waste,
Now sit and see,
Nor ride nor haste.

THE FOREST
PEAR-TREE

By woodman's edge I faint and fail;
By craftsman's edge I tell the tale.

CHESTNUT-TREE

High in the wood, high o'er the hall,
Aloft I rise when low I fall.

OAK-TREE

Unmoved I stand what wind may blow.
Swift, swift before the wind I go.

POMONA
I am the ancient Apple-Queen,
As once I was so am I now.
For evermore a hope unseen,
Betwixt the blossom and the bough.

Ah, where's the river's hidden Gold!
And where the windy grave of Troy?
Yet come I as I came of old,
From out the heart of Summer's joy.

FLORA
I am the handmaid of the earth,
I broider fair her glorious gown,
And deck her on her days of mirth
With many a garland of renown.

And while Earth's little ones are fain
And play about the Mother's hem,
I scatter every gift I gain
From sun and wind to gladden them.

THE ORCHARD

Midst bitten mead and acre shorn,
The world without is waste and worn,

But here within our orchard-close,
The guerdon of its labour shows.

O valiant Earth, O happy year
That mocks the threat of winter near,

And hangs aloft from tree to tree
The banners of the Spring to be.

TAPESTRY TREES
OAK

I am the Roof-tree and the Keel;
I bridge the seas for woe and weal.

FIR

High o'er the lordly oak I stand,
And drive him on from land to land.

ASH

I heft my brother's iron bane;
I shaft the spear, and build the wain.

YEW

Dark down the windy dale I grow,
The father of the fateful Bow.

POPLAR

The war-shaft and the milking-bowl
I make, and keep the hay-wain whole.

OLIVE

The King I bless; the lamps I trim;
In my warm wave do fishes swim.

APPLE-TREE

I bowed my head to Adam's will;
The cups of toiling men I fill.

VINE

I draw the blood from out the earth;
I store the sun for winter mirth.

ORANGE-TREE

Amidst the greenness of my night,
My odorous lamps hang round and bright.

FIG-TREE

I who am little among trees
In honey-making mate the bees.

MULBERRY-TREE

Love's lack hath dyed my berries red:
For Love's attire my leaves are shed.

PEAR-TREE

High o'er the mead-flowers' hidden feet
I bear aloft my burden sweet.

BAY

Look on my leafy boughs, the Crown
Of living song and dead renown!

THE FLOWERING ORCHARD
SILK EMBROIDERY

Lo silken my garden,
and silken my sky,
And silken my apple-boughs
hanging on high;
All wrought by the Worm
in the peasant carle's cot
On the Mulberry leafage
when summer was hot!

THE END OF MAY
How the wind howls this morn
About the end of May,
And drives June on apace
To mock the world forlorn
And the world's joy passed away

And my unlonged-for face!
The world's joy passed away;
For no more may I deem
That any folk are glad
To see the dawn of day
Sunder the tangled dream
Wherein no grief they had.
Ah, through the tangled dream
Where others have no grief
Ever it fares with me
That fears and treasons stream
And dumb sleep slays belief
Whatso therein may be.
Sleep slayeth all belief
Until the hopeless light
Wakes at the birth of June
More lying tales to weave,
More love in woe's despite,
More hope to perish soon.

THE HALF OF LIFE GONE

The days have slain the days,
and the seasons have gone by
And brought me the summer again;
and here on the grass I lie
As erst I lay and was glad
ere I meddled with right and with wrong.
Wide lies the mead as of old,
and the river is creeping along
By the side of the elm-clad bank
that turns its weedy stream;
And grey o'er its hither lip

the quivering rashes gleam.
There is work in the mead as of old;
they are eager at winning the hay,
While every sun sets bright
and begets a fairer day.
The forks shine white in the sun
round the yellow red-wheeled wain,
Where the mountain of hay grows fast;
and now from out of the lane
Comes the ox-team drawing another,
comes the bailiff and the beer,
And thump, thump, goes the farmer's nag
o'er the narrow bridge of the weir.
High up and light are the clouds,
and though the swallows flit
So high o'er the sunlit earth,
they are well a part of it,
And so, though high over them,
are the wings of the wandering herne;
In measureless depths above him
doth the fair sky quiver and burn;
The dear sun floods the land
as the morning falls toward noon,
And a little wind is awake
in the best of the latter June.
They are busy winning the hay,
and the life and the picture they make
If I were as once I was,
I should deem it made for my sake;
For here if one need not work
is a place for happy rest,
While one's thought wends over the world

north, south, and east and west.

There are the men and the maids,
and the wives and the gaffers grey
Of the fields I know so well,
and but little changed are they
Since I was a lad amongst them;
and yet how great is the change!
Strange are they grown unto me;
yea I to myself am strange.
Their talk and their laughter mingling
with the music of the meads
Has now no meaning to me
to help or to hinder my needs,
So far from them have I drifted.
And yet amidst of them goes
A part of myself, my boy,
and of pleasure and pain he knows,
And deems it something strange,
when he is other than glad.
Lo now! the woman that stoops
and kisses the face of the lad,
And puts a rake in his hand
and laughs in his laughing face.
Whose is the voice that laughs
in the old familiar place?
Whose should it be but my love's,
if my love were yet on the earth?
Could she refrain from the fields
where my joy and her joy had birth,
When I was there and her child,
on the grass that knew her feet

'Mid the flowers that led her on
when the summer eve was sweet?

No, no, it is she no longer;
never again can she come
And behold the hay-wains creeping
o'er the meadows of her home;
No more can she kiss her son
or put the rake in his hand
That she handled a while agone
in the midst of the haymaking band.
Her laughter is gone and her life;
there is no such thing on the earth,
No share for me then in the stir,
no share in the hurry and mirth.
Nay, let me look and believe
that all these will vanish away,
At least when the night has fallen,
and that she will be there 'mid the hay,
Happy and weary with work,
waiting and longing for love.
There will she be, as of old,
when the great moon hung above,
And lightless and dead was the village,
and nought but the weir was awake;
There will she rise to meet me,
and my hands will she hasten to take,
And thence shall we wander away,
and over the ancient bridge
By many a rose-hung hedgerow,
till we reach the sun-burnt ridge
And the great trench digged by the Romans:

there then awhile shall we stand,
To watch the dawn come creeping
o'er the fragrant lovely land,
Till all the world awaketh,
and draws us down, we twain,
To the deeds of the field and the fold
and the merry summer's gain.

Ah thus, only thus shall I see her,
in dreams of the day or the night,
When my soul is beguiled of its sorrow
to remember past delight.
She is gone. She was and she is not;
there is no such thing on the earth
But e'en as a picture painted;
and for me there is void and dearth
That I cannot name or measure.
Yet for me and all these she died,
E'en as she lived for awhile,
that the better day might betide.
Therefore I live, and I shall live
till the last day's work shall fail.
Have patience now but a little
and I will tell you the tale
Of how and why she died,
And why I am weak and worn,
And have wandered away to the meadows
and the place where I was born;
But here and to-day I cannot;
for ever my thought will stray
To that hope fulfilled for a little
and the bliss of the earlier day.

Of the great world's hope and anguish
to-day I scarce can think;
Like a ghost, from the lives of the living
and their earthly deeds I shrink.
I will go adown by the water
and over the ancient bridge,
And wend in our footsteps of old
till I come to the sun-burnt ridge,
And the great trench digged by the Romans;
and thence awhile will I gaze,
And see three teeming counties
stretch out till they fade in the haze;
And in all the dwellings of man
that thence mine eyes shall see,
What man as hapless as I am
beneath the sun shall be?

O fool, what words are these?
Thou hast a sorrow to nurse,
And thou hast been bold and happy;
but these, if they utter a curse,
No sting it has and no meaning,
it is empty sound on the air.
Thy life is full of mourning,
and theirs so empty and bare,
That they have no words of complaining;
nor so happy have they been
That they may measure sorrow
or tell what grief may mean.
And thou; thou hast deeds to do,
and toil to meet thee soon;
Depart and ponder on these

through the sun-worn afternoon.

MINE AND THINE
FROM A FLEMISH POEM OF THE FOUR-
TEENTH CENTURY

Two words about the world we see,
And nought but Mine and Thine they be.
Ah! might we drive them forth and wide
With us should rest and peace abide;
All free, nought owned of goods and gear,
By men and women though it were.
Common to all all wheat and wine
Over the seas and up the Rhine.
No manslayer then the wide world o'er
When Mine and Thine are known no more.
Yea, God, well counselled for our health,
Gave all this fleeting earthly wealth
A common heritage to all,
That men might feed them therewithal,
And clothe their limbs and shoe their feet
And live a simple life and sweet.
But now so rageth greediness
That each desireth nothing less
Than all the world, and all his own;
And all for him and him alone.

THE LAY OF CHRISTINE
TRANSLATED FROM THE ICELANDIC

Of silk my gear was shapen,
Scarlet they did on me,

Then to the sea-strand was I borne
And laid in a bark of the sea.
O well were I from the World away.

Befell it there I might not drown,
For God to me was good;
The billows bare me up a-land
Where grew the fair green-wood.
O well were I from the World away.

There came a Knight a-riding
With three swains along the way,
And he took me up, the little-one,
On the sea-sand as I lay.
O well were I from the World away.

He took me up, and bare me home
To the house that was his own,
And there bode I so long with him
That I was his love alone.
O well were I from the World away.

But the very first night we lay abed
Befell his sorrow and harm,
That thither came the King's ill men,
And slew him on mine arm.
O well were I from the World away.

There slew they Adalbright the King,
Two of his swains slew they,
But the third sailed swiftly from the land
Sithence I saw him never a day.

O well were I from the World away.

O wavering hope of this world's bliss,
How shall men trow in thee?
My Grove of Gems is gone away
For mine eyes no more to see!
O well were I from the World away.

Each hour the while my life shall last
Remembereth him alone,
Such heavy sorrow have I got
From our meeting long agone.
O well were I from the World away.

O, early in the morning-tide
Men cry: "Christine the fair,
Art thou well content with that true love
Thou sittest loving there?"
O well were I from the World away.

"Ah, yea, so well I love him,
And so dear my love shall be,
That the very God of Heaven aloft
Worshippeth him and me.
O well were I from the World away.

"Ah, all the red gold I have got
Well would I give to-day,
Only for this and nothing else
From the world to win away."
O well were I from the World away.

"Nay, midst all folk upon the earth
Keep thou thy ruddy gold,
And love withal the mighty lord
That wedded thee of old."
O well were I from the World away.

HILDEBRAND AND HELLELIL
TRANSLATED FROM THE DANISH

Hellelil sitteth in bower there,
None knows my grief but God alone,
And seweth at the seam so fair,
I never wail my sorrow to any other one.

But there whereas the gold should be
With silk upon the cloth sewed she.

Where she should sew with silken thread
The gold upon the cloth she laid.

So to the Queen the word came in
That Hellelil wild work doth win.

Then did the Queen do furs on her
And went to Hellelil the fair.

"O swiftly sewest thou, Hellelil,
Yet nought but mad is thy sewing still!"

"Well may my sewing be but mad
Such evil hap as I have had.

My father was good king and lord,
Knights fifteen served before his board.

He taught me sewing royally,
Twelve knights had watch and ward of me.

Well served eleven day by day,
To folly the twelfth did me bewray.

And this same was hight Hildebrand,
The King's son of the English Land.

But in bower were we no sooner laid
Than the truth thereof to my father was said.

Then loud he cried o'er garth and hall:
'Stand up, my men, and arm ye all!

'Yea draw on mail and dally not,
Hard neck lord Hildebrand hath got!'

They stood by the door with glaive and spear;
'Hildebrand rise and hasten here!'

Lord Hildebrand stroked my white white cheek:
'O love, forbear my name to speak.

'Yea even if my blood thou see,
Name me not, lest my death thou be.'

Out from the door lord Hildebrand leapt,
And round about his good sword swept.

The first of all that he slew there
Were my seven brethren with golden hair.

Then before him stood the youngest one,
And dear he was in the days agone.

Then I cried out: 'O Hildebrand,
In the name of God now stay thine hand.

'O let my youngest brother live
Tidings hereof to my mother to give!'

No sooner was the word gone forth
Than with eight wounds fell my love to earth.

My brother took me by the golden hair,
And bound me to the saddle there.

There met me then no littlest root,
But it tore off somewhat of my foot.

No littlest brake the wild-wood bore,
But somewhat from my legs it tore.

No deepest dam we came unto
But my brother's horse he swam it through

But when to the castle gate we came,
There stood my mother in sorrow and shame.

My brother let raise a tower high,

Bestrewn with sharp thorns inwardly.

He took me in my silk shirt bare
And cast me into that tower there.

And wheresoe'er my legs I laid
Torment of the thorns I had.

Wheresoe'er on feet I stood
The prickles sharp drew forth my blood.

My youngest brother me would slay,
But my mother would have me sold away.

A great new bell my price did buy
In Mary's Church to hang on high.

But the first stroke that ever it strake
My mother's heart asunder brake."

So soon as her sorrow and woe was said,
None knows my grief but God alone,
In the arm of the Queen she sat there dead,
I never tell my sorrow to any other one.

THE SON'S SORROW
FROM THE ICELANDIC

The King has asked of his son so good,
"Why art thou hushed and heavy of mood?
O fair it is to ride abroad.
Thou playest not, and thou laughest not;

All thy good game is clean forgot."

"Sit thou beside me, father dear,
And the tale of my sorrow shalt thou hear.

Thou sendedst me unto a far-off land,
And gavest me into a good Earl's hand.

Now had this good Earl daughters seven,
The fairest of maidens under heaven.

One brought me my meat when I should dine,
One cut and sewed my raiment fine.

One washed and combed my yellow hair,
And one I fell to loving there.

Befell it on so fair a day,
We minded us to sport and play.

Down in a dale my horse bound I,
Bound on my saddle speedily.

Bright red she was as the flickering flame
When to my saddle-bow she came.

Beside my saddle-bow she stood,
'To flee with thee to my heart were good.'

Kind was my horse and good to aid,
My love upon his back I laid.

We gat us from the garth away,
And none was ware of us that day.

But as we rode along the sand
Behold a barge lay by the land.

So in that boat did we depart,
And rowed away right glad at heart.

When we came to the dark wood and the shade
To raise the tent my true-love bade.

Three sons my true-love bore me there,
And syne she died who was so dear.

A grave I wrought her with my sword,
With my fair shield the mould I poured.

First in the mould I laid my love,
Then all my sons her breast above.

And I without must lie alone;
So from the place I gat me gone."

No man now shall stand on his feet
To love that love, to woo that sweet:
O fair it is to ride abroad.

AGNES AND THE HILL-MAN
TRANSLATED FROM THE DANISH

Agnes went through the meadows a-weeping,

Fowl are a-singing.
There stood the hill-man heed thereof keeping.
Agnes, fair Agnes!
"Come to the hill, fair Agnes, with me,
The reddest of gold will I give unto thee!"

Twice went Agnes the hill round about,
Then wended within, left the fair world without.

In the hillside bode Agnes, three years thrice told o'er,
For the green earth sithence fell she longing full sore.

There she sat, and lullaby sang in her singing,
And she heard how the bells of England were ringing.

Agnes before her true-love did stand:
"May I wend to the church of the English Land?"

"To England's Church well mayst thou be gone,
So that no hand thou lay the red gold upon.

"So that when thou art come the churchyard anear,
Thou cast not abroad thy golden hair.

"So that when thou standest the church within,
To thy mother on bench thou never win.

"So that when thou hearest the high God's name,
No knee unto earth thou bow to the same."

Hand she laid on all gold that was there,
And cast abroad her golden hair.

And when the church she stood within,
To her mother on bench straight did she win.

And when she heard the high God's name,
Knee unto earth she bowed to the same.

When all the mass was sung to its end,
Home with her mother dear did she wend.

"Come, Agnes, into the hillside to me,
For thy seven small sons greet sorely for thee!"

"Let them greet, let them greet, as they have will to do;
For never again will I hearken thereto!"

Weird laid he on her, sore sickness he wrought,
Fowl are a-singing.
That self-same hour to death was she brought.
Agnes, fair Agnes!

KNIGHT AAGEN AND MAIDEN ELSE
TRANSLATED FROM THE DANISH

It was the fair knight Aagen
To an isle he went his way,
And plighted troth to Else,
Who was so fair a may.

He plighted troth to Else
All with the ruddy gold,
But or ere that day's moon came again

Low he lay in the black, black mould.

It was the maiden Else,
She was fulfilled of woe
When she heard how the fair knight Aagen
In the black mould lay alow.

Uprose the fair knight Aagen,
Coffin on back took he,
And he's away to her bower,
Sore hard as the work might be.

With that same chest on door he smote,
For the lack of flesh and skin;
"O hearken, maiden Else,
And let thy true-love in!"

Then answered maiden Else,
"Never open I my door,
But and if thou namest Jesu's name
As thou hadst might before."

"O hearken, maiden Else,
And open thou thy door,
For Jesu's name I well may name
As I had might before!"

Then uprose maiden Else,
O'er her cheek the salt tears ran,
Nor spared she into her very bower
To welcome that dead man.

O, she's taken up her comb of gold
And combed adown her hair,
And for every hair she combed adown
There fell a weary tear.

"Hearken thou, knight Aagen,
Hearken, true-love, and tell,
If down-adown in the black, black earth
Thou farest ever well?"

"O whenso thou art joyous,
And the heart is glad in thee,
Then fares it with my coffin
That red roses are with me.

"But whenso thou art sorrowful
And weary is thy mood,
Then all within my coffin
Is it dreadful with dark blood.

"Now is the red cock a-crowing,
To the earth adown must I;
Down to the earth wend all dead folk,
And I wend in company.

"Now is the black cock a-crowing,
To the earth must I adown,
For the gates of Heaven are opening now,
Thereto must I begone."

Uprose the fair knight Aagen,
Coffin on back took he,

And he's away to the churchyard now,
Sore hard as the work might be.

But so wrought maiden Else,
Because of her weary mood,
That she followed after own true love
All through the mirk wild wood.

But when the wood was well passed through,
And in the churchyard they were,
Then was the fair knight Aagen
Waxen wan of his golden hair.

And when therefrom they wended
And were the church within,
Then was the fair knight Aagen
Waxen wan of cheek and chin.

"Hearken thou, maiden Else,
Hearken, true-love, to me,
Weep no more for thine own troth-plight,
However it shall be!

"Look thou up to the heavens aloft,
To the little stars and bright,
And thou shalt see how sweetly
It fareth with the night!"

She looked up to the heavens aloft,
To the little stars bright above.
The dead man sank into his grave,
Ne'er again she saw her love.

Home then went maiden Else,
Mid sorrow manifold,
And ere that night's moon came again
She lay alow in the mould.

HAFBUR AND SIGNY
TRANSLATED FROM THE DANISH.

King Hafbur and King Siward
They needs must stir up strife,
All about the sweetling Signy
Who was so fair a wife.
O wilt thou win me then,
or as fair a maid as I be?

It was the King's son Hafbur
Woke up amid the night,
And 'gan to tell of a wondrous dream
In swift words nowise light.

"Me-dreamed I was in heaven
Amid that fair abode,
And my true-love lay upon mine arm
And we fell from cloud to cloud."

As there they sat, the dames and maids
Of his words they took no keep,
Only his mother well-beloved
Heeded his dreamful sleep.

"Go get thee gone to the mountain,

And make no long delay;
To the elve's eldest daughter
For thy dream's areding pray."

So the King's son, even Hafbur,
Took his sword in his left hand,
And he's away to the mountain
To get speech of that Lily-wand.

He beat thereon with hand all bare,
With fingers small and fine,
And there she lay, the elve's daughter,
And well wotted of that sign.

"Bide hail, Elve's sweetest daughter,
As on skins thou liest fair,
I pray thee by the God of Heaven
My dream arede thou clear.

"Me-dreamed I was in heaven,
Yea amid that fair abode,
And my true-love lay upon mine arm
And we fell from cloud to cloud."

"Whereas thou dreamed'st thou wert in heaven,
So shalt thou win that may;
Dreamed'st thou of falling through the clouds,
So falls for her thy life away."

"And if it lieth in my luck
To win to me that may,
In no sorrow's stead it standeth me

For her to cast my life away."

Lord Hafbur lets his hair wax long,
And will have the gear of mays,
And he rideth to King Siward's house
And will well learn weaving ways.

Lord Hafbur all his clothes let shape
In such wise as maidens do,
And thus he rideth over the land
King Siward's daughter to woo.

Now out amid the castle-garth
He cast his cloak aside,
And goeth forth to the high-bower
Where the dames and damsels abide.

Hail, sit ye there, dames and damsels,
Maids and queens kind and fair,
And chiefest of all to the Dane-King's daughter
If she abideth here!

"Hail, sittest thou, sweet King's daughter,
A-spinning the silken twine,
It is King Hafbur sends me hither
To learn the sewing fine."

Hath Hafbur sent thee here to me?
Then art thou a welcome guest,
And all the sewing that I can

Shall I learn thee at my best.

"And all the sewing that I can
I shall learn thee lovingly,
Out of one bowl shalt thou eat with me,
And by my nurse shalt thou lie."

"King's children have I eaten with,
And lain down by their side:
Must I lie abed now with a very nurse?
Then woe is me this tide!"

"Nay, let it pass, fair maiden!
Of me gettest thou no harm,
Out of one bowl shalt thou eat with me
And sleep soft upon mine arm."

There sat they, all the damsels,
And sewed full craftily;
But ever the King's son Hafbur
With nail in mouth sat he.

They sewed the hart, they sewed the hind,
As they run through the wild-wood green,
Never gat Hafbur so big a bowl
But the bottom soon was seen.

In there came the evil nurse
In the worst tide that might be:
"Never saw I fair maiden
Who could sew less craftily.

"Never saw I fair maiden
Seam worse the linen fine,
Never saw I noble maiden
Who better drank the wine."

This withal spake the evil nurse,
The nighest that she durst:
"Never saw I yet fair maiden
Of drink so sore athirst.

"So little a seam as ever she sews
Goes the needle into her mouth,
As big a bowl as ever she gets
Out is it drunk forsooth.

"Ne'er saw I yet in maiden's head
Two eyes so bright and bold,
And those two hands of her withal
Are hard as the iron cold."

"Hearken, sweet nurse, whereso thou art,
Why wilt thou mock me still?
Never cast I one word at thee,
Went thy sewing well or ill.

"Still wilt thou mock, still wilt thou spy;
Nought such thou hast of me,
Whether mine eyes look out or look in
Nought do they deal with thee."

O it was Hafbur the King's son
Began to sew at last;

He sowed the hart, and he sewed the hind,
As they flee from the hound so fast.

He sewed the lily, and he sewed the rose,
And the little fowls of the air;
Then fell the damsels a-marvelling,
For nought had they missed him there.

Day long they sewed till the evening,
And till the long night was deep,
Then up stood dames and maidens
And were fain in their beds to sleep.

So fell on them the evening-tide,
O'er the meads the dew drave down,
And fain was Signy, that sweet thing,
With her folk to bed to be gone.

Therewith asked the King's son Hafbur,
"And whatten a bed for me?"
"O thou shalt sleep in the bower aloft,
And blue shall thy bolster be."

She went before, sweet Signy,
O'er the high-bower's bridge aright,
And after her went Hafbur
Laughing from heart grown light.

Then kindled folk the waxlights,
That were so closely twined,
And after them the ill nurse went
With an ill thought in her mind.

The lights were quenched, the nurse went forth,
They deemed they were alone:
Lord Hafbur drew off his kirtle red,
Then first his sword outshone.

Lord Hafbur mid his longing sore
Down on the bed he sat:
I tell you of my soothfastness,
His byrny clashed thereat.

Then spake the darling Signy,
Out of her heart she said,
"Never saw I so rough a shirt
Upon so fair a maid."

She laid her hand on Hafbur's breast
With the red gold all a-blaze:
"Why wax thy breasts in no such wise
As they wax in other mays?"

"The wont it is in my father's land
For maids to ride to the Thing,
Therefore my breasts are little of growth
Beneath the byrny-ring."

And there they lay through the night so long,
The King's son and the may,
In talk full sweet, but little of sleep,
So much on their minds there lay.

476

"Hearken, sweet maiden Signy,
As here alone we lie,
Who is thy dearest in the world,
And lieth thine heart most nigh?"

"O there is none in all the world
Who lieth so near to my heart
As doth the bold King Hafbur:
Ne'er in him shall I have a part.

"As doth the bold King Hafbur
That mine eyes shall never know:
Nought but the sound of his gold-wrought horn
As he rides to the Thing and fro."

"O, is it Hafbur the King's son
That thy loved heart holdeth dear?
Turn hither, O my well-beloved,
To thy side I lie so near."

"If thou art the King's son Hafbur,
Why wilt thou shame me, love,
Why ridest thou not to my father's garth
With hound, and with hawk upon glove?"

"Once was I in thy father's garth,
With hound and hawk and all;
And with many mocks he said me nay,
In such wise did our meeting fall."

All the while they talked together
They deemed alone they were,
But the false nurse ever stood close without,
And nought thereof she failed to hear.

O shame befall that evil nurse,
Ill tidings down she drew,
She stole away his goodly sword,
But and his byrny new.

She took to her his goodly sword,
His byrny blue she had away,
And she went her ways to the high bower
Whereas King Siward lay.

"Wake up, wake up, King Siward!
Over long thou sleepest there,
The while the King's son Hafbur
Lies abed by Signy the fair."

"No Hafbur is here, and no King's son,
That thou shouldst speak this word;
He is far away in the east-countries,
Warring with knight and lord.

"Hold thou thy peace, thou evil nurse,
And lay on her no lie,
Or else tomorn ere the sun is up
In the bale-fire shall ye die."

"O hearken to this, my lord and king,

And trow me nought but true;
Look here upon his bright white sword,
But and his byrny blue!"

Then mad of mind waxed Siward,
Over all the house 'gan he cry,
"Rise up, O mighty men of mine,
For a hardy knight is anigh:

"Take ye sword and shield in hand,
And look that they be true;
For Hafbur the King hath guested with us;
Stiffnecked he is, great deeds to do."

So there anigh the high-bower door
They stood with spear and glaive
"Rise up, rise up, Young Hafbur,
Out here we would thee have!"

That heard the goodly Signy,
And she wrang her hands full sore:
"Hearken and heed, O Hafbur,
Who stand without by the door!"

Thank and praise to the King's son Hafbur,
Manly he played and stout!
None might lay hand upon him
While the bed-post yet held out.

But they took him, the King's son Hafbur,
And set him in bolts new wrought;
Then lightly he rent them asunder,

As though they were leaden and nought.

Out and spake the ancient nurse,
And she gave a rede of ill;
"Bind ye him but in Signy's hair.
So shall hand and foot lie still.

"Take ye but one of Signy's hairs
Hafbur's hands to bind,
Ne'er shall he rend them asunder,
His heart to her is so kind."

Then took they two of Signy's hairs
Bonds for his hands to be,
Nor might he rive them asunder,
So dear to his heart was she.

Then spake the sweetling Signy
As the tears fast down her cheek did fall:
"O rend it asunder, Hafbur,
That gift to thee I give withal."

Now sat the-King's son Hafbur
Amidst the castle-hall,
And thronged to behold him man and maid,
But the damsels chiefest of all.

They took him, the King's son Hafbur,
Laid bolts upon him in that place,
And ever went Signy to and fro,

The weary tears fell down apace.

She speaketh to him in sorrowful mood:
"This will I, Hafbur, for thee,
Piteous prayer for thee shall make
My mother's sisters three.

"For my father's mind stands fast in this,
To do thee to hang upon the bough
On the topmost oak in the morning-tide
While the sun is yet but low."

But answered thereto young Hafbur
Out of a wrathful mind:
"Of all heeds I heeded, this was the last,
To be prayed for by womankind.

"But hearken, true-love Signy,
Good heart to my asking turn,
When thou seest me swing on oaken-bough
Then let thy high-bower burn."

Then answered the noble Signy,
So sore as she must moan,
"God to aid, King's son Hafbur,
Well will I grant thy boon."

They followed him, King Hafbur,
Thick thronging from the castle-bent:
And all who saw him needs must greet

And in full piteous wise they went.

But when they came to the fair green mead
Where Hafbur was to die,
He prayed them hold a little while:
For his true-love would he try.

"O hang me up my cloak of red,
That sight or my ending let me see.
Perchance yet may King Siward rue
My hanging on the gallows tree."

Now of the cloak was Signy ware
And sorely sorrow her heart did rive,
She thought: "The ill tale all is told,
No longer is there need to live."

Straightway her damsels did she call
As weary as she was of mind:
"Come, let us go to the bower aloft
Game and glee for a while to find."

Yea and withal spake Signy,
She spake a word of price:
"To-day shall I do myself to death
And meet Hafbur in Paradise.

"And whoso there be in this our house
Lord Hafbur's death that wrought,
Good reward I give them now
To red embers to be brought.

"So many there are in the King's garth
Of Hafbur's death shall be glad;
Good reward for them to lose
The trothplight mays they had."

She set alight to the bower aloft
And it burned up speedily,
And her good love and her great heart
Might all with eyen see.

It was the King's son Hafbur
O'er his shoulder cast his eye,
And beheld how Signy's house of maids
On a red low stood on high.

"Now take ye down my cloak of red.
Let it lie on the earth a-cold;
Had I ten lives of the world for one,
Nought of them all would I hold."

King Siward looked out of his window fair
In fearful mood enow,
For he saw Hafbur hanging on oak
And Signy's bower on a low.

Out then spake a little page
Was clad in kirtle red:
"Sweet Signy burns in her bower aloft,
With all her mays unwed."

Therewithal spake King Siward
From rueful heart unfain;
"Ne'er saw I two King's children erst
Such piteous ending gain.

"But had I wist or heard it told
That love so strong should be,
Ne'er had I held those twain apart
For all Denmark given me.

"O hasten and run to Signy's bower
For the life of that sweet thing;
Hasten and run to the gallows high,
No thief is Hafbur the King."

But when they came to Signy's bower
Low it lay in embers red;
And when they came to the gallows tree,
Hafbur was stark and dead.

They took him the King's son Hafbur,
Swathed him in linen white,
And laid him in the earth of Christ
By Signy his delight.
O wilt thou win me then,
or as fair a maid as I be?

GOLDILOCKS AND GOLDILOCKS

It was Goldilocks woke up in the morn
At the first of the shearing of the corn.

There stood his mother on the hearth

And of new-leased wheat was little dearth.

There stood his sisters by the quern,
For the high-noon cakes they needs must earn.

"O tell me Goldilocks my son,
Why hast thou coloured raiment on?"

"Why should I wear the hodden grey
When I am light of heart to-day?"

"O tell us, brother, why ye wear
In reaping-tide the scarlet gear?

Why hangeth the sharp sword at thy side
When through the land 'tis the hook goes wide?"

"Gay-clad am I that men may know
The freeman's son where'er I go.

The grinded sword at side I bear
Lest I the dastard's word should hear."

"O tell me Goldilocks my son,
Of whither away thou wilt be gone?"

"The morn is fair and the world is wide,
And here no more will I abide."

"O Brother, when wilt thou come again?"
"The autumn drought, and the winter rain,

The frost and the snow, and St. David's wind,
All these that were time out of mind,

All these a many times shall be
Ere the Upland Town again I see."

"O Goldilocks my son, farewell,
As thou wendest the world 'twixt home and hell!"

"O brother Goldilocks, farewell,
Come back with a tale for men to tell!"

So 'tis wellaway for Goldilocks,
As he left the land of the wheaten shocks.

He's gotten him far from the Upland Town,
And he's gone by Dale and he's gone by Down.

He's come to the wild-wood dark and drear,
Where never the bird's song doth he hear.

He has slept in the moonless wood and dim
With never a voice to comfort him.

He has risen up under the little light
Where the noon is as dark as the summer night.

Six days therein has he walked alone
Till his scrip was bare and his meat was done.

On the seventh morn in the mirk, mirk wood,
He saw sight that he deemed was good.

It was as one sees a flower a-bloom
In the dusky heat of a shuttered room.

He deemed the fair thing far aloof,
And would go and put it to the proof.

But the very first step he made from the place
He met a maiden face to face.

Face to face, and so close was she
That their lips met soft and lovingly.

Sweet-mouthed she was, and fair he wist;
And again in the darksome wood they kissed.

Then first in the wood her voice he heard,
As sweet as the song of the summer bird.

"O thou fair man with the golden head.
What is the name of thee?" she said.

"My name is Goldilocks," said he;
"O sweet-breathed, what is the name of thee?"

"O Goldilocks the Swain," she said,
"My name is Goldilocks the Maid."

He spake, "Love me as I love thee,
And Goldilocks one flesh shall be."

She said, "Fair man, I wot not how
Thou lovest, but I love thee now.

But come a little hence away,
That I may see thee in the day.

For hereby is a wood-lawn clear
And good for awhile for us it were."

Therewith she took him by the hand
And led him into the lighter land.

There on the grass they sat adown.
Clad she was in a kirtle brown.

In all the world was never maid
So fair, so evilly arrayed.

No shoes upon her feet she had,
And scantly were her shoulders clad;

Through her brown kirtle's rents full wide
Shone out the sleekness of her side.

An old scrip hung about her neck,
Nought of her raiment did she reck.

No shame of all her rents had she;
She gazed upon him eagerly.

She leaned across the grassy space
And put her hands about his face.

She said: "O hunger-pale art thou,
Yet shalt thou eat though I hunger now."

She took him apples from her scrip,
She kissed him, cheek and chin and lip.

She took him cakes of woodland bread:
"Whiles am I hunger-pinched," she said.

She had a gourd and a pilgrim shell;
She took him water from the well.

She stroked his breast and his scarlet gear;
She spake, "How brave thou art and dear!"

Her arms about him did she wind;
He felt her body dear and kind.

"O love," she said, "now two are one,
And whither hence shall we be gone?"

"Shall we fare further than this wood,"
Quoth he, "I deem it dear and good?"

She shook her head, and laughed, and spake;
"Rise up! For thee, not me, I quake.

Had she been minded me to slay
Sure she had done it ere to-day.

But thou: this hour the crone shall know
That thou art come, her very foe.

No minute more on tidings wait,
Lest e'en this minute be too late."

She led him from the sunlit green,
Going sweet-stately as a queen.

There in the dusky wood, and dim,
As forth they went, she spake to him:

"Fair man, few people have I seen
Amidst this world of woodland green:

But I would have thee tell me now
If there be many such as thou."

"Betwixt the mountains and the sea,
O Sweet, be many such," said he.

Athwart the glimmering air and dim
With wistful eyes she looked on him.

"But ne'er an one so shapely made
Mine eyes have looked upon," she said.

He kissed her face, and cried in mirth:

"Where hast thou dwelt then on the earth?"

"Ever," she said, "I dwell alone
With a hard-handed cruel crone.

And of this crone am I the thrall
To serve her still in bower and hall;

And fetch and carry in the wood,
And do whate'er she deemeth good.

But whiles a sort of folk there come
And seek my mistress at her home;

But such-like are they to behold
As make my very blood run cold.

Oft have I thought, if there be none
On earth save these, would all were done!

Forsooth, I knew it was not so,
But that fairer folk on earth did grow.

But fain and full is the heart in me
To know that folk are like to thee."

Then hand in hand they stood awhile
Till her tears rose up beneath his smile.

And he must fold her to his breast
To give her heart a while of rest.

Till sundered she and gazed about,
And bent her brows as one in doubt.

She spake: "The wood is growing thin,
Into the full light soon shall we win.

Now crouch we that we be not seen,
Under yon bramble-bushes green."

Under the bramble-bush they lay
Betwixt the dusk and the open day.

"O Goldilocks my love, look forth
And let me know what thou seest of worth."

He said: "I see a house of stone,
A castle excellently done."

"Yea," quoth she, "There doth the mistress dwell.
What next thou seest shalt thou tell."

"What lookest thou to see come forth?"
"Maybe a white bear of the North."

"Then shall my sharp sword lock his mouth."
"Nay," she said, "or a worm of the South."

"Then shall my sword his hot blood cool."
"Nay, or a whelming poison-pool."

"The trees its swelling flood shall stay,
And thrust its venomed lip away."

"Nay, it may be a wild-fire flash
To burn thy lovely limbs to ash."

"On mine own hallows shall I call,
And dead its flickering flame shall fall."

"O Goldilocks my love, I fear
That ugly death shall seek us here.

Look forth, O Goldilocks my love.
That I thine hardy heart may prove.

What cometh down the stone-wrought stair
That leadeth up to the castle fair?"

"Adown the doorward stair of stone
There cometh a woman all alone."

"Yea, that forsooth shall my mistress be:
O Goldilocks, what like is she?"

"O fair she is of her array,
As hitherward she wends her way."

"Unlike her wont is that indeed:
Is she not foul beneath her weed?"

"O nay, nay! But most wondrous fair
Of all the women earth doth bear."

"O Goldilocks, my heart, my heart!
Woe, woe! for now we drift apart."

But up he sprang from the bramble-side,
And "O thou fairest one!" he cried:

And forth he ran that Queen to meet,
And fell before her gold-clad feet.

About his neck her arms she cast,
And into the fair-built house they passed.

And under the bramble-bushes lay
Unholpen, Goldilocks the may.

Thenceforth a while of time there wore,
And Goldilocks came forth no more.

Throughout that house he wandered wide,
Both up and down, from side to side.

But never he saw an evil crone,
But a full fair Queen on a golden throne.

Never a barefoot maid did he see,
But a gay and gallant company.

He sat upon the golden throne,
And beside him sat the Queen alone.

Kind she was, as she loved him well,
And many a merry tale did tell.

But nought he laughed, nor spake again,
For all his life was waste and vain.

Cold was his heart, and all afraid
To think on Goldilocks the Maid.

Withal now was the wedding dight
When he should wed that lady bright.

The night was gone, and the day was up
When they should drink the bridal cup.

And he sat at the board beside the Queen,
Amidst of a guest-folk well beseen.

But scarce was midmorn on the hall,
When down did the mirk of midnight fall.

Then up and down from the board they ran,
And man laid angry hand on man.

There was the cry, and the laughter shrill,
And every manner word of ill.

Whoso of men had hearkened it,
Had deemed he had woke up over the Pit.

Then spake the Queen o'er all the crowd,
And grim was her speech, and harsh, and loud:

"Hold now your peace, ye routing swine,
While I sit with mine own love over the wine!

For this dusk is the very deed of a foe,
Or under the sun no man I know."

And hard she spake, and loud she cried
Till the noise of the bickering guests had died.

Then again she spake amidst of the mirk,
In a voice like an unoiled wheel at work:

"Whoso would have a goodly gift,
Let him bring aback the sun to the lift.

Let him bring aback the light and the day,
And rich and in peace he shall go his way."

Out spake a voice was clean and clear:
"Lo, I am she to dight your gear;

But I for the deed a gift shall gain,
To sit by Goldilocks the Swain.

I shall sit at the board by the bridegroom's side,
And be betwixt him and the bride.

I shall eat of his dish, and drink of his cup,

Until for the bride-bed ye rise up."

Then was the Queen's word wailing-wild:
"E'en so must it be, thou Angel's child.

Thou shalt sit by my groom till the dawn of night,
And then shalt thou wend thy ways aright."

Said the voice, "Yet shalt thou swear an oath
That free I shall go though ye be loth."

"How shall I swear?" the false Queen spake:
"Wherewith the sure oath shall I make?"

"Thou shalt swear by the one eye left in thine head,
And the throng of the ghosts of the evil dead."

She swore the oath, and then she spake:
"Now let the second dawn awake."

And e'en therewith the thing was done;
There was peace in the hall, and the light of the sun.

And again the Queen was calm and fair,
And courteous sat the guest-folk there.

Yet unto Goldilocks it seemed
As if amidst the night he dreamed;

As if he sat in a grassy place,
While slim hands framed his hungry face;

As if in the clearing of the wood
One gave him bread and apples good;

And nought he saw of the guest-folk gay,
And nought of all the Queen's array.

Yet saw he betwixt board and door,
A slim maid tread the chequered floor.

Her gown of green so fair was wrought,
That clad her body seemed with nought

But blossoms of the summer-tide,
That wreathed her, limbs and breast and side.

And, stepping towards him daintily,
A basket in her hand had she.

And as she went, from head to feet,
Surely was she most dainty-sweet.

Love floated round her, and her eyes
Gazed from her fairness glad and wise;

But babbling-loud the guests were grown;
Unnoted was she and unknown.

Now Goldilocks she sat beside,
But nothing changed was the Queenly bride;

Yea too, and Goldilocks the Swain
Was grown but dull and dazed again.

The Queen smiled o'er the guest-rich board,
Although his wine the Maiden poured;

Though from his dish the Maiden ate,
The Queen sat happy and sedate.

But now the Maiden fell to speak
From lips that well-nigh touched his cheek:

"O Goldilocks, dost thou forget?
Or mindest thou the mirk-wood yet?

Forgettest thou the hunger-pain
And all thy young life made but vain?

How there was nought to help or aid,
But for poor Goldilocks the Maid?"

She murmured, "Each to each we two,
Our faces from the wood-mirk grew.

Hast thou forgot the grassy place,
And love betwixt us face to face?

Hast thou forgot how fair I deemed
Thy face? How fair thy garment seemed?

Thy kisses on my shoulders bare,
Through rents of the poor raiment there?

My arms that loved thee nought unkissed
All o'er from shoulder unto wrist?

Hast thou forgot how brave thou wert,
Thou with thy fathers' weapon girt;

When underneath the bramble-bush
I quaked like river-shaken rash,

Wondering what new-wrought shape of death
Should quench my new love-quickened breath?

Or else: forget'st thou, Goldilocks,
Thine own land of the wheaten shocks?

Thy mother and thy sisters dear,
Thou said'st would bide thy true-love there?

Hast thou forgot? Hast thou forgot?
O love, my love, I move thee not."

Silent the fair Queen sat and smiled,
And heeded nought the Angel's child,

For like an image fashioned fair
Still sat the Swain with empty stare.

These words seemed spoken not, but writ
As foolish tales through night-dreams flit.

Vague pictures passed before his sight,
As in the first dream of the night.

But the Maiden opened her basket fair,
And set two doves on the table there.

And soft they cooed, and sweet they billed
Like man and maid with love fulfilled.

Therewith the Maiden reached a hand
To a dish that on the board did stand;

And she crumbled a share of the spice-loaf brown,
And the Swain upon her hand looked down;

Then unto the fowl his eyes he turned;
And as in a dream his bowels yearned

For somewhat that he could not name;
And into his heart a hope there came.

And still he looked on the hands of the Maid,
As before the fowl the crumbs she laid.

And he murmured low, "O Goldilocks!
Were we but amid the wheaten shocks!"

Then the false Queen knit her brows and laid
A fair white hand by the hand of the Maid.

He turned his eyes away thereat,
And closer to the Maiden sat.

But the queen-bird now the carle-bird fed
Till all was gone of the sugared bread.

Then with wheedling voice for more he craved,
And the Maid a share from the spice-loaf shaved;

And the crumbs within her hollow hand
She held where the creeping doves did stand.

But Goldilocks, he looked and longed,
And saw how the carle the queen-bird wronged.

For when she came to the hand to eat
The hungry queen-bird thence he beat.

Then Goldilocks the Swain spake low:
"Foul fall thee, bird, thou doest now

As I to Goldilocks, my sweet,
Who gave my hungry mouth to eat."

He felt her hand as he did speak,
He felt her face against his cheek.

He turned and stood in the evil hall,
And swept her up in arms withal.

Then was there hubbub wild and strange,
And swiftly all things there 'gan change.

The fair Queen into a troll was grown,
A one-eyed, bow-backed, haggard crone.

And though the hall was yet full fair,
And bright the sunshine streamed in there,

On evil shapes it fell forsooth:
Swine-heads; small red eyes void of ruth;

And bare-boned bodies of vile things,
And evil-feathered bat-felled wings.

And all these mopped and mowed and grinned,
And sent strange noises down the wind.

There stood those twain unchanged alone
To face the horror of the crone;

She crouched against them by the board;
And cried the Maid: "Thy sword, thy sword!

Thy sword, O Goldilocks! For see
She will not keep her oath to me."

Out flashed the blade therewith. He saw
The foul thing sidelong toward them draw,

Holding within her hand a cup

Wherein some dreadful drink seethed up.

Then Goldilocks cried out and smote,
And the sharp blade sheared the evil throat.

The head fell noseling to the floor;
The liquor from the cup did pour,

And ran along a sparkling flame
That nigh unto their footsoles came.

Then empty straightway was the hall,
Save for those twain, and she withal.

So fled away the Maid and Man,
And down the stony stairway ran.

Fast fled they o'er the sunny grass,
Yet but a little way did pass

Ere cried the Maid: "Now cometh forth
The snow-white ice-bear of the North;

Turn, Goldilocks, and heave up sword!"
Then fast he stood upon the sward,

And faced the beast, that whined and cried,
And shook his head from side to side.

But round him the Swain danced and leaped,

And soon the grisly head he reaped.

And then the ancient blade he sheathed,
And ran unto his love sweet-breathed;

And caught her in his arms and ran
Fast from that house, the bane of man.

Yet therewithal he spake her soft
And kissed her over oft and oft,

Until from kissed and trembling mouth
She cried: "The Dragon of the South!"

He set her down and turned about,
And drew the eager edges out.

And therewith scaly coil on coil
Reared 'gainst his face the mouth aboil:

The gaping jaw and teeth of dread
Was dark 'twixt heaven and his head.

But with no fear, no thought, no word,
He thrust the thin-edged ancient sword.

And the hot blood ran from the hairy throat,
And set the summer grass afloat.

Then back he turned and caught her hand,

And never a minute did they stand.

But as they ran on toward the wood,
He deemed her swift feet fair and good.

She looked back o'er her shoulder fair:
"The whelming poison-pool is here;

And now availeth nought the blade:
O if my cherished trees might aid!

But now my feet fail. Leave me then!
And hold my memory dear of men."

He caught her in his arms again;
Of her dear side was he full fain.

Her body in his arms was dear:
"Sweet art thou, though we perish here!"

Like quicksilver came on the flood:
But lo, the borders of the wood!

She slid from out his arms and stayed;
Round a great oak her arms she laid.

"If e'er I saved thee, lovely tree,
From axe and saw, now succour me:

Look how the venom creeps anigh,

Help! lest thou see me writhe and die."

She crouched beside the upheaved root,
The bubbling venom touched her foot;

Then with a sucking gasping sound
It ebbed back o'er the blighted ground.

Up then she rose and took his hand
And never a moment did they stand.

"Come, love," she cried, "the ways I know,
How thick soe'er the thickets grow.

O love, I love thee! O thine heart!
How mighty and how kind thou art!"

Therewith they saw the tree-dusk lit,
Bright grey the great boles gleamed on it.

"O flee," she said, "the sword is nought
Against the flickering fire-flaught."

"But this availeth yet," said he,
"That Hallows All our love may see."

He turned about and faced the glare:
"O Mother, help us, kind and fair!

Now help me, true St. Nicholas,

If ever truly thine I was!"

Therewith the wild-fire waned and paled,
And in the wood the light nigh failed;

And all about 'twas as the night.
He said: "Now won is all our fight,

And now meseems all were but good
If thou mightst bring us from the wood."

She fawned upon him, face and breast;
She said: "It hangs 'twixt worst and best.

And yet, O love, if thou be true,
One thing alone thou hast to do."

Sweetly he kissed her, cheek and chin:
"What work thou biddest will I win."

"O love, my love, I needs must sleep;
Wilt thou my slumbering body keep,

And, toiling sorely, still bear on
The love thou seemest to have won?"

"O easy toil," he said, "to bless
Mine arms with all thy loveliness."

She smiled; "Yea, easy it may seem,
But harder is it than ye deem.

For hearken! Whatso thou mayst see,
Piteous as it may seem to thee,

Heed not nor hearken! bear me forth,
As though nought else were aught of worth.

For all earth's wealth that may be found
Lay me not sleeping on the ground,

To help, to hinder, or to save!
Or there for me thou diggest a grave."

He took her body on his arm,
Her slumbering head lay on his barm.

Then glad he bore her on the way,
And the wood grew lighter with the day.

All still it was, till suddenly
He heard a bitter wail near by.

Yet on he went until he heard
The cry become a shapen word:

"Help me, O help, thou passer by!
Turn from the path, let me not die!

I am a woman; bound and left
To perish; of all help bereft."

Then died the voice out in a moan;
He looked upon his love, his own,

And minding all she spake to him
Strode onward through the wild-wood dim.

But lighter grew the woodland green
Till clear the shapes of things were seen.

And therewith wild halloos he heard,
And shrieks, and cries of one afeard.

Nigher it grew and yet more nigh
Till burst from out a brake near by

A woman bare of breast and limb,
Who turned a piteous face to him

E'en as she ran: for hard at heel
Followed a man with brandished steel,

And yelling mouth. Then the Swain stood
One moment in the glimmering wood

Trembling, ashamed: Yet now grown wise
Deemed all a snare for ears and eyes.

So onward swiftlier still he strode
And cast all thought on his fair load.

And yet in but a little space
Back came the yelling shrieking chase,

And well-nigh gripped now by the man,
Straight unto him the woman ran;

And underneath the gleaming steel
E'en at his very feet did kneel.

She looked up; sobs were all her speech,
Yet sorely did her face beseech.

While o'er her head the chaser stared,
Shaking aloft the edges bared.

Doubted the Swain, and a while did stand
As she took his coat-lap in her hand.

Upon his hand he felt her breath
Hot with the dread of present death.

Sleek was her arm on his scarlet coat,
The sobbing passion rose in his throat.

But e'en therewith he looked aside
And saw the face of the sleeping bride.

Then he tore his coat from the woman's hand,
And never a moment there did stand.

But swiftly thence away he strode
Along the dusky forest road.

And there rose behind him laughter shrill,

And then was the windless wood all still,

He looked around o'er all the place,
But saw no image of the chase.

And as he looked the night-mirk now
O'er all the tangled wood 'gan flow.

Then stirred the sweetling that he bore,
And she slid adown from his arms once more.

Nought might he see her well-loved face;
But he felt her lips in the mirky place.

"'Tis night," she said, "and the false day's gone,
And we twain in the wild-wood all alone.

Night o'er the earth; so rest we here
Until to-morrow's sun is clear.

For overcome is every foe
And home to-morrow shall we go."

So 'neath the trees they lay, those twain,
And to them the darksome night was gain.

But when the morrow's dawn was grey
They woke and kissed whereas they lay.

And when on their feet they came to stand
Swain Goldilocks stretched out his hand.

And he spake: "O love, my love indeed,
Where now is gone thy goodly weed?

For again thy naked feet I see,
And thy sweet sleek arms so kind to me.

Through thy rent kirtle once again
Thy shining shoulder showeth plain."

She blushed as red as the sun-sweet rose:
"My garments gay were e'en of those

That the false Queen dight to slay my heart;
And sore indeed was their fleshly smart.

Yet must I bear them, well-beloved,
Until thy truth and troth was proved

And this tattered coat is now for a sign
That thou hast won me to be thine.

Now wilt thou lead along thy maid
To meet thy kindred unafraid."

As stoops the falcon on the dove
He cast himself about her love.

He kissed her over, cheek and chin,
He kissed the sweetness of her skin.

Then hand in hand they went their way
Till the wood grew light with the outer day.

At last behind them lies the wood,
And before are the Upland Acres good.

On the hill's brow awhile they stay
At midmorn of the merry day.

He sheareth a deal from his kirtle meet,
To make her sandals for her feet.

He windeth a wreath of the beechen tree,
Lest men her shining shoulders see.

And a wreath of woodbine sweet, to hide
The rended raiment of her side;

And a crown of poppies red as wine,
Lest on her head the hot sun shine.

She kissed her love withal and smiled:
"Lead forth, O love, the Woodland Child!

Most meet and right meseems it now
That I am clad with the woodland bough.

For betwixt the oak-tree and the thorn
Meseemeth erewhile was I born.

And if my mother aught I knew,
It was of the woodland folk she grew.

And O that thou art well at ease

To wed the daughter of the trees!"

Now Goldilocks and Goldilocks
Go down amidst the wheaten shocks,

But when anigh to the town they come,
Lo there is the wain a-wending home,

And many a man and maid beside,
Who tossed the sickles up, and cried:

"O Goldilocks, now whither away?
And what wilt thou with the woodland may?"

"O this is Goldilocks my bride,
And we come adown from the wild-wood side,

And unto the Fathers' House we wend
To dwell therein till life shall end."

"Up then on the wain, that ye may see
From afar how thy mother bideth thee.

That ye may see how kith and kin
Abide thee, bridal brave to win."

So Goldilocks and Goldilocks
Sit high aloft on the wheaten shocks,

And fair maids sing before the wain,
For all of Goldilocks are fain.

But when they came to the Fathers' door,
There stood his mother old and hoar.

Yet was her hair with grey but blent,
When forth from the Upland Town he went.

There by the door his sisters stood:
Full fair they were and fresh of blood;

Little they were when he went away;
Now each is meet for a young man's may.

"O tell me, Goldilocks, my son,
What are the deeds that thou hast done?"

"I have wooed me a wife in the forest wild,
And home I bring the Woodland Child."

"A little deed to do, O son,
So long a while as thou wert gone."

"O mother, yet is the summer here
Now I bring aback my true-love dear.

And therewith an Evil Thing have I slain;
Yet I come with the first-come harvest-wain."

"O Goldilocks, my son, my son!
How good is the deed that thou hast done?

But how long the time that is worn away!
Lo! white is my hair that was but grey.

And lo these sisters here, thine own,
How tall, how meet for men-folk grown!

Come, see thy kin in the feasting-hall,
And tell me if thou knowest them all!

O son, O son, we are blithe and fain;
But the autumn drought, and the winter rain,

The frost and the snow, and St. David's wind,
All these that were, time out of mind,

All these a many times have been
Since thou the Upland Town hast seen."

Then never a word spake Goldilocks
Till they came adown from the wheaten shocks.

And there beside his love he stood
And he saw her body sweet and good.

Then round her love his arms he cast:
"The years are as a tale gone past.

But many the years that yet shall be
Of the merry tale of thee and me.

Come, love, and look on the Fathers' Hall,
And the folk of the kindred one and all!

For now the Fathers' House is kind,
And all the ill is left behind.

And Goldilocks and Goldilocks
Shall dwell in the land of the Wheaten Shocks."

LOVE IS ENOUGH
OR
THE FREEING OF PHARAMOND

DRAMATIS PERSONAE

GILES,
JOAN, his Wife,
Peasant-folk.

THE EMPEROR.
THE EMPRESS.
THE MAYOR.

A COUNCILLOR.
MASTER OLIVER, King Pharamond's Foster-father.
A NORTHERN LORD.
KING PHARAMOND.
AZALAIS, his Love.
KING THEOBALD.
HONORIUS, the Councillor.

LOVE.

LOVE IS ENOUGH

ARGUMENT

This story, which is told by way of a morality set before an Emperor and Empress newly wedded, showeth of a King whom nothing but Love might satisfy, who left all to seek Love, and, having found it, found this also, that he had enough, though he lacked all else.

In the streets of a great town where the people are gathered together thronging to see the Emperor and Empress pass.

GILES
Look long, Joan, while I hold you so,
For the silver trumpets come arow.

JOAN
O the sweet sound! the glorious sight!
O Giles, Giles, see this glittering Knight!

GILES
Nay 'tis the Marshalls'-sergeant, sweet—
—Hold, neighbour, let me keep my feet!—
There, now your head is up again;
Thus held up have you aught of pain?

JOAN
Nay, clear I see, and well at ease!

God's body! what fair Kings be these?

GILES
The Emperor's chamberlains, behold
Their silver shoes and staves of gold.
Look, look! how like some heaven come down
The maidens go with girded gown!

JOAN
Yea, yea, and this last row of them
Draw up their kirtles by the hem,
And scatter roses e'en like those
About my father's garden-close.

GILES
Ah! have I hurt you? See the girls
Whose slim hands scatter very pearls.

JOAN
Hold me fast, Giles! here comes one
Whose raiment flashes down the sun.

GILES
O sweet mouth! O fair lids cast down!
O white brow! O the crown, the crown!

JOAN
How near! if nigher I might stand
By one ell, I could touch his hand.

GILES
Look, Joan! if on this side she were

Almost my hand might touch her hair.

JOAN
Ah me! what is she thinking on?

GILES
Is he content now all is won?

JOAN
And does she think as I thought, when
Betwixt the dancing maids and men,
Twixt the porch rose-boughs blossomed red
I saw the roses on my bed?

GILES
Hath he such fear within his heart
As I had, when the wind did part
The jasmine-leaves, and there within
The new-lit taper glimmered thin?

THE MUSIC
(As the EMPEROR and EMPRESS enter.)
LOVE IS ENOUGH; though the World be a-waning
And the woods have no voice but the voice of complain-
ing,
   Though the sky be too dark for dim eyes to discover
   The gold-cups and daisies fair blooming thereunder;
   Though the hills be held shadows, and the sea a dark
wonder,
   And this day draw a veil over all deeds passed over,
   Yet their hands shall not tremble, their feet shall not fal-
ter,

The void shall not weary, the fear shall not alter
These lips and these eyes of the loved and the lover.

THE EMPEROR

The spears flashed by me, and the swords swept round,
And in war's hopeless tangle was I bound,
But straw and stubble were the cold points found,
For still thy hands led down the weary way.

THE EMPRESS

Through hall and street they led me as a queen,
They looked to see me proud and cold of mien,
I heeded not though all my tears were seen,
For still I dreamed of thee throughout the day.

THE EMPEROR

Wild over bow and bulwark swept the sea
Unto the iron coast upon our lee,
Like painted cloth its fury was to me,
For still thy hands led down the weary way.

THE EMPRESS

They spoke to me of war within the land,
They bade me sign defiance and command;
I heeded not though thy name left my hand,
For still I dreamed of thee throughout the day.

THE EMPEROR

But now that I am come, and side by side
We go, and men cry gladly on the bride
And tremble at the image of my pride,

Where is thy hand to lead me down the way?

THE EMPRESS
But now that thou art come, and heaven and earth
Are laughing in the fulness of their mirth,
A shame I knew not in my heart has birth—
—Draw me through dreams unto the end of day!

THE EMPEROR
Behold, behold, how weak my heart is grown
Now all the heat of its desire is known!
Pearl beyond price I fear to call mine own,
Where is thy hand to lead me down the way?

THE EMPRESS
Behold, behold, how little I may move!
Think in thy heart how terrible is Love,
O thou who know'st my soul as God above—
—Draw me through dreams unto the end of day!

The stage for the play in another part of the street, and
the people thronging all about.

GILES
Here, Joan, this is so good a place
'Tis worth the scramble and the race!
There is the Empress just sat down,
Her white hands on her golden gown,
While yet the Emperor stands to hear
The welcome of the bald-head Mayor
Unto the show; and you shall see
The player-folk come in presently.

The king of whom is e'en that one,
Who wandering but a while agone
Stumbled upon our harvest-home
That August when you might not come.
Betwixt the stubble and the grass
Great mirth indeed he brought to pass.
But liefer were I to have seen
Your nimble feet tread down the green
In threesome dance to pipe and fife.

JOAN
Thou art a dear thing to my life,
And nought good have I far to seek—
But hearken! for the Mayor will speak.

THE MAYOR
Since your grace bids me speak without stint or sparing
A thing little splendid I pray you to see:
Early is the day yet, for we near the dawning
Drew on chains dear-bought, and gowns done with gold;
So may ye high ones hearken an hour
A tale that our hearts hold worthy and good,
Of Pharamond the Freed, who, a king feared and hon-
oured,
Fled away to find love from his crown and his folk.
E'en as I tell of it somewhat I tremble
Lest we, fearful of treason to the love that fulfils you,
Should seem to make little of the love that ye give us,
Of your lives full of glory, of the deeds that your lifetime
Shall gleam with for ever when we are forgotten.
Forgive it for the greatness of that Love who compels
us.—

Hark! in the minster-tower minish the joy-bells,
And all men are hushed now these marvels to hear.

THE EMPEROR (to the MAYOR)
We thank your love, that sees our love indeed
Toward you, toward Love, toward life of toil and need:
We shall not falter though your poet sings
Of all defeat, strewing the crowns of kings
About the thorny ways where Love doth wend,
Because we know us faithful to the end
Toward you, toward Love, toward life of war and deed,
And well we deem your tale shall help our need.

(To the EMPRESS)
So many hours to pass before the sun
Shall blush ere sleeping, and the day be done!
How thinkest thou, my sweet, shall such a tale
For lengthening or for shortening them avail?

THE EMPRESS
Nay, dreamland has no clocks the wise ones say,
And while our hands move at the break of day
We dream of years: and I am dreaming still
And need no change my cup of joy to fill:
Let them say on, and I shall hear thy voice
Telling the tale, and in its love rejoice.

THE MUSIC
(As the singers enter and stand before the curtain, the
player-king and player-maiden in the midst.)
    LOVE IS ENOUGH: have no thought for to-morrow
If ye lie down this even in rest from your pain,

Ye who have paid for your bliss with great sorrow:
For as it was once so it shall be again.
Ye shall cry out for death as ye stretch forth in vain.

Feeble hands to the hands that would help but they may
not,
    Cry out to deaf ears that would hear if they could;
    Till again shall the change come, and words your lips say
not
    Your hearts make all plain in the best wise they would
    And the world ye thought waning is glorious and good:

And no morning now mocks you and no nightfall is
weary,
    The plains are not empty of song and of deed:
    The sea strayeth not, nor the mountains are dreary;
    The wind is not helpless for any man's need,
    Nor falleth the rain but for thistle and weed.

O surely this morning all sorrow is hidden,
All battle is hushed for this even at least;
And no one this noontide may hunger, unbidden
To the flowers and the singing and the joy of your feast
Where silent ye sit midst the world's tale increased.

Lo, the lovers unloved that draw nigh for your blessing!
For your tale makes the dreaming whereby yet they live
The dreams of the day with their hopes of redressing,
The dreams of the night with the kisses they give,
The dreams of the dawn wherein death and hope strive.

Ah, what shall we say then, but that earth threatened

often
  Shall live on for ever that such things may be,
  That the dry seed shall quicken, the hard earth shall soft-
en,
  And the spring-bearing birds flutter north o'er the sea,
  That earth's garden may bloom round my love's feet and
me?

THE EMPEROR

Lo you, my sweet, fair folk are one and all
And with good grace their broidered robes do fall,
And sweet they sing indeed: but he, the King,
Look but a little how his fingers cling
To her's, his love that shall be in the play—
His love that hath been surely ere to-day:
And see, her wide soft eyes cast down at whiles
Are opened not to note the people's smiles
But her love's lips, and dreamily they stare
As though they sought the happy country, where
They two shall be alone, and the world dead.

THE EMPRESS

Most faithful eyes indeed look from the head
The sun has burnt, and wind and rain has beat,
Well may he find her slim brown fingers sweet.
And he—methinks he trembles, lest he find
That song of his not wholly to her mind.
Note how his grey eyes look askance to see
Her bosom heaving with the melody
His heart loves well: rough with the wind and rain
His cheek is, hollow with some ancient pain;

The sun has burned and blanched his crispy hair,
And over him hath swept a world of care
And left him careless, rugged, and her own;
Still fresh desired, still strange and new, though known.

THE EMPEROR
His eyes seem dreaming of the mysteries
Deep in the depths of her familiar eyes,
Tormenting and alluring; does he dream,
As I ofttime this morn, how they would seem
Loved but unloving?—Nay the world's too sweet
That we the ghost of such a pain should meet—
Behold, she goes, and he too, turning round,
Remembers that his love must yet be found,
That he is King and loveless in this story
Wrought long ago for some dead poet's glory.
[Exeunt players behind the curtain.

Enter before the curtain LOVE crowned as a King.

LOVE
All hail, my servants! tremble ye, my foes!
A hope for these I have, a fear for those
Hid in this tale of Pharamond the Freed.
To-day, my Faithful, nought shall be your need
Of tears compassionate:—although full oft
The crown of love laid on my bosom soft
Be woven of bitter death and deathless fame,
Bethorned with woe, and fruited thick with shame.
—This for the mighty of my courts I keep,
Lest through the world there should be none to weep
Except for sordid loss; and not to gain

But satiate pleasure making mock of pain.
—Yea, in the heaven from whence my dreams go forth
Are stored the signs that make the world of worth:
There is the wavering wall of mighty Troy
About my Helen's hope and Paris' joy:
There lying neath the fresh dyed mulberry-tree
The sword and cloth of Pyramus I see:
There is the number of the joyless days
Wherein Medea won no love nor praise:
There is the sand my Ariadne pressed;
The footprints of the feet that knew no rest
While o'er the sea forth went the fatal sign:
The asp of Egypt, the Numidian wine,
My Sigurd's sword, my Brynhild's fiery bed,
The tale of years of Gudrun's drearihead,
And Tristram's glaive, and Iseult's shriek are here,
And cloister-gown of joyless Guenevere.

Save you, my Faithful! how your loving eyes
Grow soft and gleam with all these memories!
But on this day my crown is not of death:
My fire-tipped arrows, and my kindling breath
Are all the weapons I shall need to-day.
Nor shall my tale in measured cadence play
About the golden lyre of Gods long gone,
Nor dim and doubtful 'twixt the ocean's moan
Wail out about the Northern fiddle-bow,
Stammering with pride or quivering shrill with woe.
Rather caught up at hazard is the pipe
That mixed with scent of roses over ripe,
And murmur of the summer afternoon,
May charm you somewhat with its wavering tune

'Twixt joy and sadness: whatsoe'er it saith,
I know at least there breathes through it my breath

OF PHARAMOND THE FREED
Scene: In the Kings Chamber of Audience.
MASTER OLIVER and many LORDS and COUN-
CILLORS.

A COUNCILLOR
Fair Master Oliver, thou who at all times
Mayst open thy heart to our lord and master,
Tell us what tidings thou hast to deliver;
For our hearts are grown heavy, and where shall we turn
to
If thus the king's glory, our gain and salvation,
Must go down the wind amid gloom and despairing?

MASTER OLIVER
Little may be looked for, fair lords, in my story,
To lighten your hearts of the load lying on them.
For nine days the king hath slept not an hour,
And taketh no heed of soft words or beseeching.
Yea, look you, my lords, if a body late dead
In the lips and the cheeks should gain some little colour,
And arise and wend forth with no change in the eyes,
And wander about as if seeking its soul—
Lo, e'en so sad is my lord and my master;
Yea, e'en so far hath his soul drifted from us.

A COUNCILLOR
What say the leeches? Is all their skill left them?

MASTER OLIVER

Nay, they bade lead him to hunt and to tilting,
To set him on high in the throne of his honour
To judge heavy deeds: bade him handle the tiller,
And drive through the sea with the wind at its wildest;
All things he was wont to hold kingly and good.
So we led out his steed and he straight leapt upon him
With no word, and no looking to right nor to left,
And into the forest we fared as aforetime:
Fast on the king followed, and cheered without stinting
The hounds to the strife till the bear stood at bay;
Then there he alone by the beech-trees alighted;
Barehanded, unarmoured, he handled the spear-shaft,
And blew up the death on the horn of his father;
Yet still in his eyes was no look of rejoicing,
And no life in his lips; but I likened him rather
To King Nimrod carved fair on the back of the high-seat
When the candles are dying, and the high moon is
streaming
Through window and luffer white on the lone pavement
Whence the guests are departed in the hall of the pal-
ace.—
—Rode we home heavily, he with his rein loose,
Feet hanging free from the stirrups, and staring
At a clot of the bear's blood that stained his green kir-
tle;—
Unkingly, unhappy, he rode his ways homeward.

A COUNCILLOR

Was this all ye tried, or have ye more tidings?
For the wall tottereth not at first stroke of the ram.

MASTER OLIVER

Nay, we brought him a-board the Great Dragon one dawning,

When the cold bay was flecked with the crests of white billows

And the clouds lay alow on the earth and the sea;

He looked not aloft as they hoisted the sail,

But with hand on the tiller hallooed to the shipmen

In a voice grown so strange, that it scarce had seemed stranger

If from the ship Argo, in seemly wise woven

On the guard-chamber hangings, some early grey dawning

Great Jason had cried, and his golden locks wavered.

Then e'en as the oars ran outboard, and dashed

In the wind-scattered foam and the sails bellied out,

His hand dropped from the tiller, and with feet all uncertain

And dull eye he wended him down to the midship,

And gazing about for the place of the gangway

Made for the gate of the bulwark half open,

And stood there and stared at the swallowing sea,

Then turned, and uncertain went wandering back sternward,

And sat down on the deck by the side of the helmsman,

Wrapt in dreams of despair; so I bade them turn shoreward,

And slowly he rose as the side grated stoutly

'Gainst the stones of the quay and they cast forth the hawser.—

Unkingly, unhappy, he went his ways homeward.

A COUNCILLOR
But by other ways yet had thy wisdom to travel;
How else did ye work for the winning him peace?

MASTER OLIVER
We bade gather the knights for the goodliest tilting,
There the ladies went lightly in glorious array;
In the old arms we armed him whose dints well he knew
That the night dew had dulled and the sea salt had sul-
lied:
On the old roan yet sturdy we set him astride;
So he stretched forth his hand to lay hold of the spear
Neither laughing nor frowning, as lightly his wont was
When the knights are awaiting the voice of the trumpet.
It awoke, and back beaten from barrier to barrier
Was caught up by knights' cries, by the cry of the king.—
—Such a cry as red Mars in the Council-room window
May awake with some noon when the last horn is wind-
ed,
And the bones of the world are dashed grinding together.
So it seemed to my heart, and a horror came o'er me,
As the spears met, and splinters flew high o'er the field,
And I saw the king stay when his course was at swiftest,
His horse straining hard on the bit, and he standing
Stiff and stark in his stirrups, his spear held by the mid-
most,
His helm cast a-back, his teeth set hard together;
E'en as one might, who, riding to heaven, feels round him
The devils unseen: then he raised up the spear
As to cast it away, but therewith failed his fury,
He dropped it, and faintly sank back in the saddle,
And, turning his horse from the press and the turmoil,

Came sighing to me, and sore grieving I took him
And led him away, while the lists were fallen silent
As a fight in a dream that the light breaketh through.—
To the tune of the clinking of his fight-honoured armour
Unkingly, unhappy, he went his ways homeward.

A COUNCILLOR
What thing worse than the worst in the budget yet lieth?

MASTER OLIVER
To the high court we brought him, and bade him to hearken
The pleading of his people, and pass sentence on evil.
His face changed with great pain, and his brow grew all furrowed,
As a grim tale was told there of the griefs of the lowly;
Till he took up the word, mid the trembling of tyrants,
As his calm voice and cold wrought death on ill doers—
—E'en so might King Minos in marble there carven
Mid old dreaming of Crete give doom on the dead,
When the world and its deeds are dead too and buried.—
But lo, as I looked, his clenched hands were loosened,
His lips grew all soft, and his eyes were beholding
Strange things we beheld not about and above him.
So he sat for a while, and then swept his robe round him
And arose and departed, not heeding his people,
The strange looks, the peering, the rustle and whisper;
But or ever he gained the gate that gave streetward,
Dull were his eyes grown, his feet were grown heavy,
His lips crooned complaining, as onward he stumbled;—
Unhappy, unkingly, he went his ways homeward.

A COUNCILLOR
Is all striving over then, fair Master Oliver?

MASTER OLIVER
All mine, lords, for ever! help who may help henceforth
I am but helpless: too surely meseemeth
He seeth me not, and knoweth no more
Me that have loved him. Woe worth the while, Phara-
mond,
    That men should love aught, love always as I loved!
    Mother and sister and the sweetling that scorned me,
    The wind of the autumn-tide over them sweepeth,
    All are departed, but this one, the dear one—
    I should die or he died and be no more alone,
    But God's hatred hangs round me, and the life and the
glory
    That grew with my waning life fade now before it,
    And leaving no pity depart through the void.

A COUNCILLOR
This is a sight full sorry to see
These tears of an elder! But soft now, one cometh.

MASTER OLIVER
The feet of the king: will ye speak or begone?

A NORTHERN LORD
I will speak at the least, whoever keeps silence,
For well it may be that the voice of a stranger
Shall break through his dreaming better than thine;
And lo now a word in my mouth is a-coming,
That the king well may hearken: how sayst thou, fair

master,
    Whose name now I mind not, wilt thou have me essay it?

MASTER OLIVER

Try whatso thou wilt, things may not be worser. [Enter
KING.
    Behold, how he cometh weighed down by his woe!
(To the KING)
All hail, lord and master! wilt thou hearken a little
These lords high in honour whose hearts are full heavy
Because thy heart sickeneth and knoweth no joy?—
(To the COUNCILLORS)
Ah, see you! all silent, his eyes set and dreary,
His lips moving a little—how may I behold it?

THE NORTHERN LORD

May I speak, king? dost hearken? many matters I have
To deal with or death. I have honoured thee duly
Down in the north there; a great name I have held thee;
Rough hand in the field, ready righter of wrong,
Reckless of danger, but recking of pity.
But now—is it false what the chapmen have told us,
And are thy fair robes all thou hast of a king?
Is it bragging and lies, that thou beardless and tender
Weptst not when they brought thy slain father before
thee,
    Trembledst not when the leaguer that lay round thy city
Made a light for these windows, a noise for thy pillow?
Is it lies what men told us of thy singing and laughter
As thou layst in thy lair fled away from lost battle?
Is it lies how ye met in the depths of the mountains,
    And a handful rushed down and made nought of an

army?
Those tales of your luck, like the tide at its turning,
Trusty and sure howso slowly it cometh,
Are they lies? Is it lies of wide lands in the world,
How they sent thee great men to lie low at thy footstool
In five years thenceforward, and thou still a youth?
Are they lies, these fair tidings, or what see thy lords
here—
Some love-sick girl's brother caught up by that sickness,
As one street beggar catches the pest from his neigh-
bour?

KING PHARAMOND
What words are these of lies and love-sickness?
Why am I lonely among all this brawling?
O foster-father, is all faith departed
That this hateful face should be staring upon me?

THE NORTHERN LORD
Lo, now thou awakest; so tell me in what wise
I shall wend back again: set a word in my mouth
To meet the folks' murmur, and give heart to the heavy;
For there man speaks to man that thy measure is full,
And thy five-years-old kingdom is falling asunder.
[KING draws his sword.
Yea, yea, a fair token thy sword were to send them;
Thou dost well to draw it; (KING brandishes his sword
over the
lord's head, as if to strike him): soft sound is its whistle;
Strike then, O king, for my wars are well over,
And dull is the way my feet tread to the grave!

KING PHARAMOND (sheathing his sword)
Man, if ye have waked me, I bid you be wary
Lest my sword yet should reach you; ye wot in your
northland
What hatred he winneth who waketh the shipman
From the sweet rest of death mid the welter of waves;
So with us may it fare; though I know thee full faithful,
Bold in field and in council, most fit for a king.
—Bear with me. I pray you that to none may be meted
Such a measure of pain as my soul is oppressed with.
Depart all for a little, till my spirit grows lighter,
Then come ye with tidings, and hold we fair council,
That my countries may know they have yet got a king.
[Exeunt all but OLIVER and KING.
Come, my foster-father, ere thy visage fade from me,
Come with me mid the flowers some opening to find
In the clouds that cling round me; if thou canst remem-
ber
Thine old lovingkindness when I was a king.

THE MUSIC
LOVE IS ENOUGH; it grew up without heeding
In the days when ye knew not its name nor its measure
And its leaflets untrodden by the light feet of pleasure
Had no boast of the blossom, no sign of the seeding,
As the morning and evening passed over its treasure.

And what do ye say then?—that Spring long departed
Has brought forth no child to the softness and showers;
—That we slept and we dreamed through the Summer
of flowers;
We dreamed of the Winter, and waking dead-hearted

Found Winter upon us and waste of dull hours.

Nay, Spring was o'er happy and knew not the reason,
And Summer dreamed sadly, for she thought all was
ended
In her fulness of wealth that might not be amended;
But this is the harvest and the garnering season,
And the leaf and the blossom in the ripe fruit are blend-
ed.

It sprang without sowing, it grew without heeding,
Ye knew not its name and ye knew not its measure,
Ye noted it not mid your hope and your pleasure;
There was pain in its blossom, despair in its seeding,
But daylong your bosom now nurseth its treasure.

Enter before the curtain LOVE clad as an image-maker.

LOVE
How mighty and how fierce a king is here
The stayer of falling folks, the bane of fear!
Fair life he liveth, ruling passing well,
Disdaining praise of Heaven and hate of Hell;
And yet how goodly to us Great in Heaven
Are such as he, the waning world that leaven!
How well it were that such should never die!
How well it were at least that memory
Of such should live, as live their glorious deeds!
—But which of all the Gods think ye it needs
To shape the mist of Rumour's wavering breath
Into a golden dream that fears no death?

Red Mars belike?—since through his field is thrust
The polished plough-share o'er the helmets' rust!—
Apollo's beauty?—surely eld shall spare
Smooth skin, and flashing eyes, and crispy hair!—
Nay, Jove himself?—the pride that holds the low
Apart, despised, to mighty tales must grow!—
Or Pallas?—for the world that knoweth nought,
By that great wisdom to the wicket brought,
Clear through the tangle evermore shall see!
—O Faithful, O Beloved, turn to ME!
I am the Ancient of the Days that were
I am the Newborn that To-day brings here,
I am the Life of all that dieth not;
Through me alone is sorrow unforgot.

My Faithful, knowing that this man should live,
I from the cradle gifts to him did give
Unmeet belike for rulers of the earth;
As sorrowful yearning in the midst of mirth,
Pity midst anger, hope midst scorn and hate.
Languor midst labour, lest the day wax late,
And all be wrong, and all be to begin.
Through these indeed the eager life did win
That was the very body to my soul;
Yet, as the tide of battle back did roll
Before his patience: as he toiled and grieved
O'er fools and folly, was he not deceived,
But ever knew the change was drawing nigh,
And in my mirror gazed with steadfast eye.
Still, O my Faithful, seemed his life so fair
That all Olympus might have left him there
Until to bitter strength that life was grown,

And then have smiled to see him die alone,
Had I not been.—— Ye know me; I have sent
A pain to pierce his last coat of content:
Now must he tear the armour from his breast
And cast aside all things that men deem best,
And single-hearted for his longing strive
That he at last may save his soul alive.
How say ye then, Beloved? Ye have known
The blossom of the seed these hands have sown;
Shall this man starve in sorrow's thorny brake?
Shall Love the faithful of his heart forsake?

In the King's Garden.
KING PHARAMOND, MASTER OLIVER.

MASTER OLIVER
In this quiet place canst thou speak, O my King,
Where nought but the lilies may hearken our counsel?

KING PHARAMOND
What wouldst thou have of me? why came we hither?

MASTER OLIVER
Dear lord, thou wouldst speak of the woe that weighs on
thee.

KING PHARAMOND
Wouldst thou bear me aback to the strife and the battle?
Nay, hang up my banner: 'tis all passed and over!

MASTER OLIVER

Speak but a little, lord! have I not loved thee?

KING PHARAMOND
Yea,—thou art Oliver: I saw thee a-lying
A long time ago with the blood on thy face,
When my father wept o'er thee for thy faith and thy
valour.

MASTER OLIVER
Years have passed over, but my faith hath not failed me;
Spent is my might, but my love not departed.
Shall not love help—yea, look long in my eyes!
There is no more to see if thou sawest my heart.

KING PHARAMOND
Yea, thou art Oliver, full of all kindness!
Have patience, for now is the cloud passing over—
Have patience and hearken—yet shalt thou be shamed.

MASTER OLIVER
Thou shalt shine through thy shame as the sun through
the haze
When the world waiteth gladly the warm day a-coming:
As great as thou seem'st now, I know thee for greater
Than thy deeds done and told of: one day I shall know
thee:
Lying dead in my tomb I shall hear the world praising.

KING PHARAMOND
Stay thy praise—let me speak, lest all speech depart from
me.
—There is a place in the world, a great valley

That seems a green plain from the brow of the mountains,

But hath knolls and fair dales when adown there thou goest:

There are homesteads therein with gardens about them,

And fair herds of kine and grey sheep a-feeding,

And willow-hung streams wend through deep grassy meadows,

And a highway winds through them from the outer world coming:

Girthed about is the vale by a grey wall of mountains,

Rent apart in three places and tumbled together

In old times of the world when the earth-fires flowed forth:

And as you wend up these away from the valley

You think of the sea and the great world it washes;

But through two you may pass not, the shattered rocks shut them.

And up through the third there windeth a highway,

And its gorge is fulfilled by a black wood of yew-trees.

And I know that beyond, though mine eyes have not seen it,

A city of merchants beside the sea lieth.——

I adjure thee, my fosterer, by the hand of my father,

By thy faith without stain, by the days unforgotten,

When I dwelt in thy house ere the troubles' beginning,

By thy fair wife long dead and thy sword-smitten children,

By thy life without blame and thy love without blemish,

Tell me how, tell me when, that fair land I may come to!

Hide it not for my help, for my honour, but tell me,

Lest my time and thy time be lost days and confusion!

MASTER OLIVER

O many such lands!—O my master, what ails thee?
Tell me again, for I may not remember.
—I prayed God give thee speech, and lo God hath given
it—
May God give me death! if I dream not this evil.

KING PHARAMOND

Said I not when thou knew'st it, all courage should fail
thee?
But me—my heart fails not, I am Pharamond as ever.
I shall seek and shall find—come help me, my fosterer!
—Yet if thou shouldst ask for a sign from that country
What have I to show thee—I plucked a blue milk-wort
From amidst of the field where she wandered fair-foot-
ed—
It was gone when I wakened—and once in my wallet
I set some grey stones from the way through the forest—
These were gone when I wakened—and once as I wan-
dered
A lock of white wool from a thorn-bush I gathered;
It was gone when I wakened—the name of that coun-
try—
Nay, how should I know it?—but ever meseemeth
'Twas not in the southlands, for sharp in the sunset
And sunrise the air is, and whiles I have seen it
Amid white drift of snow—ah, look up, foster-father!

MASTER OLIVER

O woe, woe is me that I may not awaken!
Or else, art thou verily Pharamond my fosterling,

The Freed and the Freer, the Wise, the World's Wonder?

KING PHARAMOND

Why fainteth thy great heart? nay, Oliver, hearken,
E'en such as I am now these five years I have been.
Through five years of striving this dreamer and dotard
Has reaped glory from ruin, drawn peace from destruc-
tion.

MASTER OLIVER

Woe's me! wit hath failed me, and all the wise counsel
I was treasuring up down the wind is a-drifting—
Yet what wouldst thou have there if ever thou find it?
Are the gates of heaven there? is Death bound there and
helpless?

KING PHARAMOND

Nay, thou askest me this not as one without knowledge,
For thou know'st that my love in that land is abiding.

MASTER OLIVER

Yea—woe worth the while—and all wisdom hath failed
me:
    Yet if thou wouldst tell me of her, I will hearken
    Without mocking or mourning, if that may avail thee.

KING PHARAMOND

Lo, thy face is grown kind—Thou rememberest the even
    When I first wore the crown after sore strife and mourn-
ing?

MASTER OLIVER

Who shall ever forget it? the dead face of thy father,
And thou in thy fight-battered armour above it,
Mid the passion of tears long held back by the battle;
And thy rent banner o'er thee and the ring of men mail-
clad,
    Victorious to-day, since their ruin but a spear-length
Was thrust away from them.—Son, think of thy glory
And e'en in such wise break the throng of these devils!

KING PHARAMOND
Five years are passed over since in the fresh dawning
On the field of that fight I lay wearied and sleepless
Till slumber came o'er me in the first of the sunrise;
Then as there lay my body rapt away was my spirit,
And a cold and thick mist for a while was about me,
And when that cleared away, lo, the mountain-walled
country
    'Neath the first of the sunrise in e'en such a spring-tide
As the spring-tide our horse-hoofs that yestereve tram-
pled:
    By the withy-wrought gate of a garden I found me
    'Neath the goodly green boughs of the apple full-blos-
somed;
    And fulfilled of great pleasure I was as I entered
The fair place of flowers, and wherefore I knew not.
Then lo, mid the birds' song a woman's voice singing.
Five years passed away, in the first of the sunrise.
[He is silent, brooding.

MASTER OLIVER
God help us if God is!—for this man, I deemed him
More a glory of God made man for our helping

Than a man that should die: all the deeds he did surely,
Too great for a man's life, have undone the doer.

KING PHARAMOND (rousing himself)
Thou art waiting, my fosterer, till I tell of her singing
And the words that she sang there: time was when I
knew them;
But too much of strife is about us this morning,
And whiles I forget and whiles I remember.
[Falls a-musing again.

MASTER OLIVER
But a night's dream undid him, and he died, and his
kingdom
By unheard-of deeds fashioned, was tumbled together,
By false men and fools to be fought for and ruined.
Such words shall my ghost see the chronicler writing
In the days that shall be:—ah—what wouldst thou, my
fosterling?
Knowest thou not how words fail us awaking
That we seemed to hear plain amid sleep and its sweet-
ness?
Nay, strive not, my son, rest awhile and be silent;
Or sleep while I watch thee: full fair is the garden,
Perchance mid the flowers thy sweet dream may find
thee,
And thou shalt have pleasure and peace for a little.—
(Aside) And my soul shall depart ere thou wak'st perad-
venture.

KING PHARAMOND
Yea, thou deemest me mad: a dream thou mayst call it,

But not such a dream as thou know'st of: nay, hearken!
For what manner of dream then is this that remembers
The words that she sang on that morning of glory;—
O love, set a word in my mouth for our meeting;
Cast thy sweet arms about me to stay my hearts beating!
Ah, thy silence, thy silence! nought shines on the dark-
ness!
   —O close-serried throng of the days that I see not!
[Falls a-musing again.

MASTER OLIVER
Thus the worse that shall be, the bad that is, bettereth.
—Once more he is speechless mid evil dreams sunken.

KING PHARAMOND (speaking very low).
Hold silence, love, speak not of the sweet day departed;
Cling close to me, love, lest I waken sad-hearted!
[Louder to OLIVER.
Thou starest, my fosterer: what strange thing beholdst
thou?
   A great king, a strong man, that thou knewest a child
once:
   Pharamond the fair babe: Pharamond the warrior;
Pharamond the king, and which hast thou feared yet?
And why wilt thou fear then this Pharamond the lover?
Shall I fail of my love who failed not of my fame?
Nay, nay, I shall live for the last gain and greatest.

MASTER OLIVER
I know not—all counsel and wit is departed,
I wait for thy will; I will do it, my master.

KING PHARAMOND

Through the boughs of the garden I followed the singing
To a smooth space of sward: there the unknown desire
Of my soul I beheld,—wrought in shape of a woman.

MASTER OLIVER

O ye warders of Troy-walls, join hands through the darkness,
Tell us tales of the Downfall, for we too are with you!

KING PHARAMOND

As my twin sister, young of years was she and slender,
Yellow blossoms of spring-tide her hands had been gathering,
But the gown-lap that held them had fallen adown
And had lain round her feet with the first of the singing;
Now her singing had ceased, though yet heaved her bosom
As with lips lightly parted and eyes of one seeking
She stood face to face with the Love that she knew not,
The love that she longed for and waited unwitting;
She moved not, I breathed not—till lo, a horn winded,
And she started, and o'er her came trouble and wonder,
Came pallor and trembling; came a strain at my heart-strings
As bodiless there I stretched hands toward her beauty,
And voiceless cried out, as the cold mist swept o'er me.
Then again clash of arms, and the morning watch calling,
And the long leaves and great twisted trunks of the chesnuts,
As I sprang to my feet and turned round to the trumpets
And gathering of spears and unfolding of banners

That first morn of my reign and my glory's beginning.

MASTER OLIVER

O well were we that tide though the world was against us.

KING PHARAMOND

Hearken yet!—through that whirlwind of danger and battle,
Beaten back, struggling forward, we fought without blemish
On my banner spear-rent in the days of my father,
On my love of the land and the longing I cherished
For a tale to be told when I, laid in the minster,
Might hear it no more; was it easy of winning,
Our bread of those days? Yet as wild as the work was,
Unforgotten and sweet in my heart was that vision,
And her eyes and her lips and her fair body's fashion
Blest all times of rest, rent the battle asunder,
Turned ruin to laughter and death unto dreaming;
And again and thrice over again did I go there
Ere spring was grown winter: in the meadows I met her,
By the sheaves of the corn, by the down-falling apples,
Kind and calm, yea and glad, yet with eyes of one seeking.
—Ah the mouth of one waiting, ere all shall be over!—
But at last in the winter-tide mid the dark forest
Side by side did we wend down the pass: the wind tangled
Mid the trunks and black boughs made wild music about us,
But her feet on the scant snow and the sound of her breathing

550

Made music much better: the wood thinned, and I saw
her,
 As we came to the brow of the pass; for the moon gleamed
 Bitter cold in the cloudless black sky of the winter.
 Then the world drew me back from my love, and depart-
ing
 I saw her sweet serious look pass into terror
 And her arms cast abroad—and lo, clashing of armour,
 And a sword in my hand, and my mouth crying loud,
 And the moon and cold steel in the doorway burst open
 And thy doughty spear thrust through the throat of the
foeman
 My dazed eyes scarce saw—thou rememberest, my fos-
terer?

MASTER OLIVER

Yea, Theobald the Constable had watched but unduly;
 We were taken unwares, and wild fleeing there was
 O'er black rock and white snow—shall such times come
again, son?

KING PHARAMOND

Yea, full surely they shall; have thou courage, my foster-
er!—
 Day came thronging on day, month thrust month aside,
 Amid battle and strife and the murder of glory,
 And still oft and oft to that land was I led
 And still through all longing I young in Love's dealings,
 Never called it a pain: though, the battle passed over,
 The council determined, back again came my craving:
 I knew not the pain, but I knew all the pleasure,
 When now, as the clouds o'er my fortune were parting,

551

I felt myself waxing in might and in wisdom;
And no city welcomed the Freed and the Freer,
And no mighty army fell back before rumour
Of Pharamond's coming, but her heart bid me thither,
And the blithest and kindest of kingfolk ye knew me.
Then came the high tide of deliverance upon us,
When surely if we in the red field had fallen
The stocks and the stones would have risen to avenge us.
—Then waned my sweet vision midst glory's fulfilment,
And still with its waning, hot waxed my desire:
And did ye not note then that the glad-hearted Phara-
mond
Was grown a stern man, a fierce king, it may be?
Did ye deem it the growth of my manhood, the harden-
ing
Of battle and murder and treason about me?
Nay, nay, it was love's pain, first named and first noted
When a long time went past, and I might not behold her.
—Thou rememberest a year agone now, when the legate
Of the Lord of the Waters brought here a broad letter
Full of prayers for good peace and our friendship thence-
forward—
—He who erst set a price on the lost head of Phara-
mond—
How I bade him stand up on his feet and be merry,
Eat his meat by my side and drink out of my beaker,
In memory of days when my meat was but little
And my drink drunk in haste between saddle and straw.
But lo! midst of my triumph, as I noted the feigning
Of the last foeman humbled, and the hall fell a murmur-
ing,
And blithely the horns blew, Be glad, spring prevaileth,

—As I sat there and changed not, my soul saw a vision:
All folk faded away, and my love that I long for
Came with raiment a-rustling along the hall pavement,
Drawing near to the high-seat, with hands held out a
little,
Till her hallowed eyes drew me a space into heaven,
And her lips moved to whisper, 'Come, love, for I weary!'
Then she turned and went from me, and I heard her feet
falling
On the floor of the hall, e'en as though it were empty
Of all folk but us twain in the hush of the dawning.
Then again, all was gone, and I sat there a smiling
On the faint-smiling legate, as the hall windows quivered
With the rain of the early night sweeping across them.
Nought slept I that night, yet I saw her without sleep-
ing:—
Betwixt midnight and morn of that summer-tide was I
Amidst of the lilies by her house-door to hearken
If perchance in her chamber she turned amid sleeping:
When lo, as the East 'gan to change, and stars faded
Were her feet on the stairs, and the door opened softly,
And she stood on the threshold with the eyes of one
seeking,
And there, gathering the folds of her gown to her girdle,
Went forth through the garden and followed the high-
way,
All along the green valley, and I ever beside her,
Till the light of the low sun just risen was falling
On her feet in the first of the pass—and all faded.
Yet from her unto me had gone forth her intent,
And I saw her face set to the heart of that city,
And the quays where the ships of the outlanders come to,

And I said: She is seeking, and shall I not seek?
The sea is her prison wall; where is my prison?
—Yet I said: Here men praise me, perchance men may love me
If I live long enough for my justice and mercy
To make them just and merciful—one who is master
Of many poor folk, a man pity moveth
Love hath dealt with in this wise, no minstrel nor dreamer.
The deeds that my hand might find for the doing
Did desire undo them these four years of fight?
And now time and fair peace in my heart have begotten
More desire and more pain, is the day of deeds done with?
Lo here for my part my bonds and my prison!—
Then with hands holding praise, yet with fierce heart belike
Did I turn to the people that I had delivered—
And the deeds of this year passed shall live peradventure!
But now came no solace of dreams in the night-tide
From that day thenceforward; yet oft in the council,
Mid the hearkening folk craving for justice or mercy,
Mid the righting of wrongs and the staying of ruin,
Mid the ruling a dull folk, who deemed all my kingship
A thing due and easy as the dawning and sunset
To the day that God made once to deal with no further—
—Mid all these a fair face, a sad face, could I fashion,
And I said, She is seeking, and shall I not seek?
—Tell over the days of the year of hope's waning;
Tell over the hours of the weary days wearing:
Tell over the minutes of the hours of thy waking,
Then wonder he liveth who fails of his longing!

MASTER OLIVER
What wouldst thou have, son, wherein I might help thee?

KING PHARAMOND
Hearken yet:—for a long time no more I beheld her
Till a month agone now at the ending of Maytide;
And then in the first of the morning I found me
Fulfilled of all joy at the edge of the yew-wood;
Then lo, her gown's flutter in the fresh breeze of morning,
And slower and statelier than her wont was aforetime
And fairer of form toward the yew-wood she wended.
But woe's me! as she came and at last was beside me
With sobbing scarce ended her bosom was heaving,
Stained with tears was her face, and her mouth was yet
quivering
With torment of weeping held back for a season.
Then swiftly my spirit to the King's bed was wafted
While still toward the sea were her weary feet wending.
—Ah surely that day of all wrongs that I hearkened
Mine own wrongs seemed heaviest and hardest to bear—
Mine own wrongs and hers—till that past year of ruling
Seemed a crime and a folly. Night came, and I saw her
Stealing barefoot, bareheaded amidst of the tulips
Made grey by the moonlight: and a long time Love gave
me
To gaze on her weeping—morn came, and I wakened—
I wakened and said: Through the World will I wander,
Till either I find her, or find the World empty.

MASTER OLIVER
Yea, son, wilt thou go? Ah thou knowest from of old time

My words might not stay thee from aught thou wert
willing;
 And e'en so it must be now. And yet hast thou asked me
 To go with thee, son, if aught I might help thee?—
 Ah me, if thy face might gladden a little
 I should meet the world better and mock at its mocking:
 If thou goest to find her, why then hath there fallen
 This heaviness on thee? is thy heart waxen feeble?

KING PHARAMOND
 O friend, I have seen her no more, and her mourning
 Is alone and unhelped—yet to-night or to-morrow
 Somewhat nigher will I be to her love and her longing.
 Lo, to thee, friend, alone of all folk on the earth
 These things have I told: for a true man I deem thee
 Beyond all men call true; yea, a wise man moreover
 And hardy and helpful; and I know thy heart surely
 That thou holdest the world nought without me thy fos-
terling.
 Come, leave all awhile! it may be as time weareth
 With new life in our hands we shall wend us back hither.

MASTER OLIVER
 Yea; triumph turns trouble, and all the world changeth,
 Yet a good world it is since we twain are together.

KING PHARAMOND
 Lo, have I not said it?—thou art kinder than all men.
 Cast about then, I pray thee, to find us a keel
 Sailing who recketh whither, since the world is so wide.
 Sure the northlands shall know of the blessings she brin-
geth,

And the southlands be singing of the tales that foretold
her.

MASTER OLIVER

Well I wot of all chapmen—and to-night weighs a dro-
mond

Sailing west away first, and then to the southlands.

Since in such things I deal oft they know me, but know
not

King Pharamond the Freed, since now first they sail
hither.

So make me thy messenger in a fair-writ broad letter

And thyself make my scrivener, and this very night sail
we.—

O surely thy face now is brightening and blesseth me!

Peer through these boughs toward the bay and the haven,

And high masts thou shalt see, and white sails hanging
ready.

[Exit OLIVER.

KING PHARAMOND

Dost thou weep now, my darling, and are thy feet wan-
dering

On the ways ever empty of what thou desirest?

Nay, nay, for thou know'st me, and many a night-tide

Hath Love led thee forth to a city unknown:

Thou hast paced through this palace from chamber to
chamber

Till in dawn and stars' paling I have passed forth before
thee:

Thou hast seen thine own dwelling nor known how to
name it:

Thine own dwelling that shall be when love is victorious.
Thou hast seen my sword glimmer amidst of the moon-
light,
As we rode with hoofs muffled through waylaying mur-
der.
Through the field of the dead hast thou fared to behold
me,
Seen me waking and longing by the watch-fires' flicker;
Thou hast followed my banner amidst of the battle
And seen my face change to the man that they fear,
Yet found me not fearful nor turned from beholding:
Thou hast been at my triumphs, and heard the tale's end-
ing
Of my wars, and my winning through days evil and wea-
ry:
For this eve hast thou waited, and wilt be peradventure
By the sea-strand to-night, for thou wottest full surely
That the word is gone forth, and the world is a-moving.
—Abide me, beloved! to-day and to-morrow
Shall be little words in the tale of our loving,
When the last morn ariseth, and thou and I meeting
From lips laid together tell tales of these marvels.

THE MUSIC
LOVE IS ENOUGH: draw near and behold me
Ye who pass by the way to your rest and your laughter,
And are full of the hope of the dawn coming after;
For the strong of the world have bought me and sold me
And my house is all wasted from threshold to rafter.
—Pass by me, and hearken, and think of me not!

Cry out and come near; for my ears may not hearken,

And my eyes are grown dim as the eyes of the dying.
Is this the grey rack o'er the sun's face a-flying?
Or is it your faces his brightness that darken?
Comes a wind from the sea, or is it your sighing?
—Pass by me, and hearken, and pity me not!

Ye know not how void is your hope and your living:
Depart with your helping lest yet ye undo me!
Ye know not that at nightfall she draweth near to me,
There is soft speech between us and words of forgiving
Till in dead of the midnight her kisses thrill through me.
—Pass by me, and hearken, and waken me not!

Wherewith will ye buy it, ye rich who behold me?
Draw out from your coffers your rest and your laughter,
And the fair gilded hope of the dawn coming after!
Nay this I sell not,—though ye bought me and sold me,—
For your house stored with such things from threshold to rafter.
—Pass by me, I hearken, and think of you not!

Enter before the curtain LOVE clad as a maker of Pictured Cloths.

LOVE
That double life my faithful king has led
My hand has untwined, and old days are dead
As in the moon the sails run up the mast.
Yea, let this present mingle with the past,
And when ye see him next think a long tide

559

Of days are gone by; for the world is wide,
And if at last these hands, these lips shall meet,
What matter thorny ways and weary feet?
A faithful king, and now grown wise in love:
Yet from of old in many ways I move
The hearts that shall be mine: him by the hand
Have I led forth, and shown his eyes the land
Where dwells his love, and shown him what she is:
He has beheld the lips that he shall kiss,
The eyes his eyes shall soften, and the cheek
His voice shall change, the limbs he maketh weak:
—All this he hath as in a picture wrought—
But lo you, 'tis the seeker and the sought:
For her no marvels of the night I make,
Nor keep my dream-smiths' drowsy heads awake;
Only about her have I shed a glory
Whereby she waiteth trembling for a story
That she shall play in,—and 'tis not begun:
Therefore from rising sun to setting sun
There flit before her half-formed images
Of what I am, and in all things she sees
Something of mine: so single is her heart
Filled with the worship of one set apart
To be my priestess through all joy and sorrow;
So sad and sweet she waits the certain morrow.
—And yet sometimes, although her heart be strong,
You may well think I tarry over-long:
The lonely sweetness of desire grows pain,
The reverent life of longing void and vain:
Then are my dream-smiths mindful of my lore:
They weave a web of sighs and weeping sore,
Of languor, and of very helplessness,

Of restless wandering, lonely dumb distress,
Till like a live thing there she stands and goes,
Gazing at Pharamond through all her woes.
Then forth they fly, and spread the picture out
Before his eyes, and how then may he doubt
She knows his life, his deeds, and his desire?
How shall he tremble lest her heart should tire?
—It is not so; his danger and his war,
His days of triumph, and his years of care,
She knows them not—yet shall she know some day
The love that in his lonely longing lay.
What, Faithful—do I lie, that overshot
My dream-web is with that which happeneth not?
Nay, nay, believe it not!—love lies alone
In loving hearts like fire within the stone:
Then strikes my hand, and lo, the flax ablaze!
—Those tales of empty striving, and lost days
Folk tell of sometimes—never lit my fire
Such ruin as this; but Pride and Vain-desire,
My counterfeits and foes, have done the deed.
Beware, beloved! for they sow the weed
Where I the wheat: they meddle where I leave,
Take what I scorn, cast by what I receive,
Sunder my yoke, yoke that I would dissever,
Pull down the house my hands would build for ever.

Scene: In a Forest among the Hills of a Foreign Land.
KING PHARAMOND, MASTER OLIVER.

KING PHARAMOND
Stretch forth thine hand, foster-father, I know thee,
And fain would be sure I am yet in the world:

Where am I now, and what things have befallen?
Why am I so weary, and yet have wrought nothing?

MASTER OLIVER
Thou hast been sick, lord, but thy sickness abateth.

KING PHARAMOND
Thou art sad unto weeping: sorry rags are thy raiment,
For I see thee a little now: where am I lying?

MASTER OLIVER
On the sere leaves thou liest, lord, deep in the wild wood

KING PHARAMOND
What meaneth all this? was I not Pharamond,
A worker of great deeds after my father,
Freer of my land from murder and wrong,
Fain of folks' love, and no blencher in battle?

MASTER OLIVER
Yea, thou wert king and the kindest under heaven.

KING PHARAMOND
Was there not coming a Queen long desired,
From a land over sea, my life to fulfil?

MASTER OLIVER
Belike it was so—but thou leftst it untold of.

KING PHARAMOND
Why weepest thou more yet? O me, which are dreams,
Which are deeds of my life mid the things I remember?

MASTER OLIVER
Dost thou remember the great council chamber,
O my king, and the lords there gathered together
With drawn anxious faces one fair morning of summer,
    And myself in their midst, who would move thee to
speech?

KING PHARAMOND
A brawl I remember, some wordy debating,
Whether my love should be brought to behold me.
Sick was I at heart, little patience I had.

MASTER OLIVER
Hast thou memory yet left thee, how an hour thereafter
We twain lay together in the midst of the pleasance
'Neath the lime-trees, nigh the pear-tree, beholding the
conduit?

KING PHARAMOND
Fair things I remember of a long time thereafter—
Of thy love and thy faith and our gladness together

MASTER OLIVER
    And the thing that we talked of, wilt thou tell me about
it?

KING PHARAMOND
We twain were to wend through the wide world together
Seeking my love—O my heart! is she living?

MASTER OLIVER

God wot that she liveth as she hath lived ever.

KING PHARAMOND

Then soon was it midnight, and moonset, as we wended
Down to the ship, and the merchant-folks' babble.
The oily green waves in the harbour mouth glistened,
Windless midnight it was, but the great sweeps were run
out,
As the cable came rattling mid rich bales on the deck,
And slow moved the black side that the ripple was lap-
ping,
And I looked and beheld a great city behind us
By the last of the moon as the stars were a-brightening,
And Pharamond the Freed grew a tale of a singer,
With the land of his fathers and the fame he had toiled
for.
Yet sweet was the scent of the sea-breeze arising;
And I felt a chain broken, a sickness put from me
As the sails drew, and merchant-folk, gathered together
On the poop or the prow, 'gan to move and begone,
Till at last 'neath the far-gazing eyes of the steersman
By the loitering watch thou and I were left lonely,
And we saw by the moon the white horses arising
Where beyond the last headland the ocean abode us,
Then came the fresh breeze and the sweep of the spray,
And the beating of ropes, and the empty sails' thunder,
As we shifted our course toward the west in the dawning;
Then I slept and I dreamed in the dark I was lying,
And I heard her sweet breath and her feet falling near
me,
And the rustle of her raiment as she sought through the
darkness,

Sought, I knew not for what, till her arms clung about
me
With a cry that was hers, that was mine as I wakened.

MASTER OLIVER
Yea, a sweet dream it was, as thy dreams were aforetime.

KING PHARAMOND
Nay not so, my fosterer: thy hope yet shall fail thee
If thou lookest to see me turned back from my folly,
Lamenting and mocking the life of my longing.
Many such have I had, dear dreams and deceitful,
When the soul slept a little from all but its search,
And lied to the body of bliss beyond telling;
Yea, waking had lied still but for life and its torment.
Not so were those dreams of the days of my kingship,
Slept my body—or died—but my soul was not sleeping,
It knew that she touched not this body that trembled
At the thought of her body sore trembling to see me;
It lied of no bliss as desire swept it onward,
Who knows through what sundering space of its prison;
It saw, and it heard, and it hoped, and was lonely,
Had no doubt and no joy, but the hope that endureth.
—Woe's me I am weary: wend we forward to-morrow?

MASTER OLIVER
Yea, well it may be if thou wilt but be patient,
And rest thee a little, while time creepeth onward.

KING PHARAMOND
But tell me, has the fourth year gone far mid my sickness?

MASTER OLIVER

Nay, for seven days only didst thou lie here a-dying,
As full often I deemed: God be thanked it is over!
But rest thee a little, lord; gather strength for the striving.

KING PHARAMOND

Yea, for once again sleep meseems cometh to struggle
With the memory of times past: come tell thou, my fos-
terer,
Of the days we have fared through, that dimly before me
Are floating, as I look on thy face and its trouble.

MASTER OLIVER

Rememberest thou aught of the lands where we wended?

KING PHARAMOND

Yea, many a thing—as the moonlit warm evening
When we stayed by the trees in the Gold-bearing Land,
Nigh the gate of the city, where a minstrel was singing
That tale of the King and his fate, o'er the cradle
Foretold by the wise of the world; that a woman
Should win him to love and to woe, and despairing
In the last of his youth, the first days of his manhood.

MASTER OLIVER

I remember the evening; but clean gone is the story:
Amid deeds great and dreadful, should songs abide by
me?

KING PHARAMOND

They shut the young king in a castle, the tale saith,
Where never came woman, and never should come,

And sadly he grew up and stored with all wisdom,
Not wishing for aught in his heart that he had not,
Till the time was come round to his twentieth birthday.
Then many fair gifts brought his people unto him,
Gold and gems, and rich cloths, and rare things and dear-bought,
And a book fairly written brought a wise man among them,
Called the Praising of Prudence; wherein there was painted
The image of Prudence:—and that, what but a woman,
E'en she forsooth that the painter found fairest;—
Now surely thou mindest what needs must come after?

MASTER OLIVER

Yea, somewhat indeed I remember the misery
Told in that tale, but all mingled it is
With the manifold trouble that met us full often,
E'en we ourselves. Of nought else hast thou memory?

KING PHARAMOND

Of many such tales that the Southland folk told us,
Of many a dream by the sunlight and moonlight;
Of music that moved me, of hopes that my heart had;
The high days when my love and I held feast together.
—But what land is this, and how came we hither?

MASTER OLIVER

Nay, hast thou no memory of our troubles that were many?
How thou criedst out for Death and how near Death came to thee?

How thou needs must dread war, thou the dreadful in
battle?
Of the pest in the place where that tale was told to us;
And how we fled thence o'er the desert of horror?
How weary we wandered when we came to the moun-
tains,
All dead but one man of those who went with us?
How we came to the sea of the west, and the city,
Whose Queen would have kept thee her slave and her
lover,
And how we escaped by the fair woman's kindness,
Who loved thee, and cast her life by for thy welfare?
Of the waste of thy life when we sailed from the South-
lands,
And the sea-thieves fell on us and sold us for servants
To that land of hard gems, where thy life's purchase
seemed
Little better than mine, and we found to our sorrow
Whence came the crown's glitter, thy sign once of glory:
Then naked a king toiled in sharp rocky crannies,
And thy world's fear was grown but the task-master's
whip,
And thy world's hope the dream in the short dead of
night?
And hast thou forgotten how again we fled from it,
And that fight of despair in the boat on the river,
And the sea-strand again and white bellying sails;
And the sore drought and famine that on ship-board fell
on us,
Ere the sea was o'erpast, and we came scarcely living
To those keepers of sheep, the poor folk and the kind?
Dost thou mind not the merchants who brought us

thence northward,
> And this land that we made in the twilight of dawning?
> And the city herein where all kindness forsook us,
> And our bitter bread sought we from house-door to
house-door.

KING PHARAMOND

As the shadow of clouds o'er the summer sea sailing
Is the memory of all now, and whiles I remember
And whiles I forget; and nought it availeth
Remembering, forgetting; for a sleep is upon me
That shall last a long while:—there thou liest, my fosterer,
As thou lay'st a while since ere that twilight of dawning;
And I woke and looked forth, and the dark sea, long
changeless,
> Was now at last barred by a dim wall that swallowed
> The red shapeless moon, and the whole sea was rolling,
> Unresting, unvaried, as grey as the void is,
> Toward that wall 'gainst the heavens as though rest were
behind it.
> Still onward we fared and the moon was forgotten,
> And colder the sea grew and colder the heavens,
> And blacker the wall grew, and grey, green-besprinkled,
> And the sky seemed to breach it; and lo at the last
> Many islands of mountains, and a city amongst them.
> White clouds of the dawn, not moving yet waning,
> Wreathed the high peaks about; and the sea beat for ever
> 'Gainst the green sloping hills and the black rocks and
beachless.
> —Is this the same land that I saw in that dawning?
> For sure if it is thou at least shalt hear tidings,
> Though I die ere the dark: but for thee, O my fosterer,

Lying there by my side, I had deemed the old vision
Had drawn forth the soul from my body to see her.
And with joy and fear blended leapt the heart in my bo-
som,
And I cried, "The last land, love; O hast thou abided?"
But since then hath been turmoil, and sickness, and
slumber,
And my soul hath been troubled with dreams that I
knew not.
And such tangle is round me life fails me to rend it,
And the cold cloud of death rolleth onward to hide me.—
—O well am I hidden, who might not be happy!
I see not, I hear not, my head groweth heavy.
[Falls back as if sleeping.

MASTER OLIVER
—O Son, is it sleep that upon thee is fallen?
Not death, O my dear one!—speak yet but a little!

KING PHARAMOND (raising himself again)
O be glad, foster-father! and those troubles past over,—
Be thou thereby when once more I remember
And sit with my maiden and tell her the story,
And we pity our past selves as a poet may pity
The poor folk he tells of amid plentiful weeping.
Hush now! as faint noise of bells over water
A sweet sound floats towards me, and blesses my slum-
ber:
If I wake never more I shall dream and shall see her.
[Sleeps.

MASTER OLIVER

Is it swooning or sleeping? in what wise shall he waken?
—Nay, no sound I hear save the forest wind wailing.
Who shall help us to-day save our yoke-fellow Death?
Yet fain would I die mid the sun and the flowers;
For a tomb seems this yew-wood ere yet we are dead.
And its wailing wind chilleth my yearning for time past,
And my love groweth cold in this dusk of the daytime.
What will be? is worse than death drawing anear us?
Flit past, dreary day! come, night-tide and resting!
Come, to-morrow's uprising with light and new tidings!
—Lo, Lord, I have borne all with no bright love before
me;
Wilt thou break all I had and then give me no blessing?

THE MUSIC
LOVE IS ENOUGH: through the trouble and tangle
From yesterdays dawning to yesterday's night
I sought through the vales where the prisoned winds
wrangle,
Till, wearied and bleeding, at end of the light
I met him, and we wrestled, and great was my might.

O great was my joy, though no rest was around me,
Though mid wastes of the world were we twain all alone,
For methought that I conquered and he knelt and he
crowned me,
And the driving rain ceased, and the wind ceased to
moan,
And through clefts of the clouds her planet outshone.

O through clefts of the clouds 'gan the world to awaken,
And the bitter wind piped, and down drifted the rain,

And I was alone—and yet not forsaken,
For the grass was untrodden except by my pain:
With a Shadow of the Night had I wrestled in vain.

And the Shadow of the Night and not Love was depart-
ed;
I was sore, I was weary, yet Love lived to seek;
So I scaled the dark mountains, and wandered sad-heart-
ed
Over wearier wastes, where e'en sunlight was bleak,
With no rest of the night for my soul waxen weak.

With no rest of the night; for I waked mid a story
Of a land wherein Love is the light and the lord,
Where my tale shall be heard, and my wounds gain a
glory,
And my tears be a treasure to add to the hoard
Of pleasure laid up for his people's reward.

Ah, pleasure laid up! haste thou onward and listen,
For the wind of the waste has no music like this,
And not thus do the rocks of the wilderness glisten:
With the host of his faithful through sorrow and bliss
My Lord goeth forth now, and knows me for his.

Enter before the curtain LOVE, with a cup of bitter
drink and his hands bloody.

LOVE
O Pharamond, I knew thee brave and strong,
And yet how might'st thou live to bear this wrong?

—A wandering-tide of three long bitter years,
Solaced at whiles by languor of soft tears,
By dreams self-wrought of night and sleep and sorrow,
Holpen by hope of tears to be to-morrow:
Yet all, alas, but wavering memories;
No vision of her hands, her lips, her eyes,
Has blessed him since he seemed to see her weep,
No wandering feet of hers beset his sleep.
Woe's me then! am I cruel, or am I grown
The scourge of Fate, lest men forget to moan?
What!—is there blood upon these hands of mine?
Is venomed anguish mingled with my wine?
—Blood there may be, and venom in the cup;
But see, Beloved, how the tears well up
From my grieved heart my blinded eyes to grieve,
And in the kindness of old days believe!
So after all then we must weep to-day—
—We, who behold at ending of the way,
These lovers tread a bower they may not miss
Whose door my servant keepeth, Earthly Bliss:
There in a little while shall they abide,
Nor each from each their wounds of wandering hide,
But kiss them, each on each, and find it sweet,
That wounded so the world they may not meet.
—Ah, truly mine! since this your tears may move,
The very sweetness of rewarded love!
Ah, truly mine, that tremble as ye hear
The speech of loving lips grown close and dear;
—Lest other sounds from other doors ye hearken,
Doors that the wings of Earthly Anguish darken.

Scene: On a Highway in a Valley near the last, with a

Mist over all things.
   KING PHARAMOND, MASTER OLIVER.

KING PHARAMOND
Hold a while, Oliver! my limbs are grown weaker
Than when in the wood I first rose to my feet.
There was hope in my heart then, and now nought but
sickness;
There was sight in my eyes then, and now nought but
blindness.
   Good art thou, hope, while the life yet tormenteth,
   But a better help now have I gained than thy goading.
   Farewell, O life, wherein once I was merry!
   O dream of the world, I depart now, and leave thee
   A little tale added to thy long-drawn-out story.
   Cruel wert thou, O Love, yet have thou and I conquered.
   —Come nearer, O fosterer, come nearer and kiss me,
   Bid farewell to thy fosterling while the life yet is in me,
   For this farewell to thee is my last word meseemeth.
   [He lies down and sleeps.

MASTER OLIVER
O my king, O my son! Ah, woe's me for my kindness,
For the day when thou drew'st me and I let thee be drawn
Into toils I knew deadly, into death thou desiredst!
And woe's me that I die not! for my body made hardy
By the battles of old days to bear every anguish!
   —Speak a word and forgive me, for who knows how long
yet
   Are the days of my life, and the hours of my loathing!
   He speaks not, he moves not; yet he draweth breath soft-
ly:

574

I have seen men a-dying, and not thus did the end come.
Surely God who made all forgets not love's rewarding,
Forgets not the faithful, the guileless who fear not.
Oh, might there be help yet, and some new life's begin-
ning!
—Lo, lighter the mist grows: there come sounds through
its dulness,
The lowing of kine, or the whoop of a shepherd,
The bell-wether's tinkle, or clatter of horse-hoofs.
A homestead is nigh us: I will fare down the highway
And seek for some helping: folk said simple people
Abode in this valley, and these may avail us—
If aught it avail us to live for a little.
—Yea, give it us, God!—all the fame and the glory
We fought for and gained once; the life of well-doing,
Fair deed thrusting on deed, and no day forgotten;
And due worship of folk that his great heart had hol-
pen;—
All I prayed for him once now no longer I pray for.
Let it all pass away as my warm breath now passeth
In the chill of the morning mist wherewith thou hidest
Fair vale and grey mountain of the land we are come to!
Let it all pass away! but some peace and some pleasure
I pray for him yet, and that I may behold it.
A prayer little and lowly,—and we in the old time
When the world lay before us, were we hard to the lowly?
Thou know'st we were kind, howso hard to be beaten;
Wilt thou help us this last time? or what hast thou hid-
den
We know not, we name not, some crown for our striving?
—O body and soul of my son, may God keep thee!
For, as lone as thou liest in a land that we see not

When the world loseth thee, what is left for its losing?
[Exit OLIVER.

THE MUSIC
LOVE IS ENOUGH: cherish life that abideth,
    Lest ye die ere ye know him, and curse and misname
him;
        For who knows in what ruin of all hope he hideth,
        On what wings of the terror of darkness he rideth?
        And what is the joy of man's life that ye blame him
        For his bliss grown a sword, and his rest grown a fire?

    Ye who tremble for death, or the death of desire,
    Pass about the cold winter-tide garden and ponder
    On the rose in his glory amidst of June's fire,
    On the languor of noontide that gathered the thunder,
    On the morn and its freshness, the eve and its wonder;
    Ye may wake it no more—shall Spring come to awaken?

    Live on, for Love liveth, and earth shall be shaken
    By the wind of his wings on the triumphing morning,
    When the dead, and their deeds that die not shall awak-
en,
    And the world's tale shall sound in your trumpet of
warning,
    And the sun smite the banner called Scorn of the Scorn-
ing,
    And dead pain ye shall trample, dead fruitless desire,
    As ye wend to pluck out the new world from the fire.

Enter before the curtain, LOVE clad as a Pilgrim.

LOVE

Alone, afar from home doth Pharamond lie,
Drawn near to death, ye deem—or what draws nigh?
Afar from home—and have ye any deeming
How far may be that country of his dreaming?
Is it not time, is it not time, say ye,
That we the day-star in the sky should see?
Patience, Beloved; these may come to live
A life fulfilled of all I have to give,
But bare of strife and story; and ye know well
How wild a tale of him might be to tell
Had I not snatched away the sword and crown;
Yea, and she too was made for world's renown,
And should have won it, had my bow not been;
These that I love were very king and queen;
I have discrowned them, shall I not crown too?
Ye know, Beloved, what sharp bitter dew,
What parching torment of unresting day
Falls on the garden of my deathless bay:
Hands that have gathered it and feet that came
Beneath its shadow have known flint and flame;
Therefore I love them; and they love no less
Each furlong of the road of past distress.
—Ah, Faithful, tell me for what rest and peace,
What length of happy days and world's increase,
What hate of wailing, and what love of laughter,
What hope and fear of worlds to be hereafter,
Would ye cast by that crown of bitter leaves?
And yet, ye say, our very heart it grieves
To see him lying there: how may he save
His life and love if he more pain must have?

And she—how fares it with her? is not earth
From winter's sorrow unto summer's mirth
Grown all too narrow for her yearning heart?
We pray thee, Love, keep these no more apart.
Ye say but sooth: not long may he endure:
And her heart sickeneth past all help or cure
Unless I hasten to the helping—see,
Am I not girt for going speedily?
—The journey lies before me long?—nay, nay,
Upon my feet the dust is lying grey,
The staff is heavy in my hand.—Ye too,
Have ye not slept? or what is this ye do,
Wearying to find the country ye are in?
[The curtain draws up and
shows the same scene
as the last, with the mist clearing, and
PHARAMOND lying there as before.
Look, look! how sun and morn at last do win
Upon the shifting waves of mist! behold
That mountain-wall the earth-fires rent of old,
Grey toward the valley, sun-gilt at the side!
See the black yew-wood that the pass doth hide!
Search through the mist for knoll, and fruited tree,
And winding stream, and highway white—and see,
See, at my feet lies Pharamond the Freed!
A happy journey have we gone indeed!
Hearken, Beloved, over-long, ye deem,
I let these lovers deal with hope and dream
Alone unholpen.—Somewhat sooth ye say:
But now her feet are on this very way
That leadeth from the city: and she saith
One beckoneth her back hitherward—even Death—

And who was that, Beloved, but even I?
Yet though her feet and sunlight are drawn nigh
The cold grass where he lieth like the dead,
To ease your hearts a little of their dread
I will abide her coming, and in speech
He knoweth, somewhat of his welfare teach.

LOVE goes on to the Stage and stands at PHARA-
MOND's head.

LOVE
HEARKEN, O Pharamond, why camest thou hither?

KING PHARAMOND
I came seeking Death; I have found him belike.

LOVE
In what land of the world art thou lying, O Pharamond?

KING PHARAMOND
In a land 'twixt two worlds: nor long shall I dwell there.

LOVE
Who am I, Pharamond, that stand here beside thee?

KING PHARAMOND
The Death I have sought—thou art welcome; I greet
thee.

LOVE
Such a name have I had, but another name have I.

KING PHARAMOND
Art thou God then that helps not until the last season?

LOVE
Yea, God am I surely: yet another name have I.

KING PHARAMOND
Methinks as I hearken, thy voice I should wot of.

LOVE
I called thee, and thou cam'st from thy glory and king-
ship.

KING PHARAMOND
I was King Pharamond, and love overcame me.

LOVE
Pharamond, thou say'st it.—I am Love and thy master.

KING PHARAMOND
Sooth didst thou say when thou call'dst thyself Death.

LOVE
Though thou diest, yet thy love and thy deeds shall I
quicken.

KING PHARAMOND
Be thou God, be thou Death, yet I love thee and dread
not.

LOVE
Pharamond, while thou livedst what thing wert thou lov-

ing?

KING PHARAMOND
A dream and a lie—and my death—and I love it.

LOVE
Pharamond, do my bidding, as thy wont was aforetime.

KING PHARAMOND
What wilt thou have of me, for I wend away swiftly?

LOVE
Open thine eyes, and behold where thou liest!

KING PHARAMOND
It is little—the old dream, the old lie is about me.

LOVE
Why faintest thou, Pharamond? is love then unworthy?

KING PHARAMOND
Then hath God made no world now, nor shall make hereafter.

LOVE
Wouldst thou live if thou mightst in this fair world, O Pharamond?

KING PHARAMOND
Yea, if she and truth were; nay, if she and truth were not.

LOVE

O long shalt thou live: thou art here in the body,
Where nought but thy spirit I brought in days bygone.
Ah, thou hearkenest!—and where then of old hast thou heard it?
[Music outside, far off.

KING PHARAMOND
O mock me not, Death; or, Life, hold me no longer!
For that sweet strain I hear that I heard once a-dreaming:
Is it death coming nigher, or life come back that brings it?
Or rather my dream come again as aforetime?

LOVE
Look up, O Pharamond! canst thou see aught about thee?

KING PHARAMOND
Yea, surely: all things as aforetime I saw them:
The mist fading out with the first of the sunlight,
And the mountains a-changing as oft in my dreaming,
And the thornbrake anigh blossomed thick with the May-tide.
[Music again.
O my heart!—I am hearkening thee whereso thou wanderest!

LOVE
Put forth thine hand, feel the dew on the daisies!

KING PHARAMOND
So their freshness I felt in the days ere hope perished.

—O me, me, my darling! how fair the world groweth!
Ah, shall I not find thee, if death yet should linger,
Else why grow I so glad now when life seems departing?
What pleasure thus pierceth my heart unto fainting?
—O me, into words now thy melody passeth.

MUSIC with singing (from without)
Dawn talks to-day
Over dew-gleaming flowers,
Night flies away
Till the resting of hours:
Fresh are thy feet
And with dreams thine eyes glistening.
Thy still lips are sweet
Though the world is a-listening.
O Love, set a word in my mouth for our meeting,
Cast thine arms round about me to stay my heart's beat-
ing!
O fresh day, O fair day, O long day made ours!

LOVE
What wilt thou say now of the gifts Love hath given?

KING PHARAMOND
Stay thy whispering, O wind of the morning—she spea-
keth.

THE MUSIC (coming nearer)
Morn shall meet noon
While the flower-stems yet move,
Though the wind dieth soon

And the clouds fade above.
Loved lips are thine
As I tremble and hearken;
Bright thine eyes shine,
Though the leaves thy brow darken.
O Love, kiss me into silence, lest no word avail me,
Stay my head with thy bosom lest breath and life fail me!
O sweet day, O rich day, made long for our love!

LOVE
Was Love then a liar who fashioned thy dreaming?

KING PHARAMOND
O fair-blossomed tree, stay thy rustling—I hearken.

THE MUSIC (coming nearer)
Late day shall greet eve,
And the full blossoms shake,
For the wind will not leave
The tall trees while they wake.
Eyes soft with bliss,
Come nigher and nigher!
Sweet mouth I kiss,
Tell me all thy desire!
Let us speak, love, together some words of our story,
That our lips as they part may remember the glory!
O soft day, O calm day, made clear for our sake!

LOVE
What wouldst thou, Pharamond? why art thou fainting?

KING PHARAMOND

And thou diest, fair daylight, now she draweth near me!

THE MUSIC (close outside)
Eve shall kiss night,
And the leaves stir like rain
As the wind stealeth light
O'er the grass of the plain.
Unseen are thine eyes
Mid the dreamy night's sleeping,
And on my mouth there lies
The dear rain of thy weeping.
Hold, silence, love, speak not of the sweet day departed,
Cling close to me, love, lest I waken sad-hearted!
O kind day, O dear day, short day, come again!

LOVE
Sleep then, O Pharamond, till her kiss shall awake thee,
For, lo, here comes the sun o'er the tops of the mountains,
And she with his light in her hair comes before him,
As solemn and fair as the dawn of the May-tide
On some isle of mid-ocean when all winds are sleeping.
O worthy is she of this hour that awaits her,
And the death of all doubt, and beginning of gladness
Her great heart shall embrace without fear or amaze-
ment.
　—He sleeps, yet his heart's beating measures her foot-
falls;
　And her heart beateth too, as her feet bear her onward:
　Breathe gently between them, O breeze of the morning!
　Wind round them unthought of, sweet scent of the blos-
soms!
　Treasure up every minute of this tide of their meeting,

O flower-bedecked Earth! with such tales of my triumph
Is your life still renewed, and spring comes back for ever
From that forge of all glory that brought forth my bless-
ing.
O welcome, Love's darling: Shall this day ever darken,
Whose dawn I have dight for thy longing triumphant?
[Exit LOVE. Enter AZALAIS.

AZALAIS
A song in my mouth, then? my heart full of gladness?
My feet firm on the earth, as when youth was beginning?
And the rest of my early days come back to bless me?—
Who hath brought me these gifts in the midst of the
May-tide?
What!—three days agone to the city I wandered,
And watched the ships warped to the Quay of the Mer-
chants;
And wondered why folk should be busy and anxious;
For bitter my heart was, and life seemed a-waning,
With no story told, with sweet longing turned torment,
Love turned to abasement, and rest gone for ever.
And last night I awoke with a pain piercing through me,
And a cry in my ears, and Death passed on before,
As one pointing the way, and I rose up sore trembling,
And by cloud and by night went before the sun's coming,
As one goeth to death,—and lo here the dawning!
And a dawning therewith of a dear joy I know not.
I have given back the day the glad greeting it gave me;
And the gladness it gave me, that too would I give
Were hands held out to crave it——Fair valley, I greet
thee,
And the new-wakened voices of all things familiar.

586

—Behold, how the mist-bow lies bright on the moun-
tain,

Bidding hope as of old since no prison endureth.

Full busy has May been these days I have missed her,

And the milkwort is blooming, and blue falls the speed-
well.

—Lo, here have been footsteps in the first of the morn-
ing,

Since the moon sank all red in the mist now departed.

—Ah! what lieth there by the side of the highway?

Is it death stains the sunlight, or sorrow or sickness?

[Going up to PHARAMOND.

—Not death, for he sleepeth; but beauty sore blemished

By sorrow and sickness, and for all that the sweeter.

I will wait till he wakens and gaze on his beauty,

Lest I never again in the world should behold him.

—Maybe I may help him; he is sick and needs tending,

He is poor, and shall scorn not our simpleness surely.

Whence came he to us-ward—what like has his life
been—

Who spoke to him last—for what is he longing?

—As one hearkening a story I wonder what cometh,

And in what wise my voice to our homestead shall bid
him.

O heart, how thou faintest with hope of the gladness

I may have for a little if there he abide.

Soft there shalt thou sleep, love, and sweet shall thy
dreams be,

And sweet thy awaking amidst of the wonder

Where thou art, who is nigh thee—and then, when thou
seest

How the rose-boughs hang in o'er the little loft window,

And the blue bowl with roses is close to thine hand,
And over thy bed is the quilt sewn with lilies,
And the loft is hung round with the green Southland hangings,
And all smelleth sweet as the low door is opened,
And thou turnest to see me there standing, and holding
Such dainties as may be, thy new hunger to stay—
Then well may I hope that thou wilt not remember
Thine old woes for a moment in the freshness and pleasure,
And that I shall be part of thy rest for a little.
And then—-who shall say—wilt thou tell me thy story,
And what thou hast loved, and for what thou hast striven?
—Thou shalt see me, and my love and my pity, as thou speakest,
And it may be thy pity shall mingle with mine.
—And meanwhile—Ah, love, what hope may my heart hold?
For I see that thou lovest, who ne'er hast beheld me.
And how should thy love change, howe'er the world changeth?
Yet meanwhile, had I dreamed of the bliss of this minute,
How might I have borne to live weary and waiting!
Woe's me! do I fear thee? else should I not wake thee,
For tending thou needest—If my hand touched thy hand
[Touching him.
I should fear thee the less.—O sweet friend, forgive it,
My hand and my tears, for faintly they touched thee!
He trembleth, and waketh not: O me, my darling!
Hope whispers that thou hear'st me through sleep, and wouldst waken,

But for dread that thou dreamest and I should be gone.
Doth it please thee in dreaming that I tremble and dread
thee,
 That these tears are the tears of one praying vainly,
 Who shall pray with no word when thou hast awakened?
 —Yet how shall I deal with my life if he love not,
 As how should he love me, a stranger, unheard of?
 —O bear witness, thou day that hast brought my love
hither!
Thou sun that burst out through the mist o'er the moun-
tains,
 In that moment mine eyes met the field of his sorrow—
 Bear witness, ye fields that have fed me and clothed me,
 And air I have breathed, and earth that hast borne me—
 Though I find you but shadows, and wrought but for fad-
ing,
 Though all ye and God fail me,—my love shall not fail!
 Yea, even if this love, that seemeth such pleasure
 As earth is unworthy of, turneth to pain;
 If he wake without memory of me and my weeping,
 With a name on his lips not mine—that I know not:
 If thus my hand leave his hand for the last time,
 And no word from his lips be kind for my comfort—
 If all speech fail between us, all sight fail me henceforth,
 If all hope and God fail me—my love shall not fail.
 —Friend, I may not forbear: we have been here together:
 My hand on thy hand has been laid, and thou trembledst.
 Think now if this May sky should darken above us,
 And the death of the world in this minute should part
us—
 Think, my love, of the loss if my lips had not kissed thee.
 And forgive me my hunger of no hope begotten! [She

kisses him.

KING PHARAMOND (awaking)
Who art thou? who art thou, that my dream I might tell
thee?
How with words full of love she drew near me, and kissed
me.
O thou kissest me yet, and thou clingest about me!
Ah, kiss me and wake me into death and deliverance!

AZALAIS (drawing away from him)
Speak no rough word, I pray thee, for a little, thou love-
liest!
But forgive me, for the years of my life have been lonely,
And thou art come hither with the eyes of one seeking.

KING PHARAMOND
Sweet dream of old days, and her very lips speaking
The words of my lips and the night season's longing.
How might I have lived had I known what I longed for!

AZALAIS
I knew thou wouldst love, I knew all thy desire—
Am I she whom thou seekest? may I draw nigh again?

KING PHARAMOND
Ah, lengthen no more the years of my seeking,
For thou knowest my love as thy love lies before me.

AZALAIS (coming near to him again)
O Love, there was fear in thine eyes as thou wakenedst;
Thy first words were of dreaming and death—but we die

not.

KING PHARAMOND

In thine eyes was a terror as thy lips' touches faded,
Sore trembled thine arms as they fell away from me;
And thy voice was grown piteous with words of beseech-
ing,
    So that still for a little my search seemed unended.
—Ah, enending, unchanging desire fulfils me!
I cry out for thy comfort as thou clingest about me.
O joy hard to bear, but for memory of sorrow,
But for pity of past days whose bitter is sweet now!
Let us speak, love, together some word of our story,
That our lips as they part may remember the glory.

AZALAIS

O Love, kiss me into silence lest no word avail me;
Stay my head with thy bosom lest breath and life fail me.

THE MUSIC

LOVE IS ENOUGH: while ye deemed him a-sleeping,
There were signs of his coming and sounds of his feet;
His touch it was that would bring you to weeping,
When the summer was deepest and music most sweet:
In his footsteps ye followed the day to its dying,
Ye went forth by his gown-skirts the morning to meet:
In his place on the beaten-down orchard-grass lying,
Of the sweet ways ye pondered yet left for life's trying.

Ah, what was all dreaming of pleasure anear you,
To the time when his eyes on your wistful eyes turned,
And ye saw his lips move, and his head bend to hear you,

As new-born and glad to his kindness ye yearned?
Ah, what was all dreaming of anguish and sorrow,
To the time when the world in his torment was burned,
And no god your heart from its prison might borrow,
And no rest was left, no to-day, no to-morrow?

All wonder of pleasure, all doubt of desire,
All blindness, are ended, and no more ye feel
If your feet tread his flowers or the flames of his fire,
If your breast meet his balms or the edge of his steel.
Change is come, and past over, no more strife, no more
learning:
Now your lips and your forehead are sealed with his seal,
Look backward and smile at the thorns and the burning.
—Sweet rest, O my soul, and no fear of returning!

Enter before the curtain LOVE, clad still as a Pilgrim.

LOVE
How is it with the Fosterer then, when he
Comes back again that rest and peace to see,
And God his latest prayer has granted now?—
Why, as the winds whereso they list shall blow,
So drifts the thought of man, and who shall say
To-morrow shall my thought be as to-day?
—My fosterling is happy, and I too;
Yet did we leave behind things good to do,
Deeds good to tell about when we are dead.
Here is no pain, but rest, and easy bread;
Yet therewith something hard to understand
Dulls the crowned work to which I set my hand.
Ah, patience yet! his longing is well won,

And I shall die at last and all be done.—
Such words unspoken the best man on earth
Still bears about betwixt the lover's mirth;
And now he hath what he went forth to find,
This Pharamond is neither dull nor blind,
And looking upon Oliver, he saith:—
My friend recked nothing of his life or death,
Knew not my anguish then, nor now my pleasure,
And by my crowned joy sets his lessened treasure.
Is risk of twenty days of wind and sea,
Of new-born feeble headless enmity,
I should have scorned once, too great gift to give
To this most faithful man that he may live?
—Yea, was that all? my faithful, you and I,
Still craving, scorn the world too utterly,
The world we want not—yet, our one desire
Fulfilled at last, what next shall feed the fire?
—I say not this to make my altar cold;
Rather that ye, my happy ones, should hold
Enough of memory and enough of fear
Within your hearts to keep its flame full clear;
Rather that ye, still dearer to my heart,
Whom words call hapless, yet should praise your part,
Wherein the morning and the evening sun
Are bright about a story never done;
That those for chastening, these for joy should cling
About the marvels that my minstrels sing.
Well, Pharamond fulfilled of love must turn
Unto the folk that still he deemed would yearn
To see his face, and hear his voice once more;
And he was mindful of the days passed o'er,
And fain had linked them to these days of love;

And he perchance was fain the world to move
While love looked on; and he perchance was fain
Some pleasure of the strife of old to gain.
Easy withal it seemed to him to land,
And by his empty throne awhile to stand
Amid the wonder, and then sit him down
While folk went forth to seek the hidden crown.
Or else his name upon the same wind borne
As smote the world with winding of his horn,
His hood pulled back, his banner flung abroad,
A gleam of sunshine on his half-drawn sword.
—Well, he and you and I have little skill
To know the secret of Fate's worldly will;
Yet can I guess, and you belike may guess,
Yea, and e'en he mid all his lordliness,
That much may be forgot in three years' space
Outside my kingdom.—Gone his godlike face,
His calm voice, and his kindness, half akin
Amid a blind folk to rebuke of sin,
Men 'gin to think that he was great and good,
But hindered them from doing as they would,
And ere they have much time to think on it
Between their teeth another has the bit,
And forth they run with Force and Fate behind.
—Indeed his sword might somewhat heal the blind,
Were I not, and the softness I have given;
With me for him have hope and glory striven
In other days when my tale was beginning;
But sweet life lay beyond then for the winning,
And now what sweetness?—blood of men to spill
Who once believed him God to heal their ill:
To break the gate and storm adown the street

Where once his coming flower-crowned girls did greet:
To deem the cry come from amidst his folk
When his own country tongue should curse his stroke—
Nay, he shall leave to better men or worse
His people's conquered homage and their curse.
So forth they go, his Oliver and he,
One thing at least to learn across the sea,
That whatso needless shadows life may borrow
Love is enough amidst of joy or sorrow.
Love is enough—My Faithful, in your eyes
I see the thought, Our Lord is overwise
Some minutes past in what concerns him not,
And us no more: is all his tale forgot?
—Ah, Well-beloved, I fell asleep e'en now,
And in my sleep some enemy did show
Sad ghosts of bitter things, and names unknown
For things I know—a maze with shame bestrown
And ruin and death; till e'en myself did seem
A wandering curse amidst a hopeless dream.
—Yet see! I live, no older than of old,
What tales soe'er of changing Time has told.
And ye who cling to all my hand shall give,
Sorrow or joy, no less than I shall live.

Scene: Before KING PHARAMOND'S Palace.

KING PHARAMOND
A long time it seems since this morn when I met them,
The men of my household and the great man they hon-
our:
Better counsel in king-choosing might I have given
Had ye bided my coming back hither, my people:

595

And yet who shall say or foretell what Fate meaneth?
For that man there, the stranger, Honorius men called
him,
    I account him the soul to King Theobald's body,
    And the twain are one king; and a goodly king may be
    For this people, who grasping at peace and good days,
    Careth little who giveth them that which they long for.
    Yet what gifts have I given them; I who this even
    Turn away with grim face from the fight that should try
me?
    It is just then, I have lost: lie down, thou supplanter,
    In thy tomb in the minster when thy life is well over,
    And the well-carven image of latten laid o'er thee
    Shall live on as thou livedst, and be worthy the praising
    Whereby folk shall remember the days of thy plenty.
    Praising Theobald the Good and the peace that he
brought them,
    But I—I shall live too, though no graven image
    On the grass of the hillside shall brave the storms' beat-
ing;
    Though through days of thy plenty the people remember
    As a dim time of war the past days of King Pharamond;
    Yet belike as time weareth, and folk turn back a little
    To the darkness where dreams lie and live on for ever,
    Even there shall be Pharamond who failed not in battle,
    But feared to overcome his folk who forgot him,
    And turned back and left them a tale for the telling,
    A song for the singing, that yet in some battle
    May grow to remembrance and rend through the ruin
    As my sword rent it through in the days gone for ever.
    So, like Enoch of old, I was not, for God took me.
    —But lo, here is Oliver, all draws to an ending—

[Enter OLIVER.
Well met, my Oliver! the clocks strike the due minute,
What news hast thou got?—thou art moody of visage.

MASTER OLIVER
In one word, 'tis battle; the days we begun with
Must begin once again with the world waxen baser.

KING PHARAMOND
Ah! battle it may be: but surely no river
Runneth back to its springing: so the world has grown
wiser
And Theobald the Constable is king in our stead,
And contenteth the folk who cried, "Save us, King Pha-
ramond!"

MASTER OLIVER
Hast thou heard of his councillor men call Honorius?
Folk hold him in fear, and in love the tale hath it.

KING PHARAMOND
Much of him have I heard: nay, more, I have seen him
With the men of my household, and the great man they
honour.
They were faring afield to some hunt or disporting,
Few faces were missing, and many I saw there
I was fain of in days past at fray or at feasting;
My heart yearned towards them—but what—days have
changed them,
They must wend as they must down the way they are
driven.

MASTER OLIVER
Yet e'en in these days there remaineth a remnant
That is faithful and fears not the flap of thy banner.

KING PHARAMOND
And a fair crown is faith, as thou knowest, my father;
Fails the world, yet that faileth not; love hath begot it,
Sweet life and contentment at last springeth from it;
No helping these need whose hearts still are with me,
Nay, rather they handle the gold rod of my kingdom.

MASTER OLIVER
Yet if thou leadest forth once more as aforetime
In faith of great deeds will I follow thee, Pharamond,
And thy latter end yet shall be counted more glorious
Than thy glorious beginning; and great shall my gain be
If e'en I must die ere the day of thy triumph.

KING PHARAMOND
Dear is thy heart mid the best and the brightest,
Yet not against these my famed blade will I bare.

MASTER OLIVER
Nay, what hast thou heard of their babble and baseness?

KING PHARAMOND
Full enough, friend—content thee, my lips shall not
speak it,
    The same hour wherein they have said that I love thee.
    Suffice it, folk need me no more: the deliverance,
    Dear bought in the days past, their hearts have forgotten,
    But faintly their dim eyes a feared face remember,

Their dull ears remember a stern voice they hated.
What then, shall I waken their fear and their hatred,
And then wait till fresh terror their memory awaketh,
With the semblance of love that they have not to give
me?
Nay, nay, they are safe from my help and my justice,
And I—I am freed, and fresh waxeth my manhood.

MASTER OLIVER
It may not be otherwise since thou wilt have it,
Yet I say it again, if thou shake out thy banner,
Some brave men will be borne unto earth peradventure,
Many dastards go trembling to meet their due doom,
And then shall come fair days and glory upon me
And on all men on earth for thy fame, O King Phara-
mond.

KING PHARAMOND
Yea, I was king once; the songs sung o'er my cradle,
Were ballads of battle and deeds of my fathers:
Yea, I was King Pharamond; in no carpeted court-room
Bore they the corpse of my father before me;
But on grass trodden grey by the hoofs of the war-steeds
Did I kneel to his white lips and sword-cloven bosom,
As from clutch of dead fingers his notched sword I
caught;
For a furlong before us the spear-wood was glistening.
I was king of this city when here where we stand now
Amidst a grim silence I mustered all men folk
Who might yet bear a weapon; and no brawl of kings
was it
That brought war on the city, and silenced the markets

And cumbered the haven with crowd of masts sailless,
But great countries arisen for our ruin and downfall.
I was king of the land, when on all roads were riding
The legates of proud princes to pray help and give service—
Yea, I was a great king at last as I sat there,
Peace spread far about me, and the love of all people
To my palace gates wafted by each wind of the heavens.
—And where sought I all this? with what price did I buy it?
Nay, for thou knowest that this fair fame and fortune
Came stealing soft-footed to give their gifts to me:
And shall I, who was king once, grow griping and weary
In unclosing the clenched fists of niggards who hold them,
These gifts that I had once, and, having, scarce heeded?
Nay, one thing I have sought, I have sought and have found it,
And thou, friend, hast helped me and seest me made happy.

MASTER OLIVER
Farewell then the last time, O land of my fathers!
Farewell, feeble hopes that I once held so mighty.
Yet no more have I need of but this word that thou sayest,
And nought have I to do but to serve thee, my master.
In what land of the world shall we dwell now henceforward?

KING PHARAMOND
In the land where my love our returning abideth,
The poor land and kingless of the shepherding people,

There is peace there, and all things this land are unlike to.

MASTER OLIVER
Before the light waneth will I seek for a passage,
Since for thee and for me the land groweth perilous:
Yea, o'er sweet smell the flowers, too familiar the folk
seem,
    Fain I grow of the salt seas, since all things are over here.

KING PHARAMOND
I am fain of one hour's farewell in the twilight,
To the times I lament not: times worser than these times,
To the times that I blame not, that brought on times
better—
    Let us meet in our hostel—be brave mid thy kindness,
Let thy heart say, as mine saith, that fair life awaits us.

MASTER OLIVER
Yea, no look in thy face is of ruin, O my master;
Thou art king yet, unchanged yet, nor is my heart chang-
ing;
    The world hath no chances to conquer thy glory.
    [Exit OLIVER

KING PHARAMOND
Full fair were the world if such faith were remembered.
If such love as thy love had its due, O my fosterer.
Forgive me that giftless from me thou departest,
With thy gifts in my hands left. I might not but take
them;
    Thou wilt not begrudge me, I will not forget thee.—
    —Long fall the shadows and night draws on apace now,

Day sighs as she sinketh back on to her pillow,
And her last waking breath is full sweet with the rose.
—In such wise depart thou, O daylight of life,
Loved once for the shadows that told of the dreamtide;
Loved still for the longing whereby I remember
That I was lone once in the world of thy making;
Lone wandering about on thy blind way's confusion,
The maze of thy paths that yet led me to love.
All is passed now, and passionless, faint are ye waxen,
Ye hours of blind seeking full of pain clean forgotten.
If it were not that e'en now her eyes I behold not.
That the way lieth long to her feet that would find me,
That the green seas delay yet her fair arms enfolding,
That the long leagues of air will not bear the cry hither
Wherewith she is crying. Come, love, for I love thee.
[A trumpet sounds.
Hark! O days grown a dream of the dream ye have won me,
Do ye draw forth the ghosts of old deeds that were nothing,
That the sound of my trumpet floats down on the even?
What shows will ye give me to grace my departure?
Hark!—the beat of the horse-hoofs, the murmur of men folk!
Am I riding from battle amidst of my faithful,
Wild hopes in my heart of the days that are coming;
Wild longing unsatisfied clinging about me;
Full of faith that the summer sun elsewhere is ripening
The fruit grown a pain for my parched lips to think of?
—Come back, thou poor Pharamond! come back for my pity!
Far afield must thou fare before the rest cometh;

In far lands are they raising the walls of thy prison,
Forging wiles for waylaying, and fair lies for lulling,
The faith and the fire of the heart the world hateth.
In thy way wax streams fordless, and choked passes path-
less,
Fever lurks in the valley, and plague passeth over
The sand of the plain, and with venom and fury
Fulfilled are the woods that thou needs must wend
through:
In the hollow of the mountains the wind is a-storing
Till the keel that shall carry thee hoisteth her sail;
War is crouching unseen round the lands thou shalt
come to,
With thy sword cast away and thy cunning forgotten.
Yea, and e'en the great lord, the great Love of thy fealty,
He who goadeth thee on, weaveth nets to cast o'er thee.
—And thou knowest it all, as thou ridest there lonely,
With the tangles and toils of to-morrow's uprising
Making ready meanwhile for more days of thy kingship.
Faithful heart hadst thou, Pharamond, to hold fast thy
treasure!
I am fain of thee: surely no shame hath destained thee;
Come hither, for thy face all unkissed would I look on!
—Stand we close, for here cometh King Theobald from
the hunting.
Enter KING THEOBALD, HONORIUS, and the
people.

KING THEOBALD
A fair day, my folk, have I had in your fellowship,
And as fair a day cometh to-morrow to greet us,
When the lord of the Golden Land bringeth us tribute:

Grace the gifts of my good-hap with your presence, I
pray you.

THE PEOPLE
God save Theobald the Good, the king of his people!

HONORIUS (aside)
Yea, save him! and send the Gold lords away satisfied,
That the old sword of Pharamond, lying asleep there
In the new golden scabbard, will yet bite as aforetime!
[They pass away into the palace court.

KING PHARAMOND
Troop past in the twilight, O pageant that served me,
Pour through the dark archway to the light that awaits
you
In the chamber of daïs where I once sat among you!
Like the shadows ye are to the shadowless glory
Of the banquet-hall blazing with gold and light go ye:
There blink for a little at your king in his bravery,
Then bear forth your faith to the blackness of night-tide,
And fall asleep fearless of memories of Pharamond,
And in dim dreams dream haply that ye too are kings
—For your dull morrow cometh that is as to-day is.
Pass on in contentment, O king, I discerned not
Through the cloak of your blindness that saw nought be-
side thee,
That feared for no pain and craved for no pleasure!
Pass on, dead-alive, to thy place! thou art worthy:
Nor shalt thou grow wearier than well-worshipped idol
That the incense winds round in the land of the heathen,
While the early and latter rains fall as God listeth,

And on earth that God loveth the sun riseth daily.
—Well art thou: for wert thou the crown of all rulers,
No field shouldst thou ripen, free no frost-bounden river,
Loose no heart from its love, turn no soul to salvation,
Thrust no tempest aside, stay no plague in mid ocean,
Yet grow unto thinking that thou wert God's brother,
Till loveless death gripped thee unloved, unlamented.
—Pass forth, weary King, bear thy crown high to-night!
Then fall asleep, fearing no cry from times bygone,
But in dim dreams dream haply that thou art desired,—
—For thy dull morrow cometh, and is as to-day is.
Ah, hold! now there flashes a link in the archway,
And its light falleth full on thy face, O Honorius,
And I know thee the land's lord, and far away fadeth
My old life of a king at the sight, O thou stranger!
For I know thee full surely the foe the heart hateth
For that barren fulfilment of all that it lacketh.
I may turn away praising that those days long departed
Departed without thee—how long had I piped then
Or e'er thou hadst danced, how long were my weeping
Ere thou hadst lamented!—What dear thing desired
Would thy heart e'er have come to know why I craved
for!
To what crime I could think of couldst thou be consent-
ing?
Yet thou—well I know thee most meet for a ruler—
—Thou lovest not mercy, yet shalt thou be merciful;
Thou joy'st not in justice, yet just shall thy dooms be;
No deep hell thou dreadest, nor dream'st of high heaven;
No gleam of love leads thee: no gift men may give thee;
For no kiss, for no comfort the lone way thou wearest,
A blind will without life, lest thou faint ere the end come.

—Yea, folly it was when I called thee my foeman;
From thee may I turn now with sword in the scabbard
Without shame or misgiving, because God hath made thee
A ruler for manfolk: pass on then unpitied!
There is darkness between us till the measure's fulfilment.
Amidst singing thou hear'st not, fair sights that thou seest not,
Think this eve on the deeds thou shalt set in men's hands
To bring fair days about for which thou hast no blessing.
Then fall asleep fearless of dead days that return not;
Yet dream if thou may'st that thou yet hast a hope!
—For thy dull morrow cometh and is as to-day is.
O sweet wind of the night, wherewith now ariseth
The red moon through the garden boughs frail, overladen,
O faint murmuring tongue of the dream-tide triumphant,
That wouldst tell me sad tales in the times long passed over,
If somewhat I sicken and turn to your freshness,
From no shame it is of earth's tangle and trouble,
And deeds done for nought, and change that forgetteth;
But for hope of the lips that I kissed on the sea-strand,
But for hope of the hands that clung trembling about me,—
And the breast that was heaving with words driven backward,
By longing I longed for, by pain of departing,
By my eyes that knew her pain, my pain that might speak not—
Yea, for hope of the morn when the sea is passed over,

And for hope of the next moon the elm-boughs shall tangle;

And fresh dawn, and fresh noon, and fresh night of desire
Still following and changing, with nothing forgotten;
For hope of new wonder each morn, when I, waking
Behold her awaking eyes turning to seek me;
For hope of fresh marvels each time the world changing
Shall show her feet moving in noontide to meet me;
For hope of fresh bliss, past all words, half forgotten,
When her voice shall break through the hushed blackness of night.

—O sweet wind of the summer-tide, broad moon a-whitening,

Bear me witness to Love, and the world he has fashioned!

It shall change, we shall change, as through rain and through sunshine

The green rod of the rose-bough to blossoming changeth:

Still lieth in wait with his sweet tale untold of
Each long year of Love, and the first scarce beginneth,
Wherein I have hearkened to the word God hath whispered,
Why the fair world was fashioned mid wonders uncounted.

Breathe soft, O sweet wind, for surely she speaketh:
Weary I wax, and my life is a-waning;
Life lapseth fast, and I faint for thee, Pharamond,
What are thou lacking if Love no more sufficeth?
—Weary not, sweet, as I weary to meet thee;
Look not on the long way but my eyes that were weeping
Faint not in love as thy Pharamond fainteth!—
—Yea, Love were enough if thy lips were not lacking.

THE MUSIC

LOVE IS ENOUGH: ho ye who seek saving,
Go no further; come hither; there have been who have
found it,
And these know the House of Fulfilment of Craving;
These know the Cup with the roses around it;
These know the World's Wound and the balm that hath
bound it:
Cry out, the World heedeth not, "Love, lead us home!"

He leadeth, He hearkeneth, He cometh to you-ward;
Set your faces as steel to the fears that assemble
Round his goad for the faint, and his scourge for the fro-
ward:
Lo his lips, how with tales of last kisses they tremble!
Lo his eyes of all sorrow that may not dissemble!
Cry out, for he heedeth, "O Love, lead us home!"

O hearken the words of his voice of compassion:
"Come cling round about me, ye faithful who sicken
Of the weary unrest and the world's passing fashion!
As the rain in mid-morning your troubles shall thicken,
But surely within you some Godhead doth quicken,
As ye cry to me heeding, and leading you home.

"Come—pain ye shall have, and be blind to the ending!
Come—fear ye shall have, mid the sky's overcasting!
Come—change ye shall have, for far are ye wending!
Come—no crown ye shall have for your thirst and your
fasting,

But the kissed lips of Love and fair life everlasting!
Cry out, for one heedeth, who leadeth you home!"

Is he gone? was he with us?—ho ye who seek savings
Go no further; come hither; for have we not found it?
Here is the House of Fulfilment of Craving;
Here is the Cup with the roses around it;
The World's Wound well healed, and the balm that hath
bound it:
Cry out! for he heedeth, fair Love that led home.

Enter before the curtain, LOVE, holding a crown and palm-branch.

LOVE
If love be real, if I whom ye behold
Be aught but glittering wings and gown of gold,
Be aught but singing of an ancient song
Made sweet by record of dead stingless wrong,
How shall we part at that sad garden's end
Through which the ghosts of mighty lovers wend?
How shall ye faint and fade with giftless hands
Who once held fast the life of all the lands?
—Beloved, if so much as this I say,
I know full well ye need it not to-day,
As with full hearts and glorious hope ablaze
Through the thick veil of what shall be ye gaze,
And lacking words to name the things ye see
Turn back with yearning speechless mouths to me.—
—Ah, not to-day—and yet the time has been
When by the bed my wings have waved unseen

Wherein my servant lay who deemed me dead;
My tears have dropped anigh the hapless head
Deep buried in the grass and crying out
For heaven to fall, and end despair or doubt:
Lo, for such days I speak and say, believe
That from these hands reward ye shall receive.
—Reward of what?—Life springing fresh again.—
Life of delight?—I say it not—Of pain?
It may be—Pain eternal?—Who may tell?
Yet pain of Heaven, beloved, and not of Hell.
—What sign, what sign, ye cry, that so it is?
The sign of Earth, its sorrow and its bliss,
Waxing and waning, steadfastness and change;
Too full of life that I should think it strange
Though death hang over it; too sure to die
But I must deem its resurrection nigh.
—In what wise, ah, in what wise shall it be?
How shall the bark that girds the winter tree
Babble about the sap that sleeps beneath,
And tell the fashion of its life and death?
How shall my tongue in speech man's longing wrought
Tell of the things whereof he knoweth nought?
Should I essay it might ye understand
How those I love shall share my promised land!
Then must I speak of little things as great,
Then must I tell of love and call it hate,
Then must I bid you seek what all men shun,
Reward defeat, praise deeds that were not done.
Have faith, and crave and suffer, and all ye
The many mansions of my house shall see
In all content: cast shame and pride away,
Let honour gild the world's eventless day,

Shrink not from change, and shudder not at crime,
Leave lies to rattle in the sieve of Time!
Then, whatsoe'er your workday gear shall stain,
Of me a wedding-garment shall ye gain
No God shall dare cry out at, when at last
Your time of ignorance is overpast;
A wedding garment, and a glorious seat
Within my household, e'en as yet be meet.
Fear not, I say again; believe it true
That not as men mete shall I measure you:
This calm strong soul, whose hidden tale found out
Has grown a spell to conquer fear and doubt,
Is he not mine? yea, surely—mine no less
This well mocked clamourer out of bitterness:
The strong one's strength, from me he had it not;
Let the world keep it that his love forgot;
The weak one's weakness was enough to save,
Let the world hide it in his honour's grave!
For whatso folly is, or wisdom was
Across my threshold naked all must pass.
Fear not; no vessel to dishonour born
Is in my house; there all shall well adorn
The walls whose stones the lapse of Time has laid.
Behold again; this life great stories made;
All cast aside for love, and then and then
Love filched away; the world an adder-den,
And all folk foes: and one, the one desire—
—How shall we name it?—grown a poisoned fire,
God once, God still, but God of wrong and shame
A lying God, a curse without a name.
So turneth love to hate, the wise world saith.
—Folly—I say 'twixt love and hate lies death,

They shall not mingle: neither died this love,
But through a dreadful world all changed must move
With earthly death and wrong, and earthly woe
The only deeds its hand might find to do.
Surely ye deem that this one shall abide
Within the murmuring palace of my pride.
But lo another, how shall he have praise?
Through flame and thorns I led him many days
And nought he shrank, but smiled and followed close,
Till in his path the shade of hate arose
'Twixt him and his desire: with heart that burned
For very love back through the thorns he turned,
His wounds, his tears, his prayers without avail
Forgotten now, nor e'en for him a tale;
Because for love's sake love he cast aside.
—Lo, saith the World, a heart well satisfied
With what I give, a barren love forgot—
—Draw near me, O my child, and heed them not!
The world thou lovest, e'en my world it is,
Thy faithful hands yet reach out for my bliss,
Thou seest me in the night and in the day
Thou canst not deem that I can go astray.
No further, saith the world 'twixt Heaven and Hell
Than 'twixt these twain.—My faithful, heed it well!
For on the great day when the hosts are met
On Armageddon's plain by spears beset,
This is my banner with my sign thereon,
That is my sword wherewith my deeds are done.
But how shall tongue of man tell all the tale
Of faithful hearts who overcome or fail,
But at the last fail nowise to be mine.
In diverse ways they drink the fateful wine

Those twain drank mid the lulling of the storm
Upon the Irish Sea, when love grown warm
Kindled and blazed, and lit the days to come,
The hope and joy and death that led them home.
—In diverse ways; yet having drunk, be sure
The flame thus lighted ever shall endure,
So my feet trod the grapes whereby it glowed.
Lo, Faithful, lo, the door of my abode
Wide open now, and many pressing in
That they the lordship of the World may win!
Hark to the murmuring round my bannered car,
And gird your weapons to you for the war!
For who shall say how soon the day shall be
Of that last fight that swalloweth up the sea?
Fear not, be ready! forth the banners go,
And will not turn again till every foe
Is overcome as though they had not been.
Then, with your memories ever fresh and green,
Come back within the House of Love to dwell;
For ye—the sorrow that no words might tell,
Your tears unheeded, and your prayers made nought
Thus and no otherwise through all have wrought,
That if, the while ye toiled and sorrowed most
The sound of your lamenting seemed all lost,
And from my land no answer came again,
It was because of that your care and pain
A house was building, and your bitter sighs
Came hither as toil-helping melodies,
And in the mortar of our gem-built wall
Your tears were mingled mid the rise and fall
Of golden trowels tinkling in the hands
Of builders gathered wide from all the lands.—

—Is the house finished? Nay, come help to build
Walls that the sun of sorrow once did gild
Through many a bitter morn and hopeless eve,
That so at last in bliss ye may believe;
Then rest with me, and turn no more to tears,
For then no more by days and months and years,
By hours of pain come back, and joy passed o'er
We measure time that was—and is no more.

JOAN
The afternoon is waxen grey
Now these fair shapes have passed away;
And I, who should be merry now
A-thinking of the glorious show,
Feel somewhat sad, and wish it were
To-morrow's mid-morn fresh and fair
About the babble of our stead.

GILES
Content thee, sweet, for nowise dead
Within our hearts the story is;
It shall come back to better bliss
On many an eve of happy spring,
Or midst of summer's flourishing.
Or think—some noon of autumn-tide
Thou wandering on the turf beside
The chestnut-wood may'st find thy song
Fade out, as slow thou goest along,
Until at last thy feet stay there
As though thou bidedst something fair,
And hearkenedst for a coming foot;
While down the hole unto the root

The long leaves flutter loud to thee
The fall of spiky nuts shall be,
And creeping wood-wale's noise above;
For thou wouldst see the wings of Love.

JOAN
Or some November eve belike
Thou wandering back with bow and tyke
From wolf-chase on the wind-swept hill
Shall find that narrow vale and still,
And Pharamond and Azalais
Amidmost of that grassy place
Where we twain met last year, whereby
Red-shafted pine-trunks rise on high,
And changeless now from year to year,
What change soever brought them there,
Great rocks are scattered all around:
—Wouldst thou be frightened at the sound
Of their soft speech? So long ago
It was since first their love did grow.

GILES
Maybe: for e'en now when he turned,
His heart's scorn and his hate outburned,
And love the more for that ablaze,
I shuddered, e'en as in the place
High up the mountains, where men say
Gods dwelt in time long worn away.

JOAN
At Love's voice did I tremble too,
And his bright wings, for all I knew

He was a comely minstrel-lad,
In dainty golden raiment clad.

GILES
Yea, yea; for though to-day he spake
Words measured for our pleasure's sake,
From well-taught mouth not overwise,
Yet did that fount of speech arise
In days that ancient folk called old.
O long ago the tale was told
To mighty men of thought and deed,
Who kindled hearkening their own need,
Set forth by long-forgotten men,
E'en as we kindle: praise we then
Tales of old time, whereby alone
The fairness of the world is shown.

JOAN
A longing yet about me clings,
As I had hearkened half-told things;
And better than the words make plain
I seem to know these lovers twain.
Let us go hence, lest there should fall
Something that yet should mar it all.

GILES
Hist—Master Mayor is drawn anigh;
The Empress speaketh presently.

THE MAYOR
May it please you, your Graces, that I be forgiven,
Over-bold, over-eager to bear forth my speech,

In which yet there speaketh the Good Town, beseeching
That ye tell us of your kindness if ye be contented
With this breath of old tales, and shadowy seemings
Of old times departed.—Overwise for our pleasure
May the rhyme be perchance; but rightly we knew not
How to change it and fashion it fresh into fairness.
And once more, your Graces, we pray your forgiveness
For the boldness Love gave us to set forth this story;
And again, that I say, all that Pharamond sought for,
Through sick dreams and weariness, now have ye found,
Mid health and in wealth, and in might to uphold us;
Midst our love who shall deem you our hope and our
treasure.
Well all is done now; so forget ye King Pharamond,
And Azalais his love, if we set it forth foully,
That fairly set forth were a sweet thing to think of
In the season of summer betwixt labour and sleeping.

THE EMPEROR
Fair Master Mayor, and City well beloved,
Think of us twain as folk no little moved
By this your kindness; and believe it not
That Pharamond the Freed shall be forgot,
By us at least: yea, more than ye may think,
This summer dream into our hearts shall sink.
Lo, Pharamond longed and toiled, nor toiled in vain,
But fame he won: he longed and toiled again,
And Love he won: 'twas a long time ago,
And men did swiftly what we now do slow,
And he, a great man full of gifts and grace,
Wrought out a twofold life in ten years' space.
Ah, fair sir, if for me reward come first,

617

Yet will I hope that ye have seen the worst
Of that my kingcraft, that I yet shall earn
Some part of that which is so long to learn.
Now of your gentleness I pray you bring
This knife and girdle, deemed a well-wrought thing;
And a king's thanks, whatso they be of worth,
To him who Pharamond this day set forth
In worthiest wise, and made a great man live,
Giving me greater gifts than I may give.

THE EMPRESS
And therewithal I pray you, Master Mayor,
Unto the seeming Azalais to bear
This chain, that she may wear it for my sake,
The memory of my pleasure to awake. [Exit MAYOR.

THE EMPEROR
Gifts such as kings give, sweet! Fain had I been
To see him face to face and his fair Queen,
And thank him friendly; asking him maybe
How the world looks to one with love left free:
It may not be, for as thine eyes say, sweet,
Few folk as friends shall unfreed Pharamond meet.
So is it: we are lonelier than those twain,
Though from their vale they ne'er depart again.

THE EMPRESS
Shall I lament it, love, since thou and I
By all the seeming pride are drawn more nigh?
Lo, love, our toil-girthed garden of desire,
How of its changeless sweetness may we tire,
While round about the storm is in the boughs